"It's a well-known fact that nearly 80% of businesses fail in the first five years. An even larger percentage of them never grow to the size that the founder hoped for. This doesn't happen because of bad products or services, but rather because of a lack of a good, strong marketing plan. Mark Satterfield's *The One Week Marketing Plan* provides an easy to follow blueprint that any business can use to quickly attract new customers and clients."

—David T. Scott,
author of *The New Rules of Lead Generation*

"One of the biggest challenges most businesses are facing is attracting more *new* clients on a consistent basis. Mark Satterfield's *The One Week Marketing Plan* helps businesses get out there by implementing a client attraction program in just five days. This is *huge*! It works and every business owner who doesn't read this book is doing themselves (and their business) a disservice."

—Jeffrey Hayzlett,
host of Bloomberg TV's *C-Suite* and *New York Times*
bestselling author of *Running the Gauntlet*

"Many business owners worry that implementing a marketing system will be too difficult, too complicated, and too expensive. What's great about Mark Satterfield's *The One Week Marketing Plan* is that it's practical and easy to implement, and doesn't cost you an arm and a leg. Every business owner needs to read this."

—Robert H. Bloom,
former U.S. CEO of Publicis Worldwide and author
of *The New Experts* and *The Inside Advantage*

"Any small business owner or advisor would be well served to read Mark Satterfield's *The One Week Marketing Plan*. It's a concise, here's-precisely-how-to-do-it approach that will get you a lot more new customers and clients. If you're serious about growing your business, you need to read this."

"Insurance producers and financial advisors face an ongoing challenge of how to attract more new prospects and clients. Mark Satterfield's *The One Week Marketing Plan* shows you how to quickly and inexpensively develop a client-attraction system that will work for you without a lot of ongoing maintenance. If you read only one business book this year, this should be it."

"If your company is seeking a better ROI on its marketing invest-ment, you'll find Mark Satterfield's *The One Week Marketing Plan* to be definitely worth reading. His approach is efficient, measur-able, and simple to execute."

"As all sales professionals know, the key to closing more sales is having more prospects to talk with. In Mark Satterfield's *The One Week Marketing Plan*, you'll learn how to set up a client attraction system in just 5 days that will keep your pipeline full. I highly recommend you get a copy."

"Brilliant. Succinct. East-to-implement. I've read well over 100 marketing books and might I say *finally* there's a book that provides the blueprint to develop quality clients with predictable success."

—**Roxanne Emmerich,**
author of the *New York Times* bestseller
Thank God It's Monday! How to Create a Workplace You
and Your Customers Love

"This is a must-buy for anyone serious about taking their business to the next level. *The One Week Marketing Plan* is like giving you the key to unlock a treasure box. It shows you exactly what you need to do to create your dream business in a simple, easy-to-implement format that only takes one week! One of the biggest challenges advisors, consultants, and small business owners experience is lack of leads or a strategy to attract their ideal clients. In *The One Week Marketing Plan*, Mark Satterfield shows you each step you need in your plan to attract more of your ideal clients without a huge budget or a lot of work. His approach is straight forward and anyone can implement it."

—**Annette Bau,**
founder of MillionaireSeries.com

The ONE WEEK MARKETING PLAN

The Set It & Forget It
Approach for Quickly
Growing Your Business

Mark Satterfield

FOUNDER AND CEO
GENTLE RAIN MARKETING, INC.

BENBELLA

BenBella Books, Inc.
DALLAS, TX

BenBella Books, Inc.
10300 N. Central Expressway
Suite #530
Dallas, TX 75231
www.benbellabooks.com
Send feedback to feedback@benbellabooks.com

Printed in the United States of America
10 9 8 7 6 5 4 3 2 1

Library of Congress Cataloging-in-Publication Data

Satterfield, Mark, 1955–
    The one week marketing plan : the set it & forget it approach for quickly growing your
business / by Mark Satterfield.
       pages cm
    Includes bibliographical references and index.
    ISBN 978-1-939529-78-7 (trade cloth : alk. paper)—ISBN 978-1-939529-79-4 (elec-
tronic) 1. Marketing—Management. 2. Marketing. I. Title.
    HF5415.13.S274 2014
    658.8'02—dc23

                                                                                2013047393

Editing by Jennifer Canzoneri
Copyediting by Stacia Seaman
Proofreading by Brittany Dowdle and Amy Zarkos
Cover design by Jarrod Taylor
Text design and composition by John Reinhardt Book Design
Printed by by Bang Printing

Distributed by Perseus Distribution
www.perseusdistribution.com

To place orders through Perseus Distribution:
Tel: (800) 343-4499
Fax: (800) 351-5073
E-mail: orderentry@perseusbooks.com

Significant discounts for bulk sales are available.
Please contact Glenn Yeffeth at glenn@benbellabooks.com or (214) 750-3628.

Register your book at:
www.TheOneWeekMarketingPlan.com
and receive the companion video series
for FREE.

Register today and you'll receive
additional case studies, tips, tactics, and ideas for:

- attracting more targeted prospects,
- converting large percentages of them into paying clients
- micro-targeting a niche,
- putting together content for your website to engage new prospects,
- creating an irresistible offer that will motivate prospective clients to eagerly contact you,
- branding your business and differentiate yourself from your competition,
- getting clients to call you, rather than you chasing after them,
- and much more!

Thanks,
Mark Satterfield
Gentle Rain Marketing Inc.
www.GentleRainMarketing.com

To my wife, Marian, for all her love, support, and encouragement

CONTENTS

Why You Need the One Week Marketing Plan

There's a rock in my pool room with the word "Patience" carved into it. I think my sensei gave it to me, or it could have been my wife, or my neighbor...apparently there's a long list of people who feel this is something I need to work on.

If truth be told, I don't think I'm alone. I imagine there's lots of stuff you would do, if only it was simpler. Me too.

Unfortunately, simple answers usually only exist for simple problems. I'm sure there are exceptions, but I find that the more challenging the problem, the more we have to think "deep into the game," as the chess masters say.

For example, let's take the topic of getting more new clients.

On the surface the answer should be simple: Just ask them.

"Hey you. I realize we've never met, and you don't know me, but wanna buy my stuff?"

Okay, perhaps we say it a bit more elegantly, but haven't you been guilty of that? I know I have.

It's what's called selling to strangers.

1

Does it work? Sure—if you're willing to talk to enough people. It sort of reminds me of my strategy in the '70s of going up to women in the disco and asking them to go out with me.

Did it work? Sure. All right . . . occasionally. But what about the quality, you ask? Well . . . that was a bit suspect.

The problem is that if our strategy is basically asking strangers to do business with us, not only do we get a lot of rejection, but we also have no filter on the types of clients we eventually wind up with.

Granted, if you have no clients, the idea of having *any* clients, regardless of how bad, sounds good. But I think it's important to remember that the goal is to have both quality and quantity.

So how do we accomplish this?

The key is having a system to follow. I don't know about you, but when I have a plan, when I know what the next steps are, then I'm much more likely to stay the course. I'll see something through to the end. Conversely, when I've only figured out one step in the process, then I'm very likely to give up (or get distracted) after I do just that one thing.

So if your marketing effort has been filled with good intentions but little tangible results, I've got something for you. It's called the One Week Marketing Plan, and over the next five days we're going to work together to eliminate the need for you to chase after clients once and for all.

At the risk of stating the obvious, the success of any company depends upon having a consistent flow of new prospective clients. Unfortunately, far too many businesses rely solely on their existing clients and referrals as their primary methods for getting new business. While this may prove to be a successful strategy in the short term, it invariably leads to the "feast or famine" roller coaster that so many businesses experience.

Here's what I believe.

1. Marketing doesn't *have* to be expensive, time-consuming, or confusing.
2. You *can* have a highly effective marketing system up and running, doing what it's supposed to be doing in a week.
3. The key is to focus on a *system* rather than a series of unconnected activities.
4. Ultimately, successful marketing is all about developing relationships first and selling things second.
5. Anyone can do this.

This book will show you precisely how to set up your marketing system. The key is to follow the steps. Don't worry about step #4 until you've finished step #1. It would seem obvious, but many people fall into this trap.

The bottom line is that if you do what I tell you to do, you will never again have to worry about where your next client is coming from.

I realize that's a rather bold statement, so who am I to make that claim?

In many ways I'm not terribly different from you. For years I struggled with those feast-or-famine business cycles and wondered if there would ever come a time when I could stop chasing after clients and have them seek me out.

Looking back twenty years ago to when I first started my own business, I'll be the first to admit that the transition from corporate life to entrepreneurship was not easy.

One of the things that took me by surprise (although it shouldn't have) was that while I had a relatively impressive résumé with Pepsi and Kraft Foods, I discovered that I really didn't have a large network of contacts. Pretty much everyone I knew worked where I had worked. Thus, it wasn't long before I had lapped the track more than a few times hitting up my meager list of contacts for leads and referrals.

Like most people, I heard that networking events were a good way to meet prospective clients, so I joined a few groups, went to Chamber of Commerce meetings, and even tested a couple of Rotary groups. The problem was that I'm just not real good at "meet and mingle" events, so I never got much out of them. Most everyone I met *said* they got a lot of business from these things, but for some reason these types of events never worked for me—I found myself falling into that trap of hanging out with the few people I already knew.

I was getting a bit desperate when I borrowed an old cassette program from my cousin Jerry. It was Dan Kennedy's *Magnetic Marketing*, and it was my introduction to what's referred to as direct-response marketing. Simply put, this is marketing in which you attract new prospects by offering them something for free and then follow up with ongoing messages to build trust and convert them into paying clients. It's a type of marketing in which you can immediately track your results, so you don't waste your valuable marketing dollars.

To be honest, I first resisted direct-response marketing because the examples I read about focused on restaurant owners and plumbers. I thought that my clients were different—they're too sophisticated for this type of marketing.

But I really liked the idea of using free information to get prospects to raise their hands, and then using a planned drip-marketing sequence to build credibility and eventually turn these prospects into customers and clients. I figured that I really didn't have anything to lose, so I modified what I learned to focus on my niche, which was consultants and others who offer valuable advice and services.

Anyway, to make a long story short, it worked. Really well, as a matter of fact. I went from making $45,000 to $97,000 the following year. For someone like me, who had $1,800 in my checking account, that was a huge leap forward.

And it got better.

I kept experimenting with ideas; some didn't work—but a lot of them did, and in two years my business was up to around $250,000. That was in 2002, and as you may recall, this was when the Internet really started to take off. All of a sudden websites became a lot easier (and cheaper) to create. Now there were these programs called autoresponders that enabled someone like me (who had absolutely no technical skills whatsoever) to automate almost the entire marketing system.

My income increased by 50%. And then it did it again.

I'll admit this was pretty great. Instead of having to go out and try to strike up conversations with strangers at networking events, I literally had a waiting list of clients. Which meant that I could raise my fees, and even more importantly, choose whom I wanted to work with.

Anyway, that was my life for the next three years, and it was great.

But things change, and in my case the change came in the form of an international management consulting firm that was going through a tough patch. Surprisingly, for a billion-dollar firm, they didn't really do any marketing. Virtually all of their business came from referrals and repeat assignments.

This worked fine until a number of their long-term clients didn't renew their contracts and the referrals started to dry up. Then they started to get worried about how they were going to fill their pipeline back up with new business.

One of their senior partners read an article I wrote about my marketing method, liked my non-hard-selling approach, and asked me to fly up to New York to meet with him and some of the other partners.

That conversation led to a five-year engagement in which I trained 275 of the 350 partners on what we're going to be covering over the next five days.

Did it work? Obviously I wouldn't be telling you this story if the answer was "no," and to be totally honest, the success they achieved was mostly due to their willingness to implement what I taught and embrace new ideas and approaches.

That's when word got out about me.

It was a pretty heady period of time. But there was a price.

A lot of my work was in Europe. In the beginning it was terribly glamorous, and I wouldn't trade the experience for anything. But it does wear on you. The eleventh time you go to Düsseldorf, it really becomes little more than just a v-e-r-y long consulting trip.

Plus, while I enjoyed working with some of the world's top consulting firms, I had a desire to teach and apply this marketing methodology on a more intimate canvas—working with smaller companies who really wanted to make a mark in a particular niche. That's what got me the most excited.

Which leads me to where I am today. My clients are in consulting, insurance, financial services, real estate, training, and fifteen other niche businesses.

The one thing they all have in common is a desire to have a waiting list of clients without cold calling or hard selling. Probably much like you, they don't have lots of time or money to invest in marketing, but they have a strong desire to attract more consistent streams of new clients.

In the coming chapters, I'll help you identify your most hyper-responsive niche market and show you how to get them to "raise their hands" and express an initial interest in who you are and what you offer. Then I'll show you how to convert them from idle prospects into paying clients through a series of automated messages. If you're not a writer, don't worry—I'll provide you with templates that will make this whole process easy to implement.

As these prospects enter your "drip communication" system, you will begin to build a relationship with them. They'll feel as if they know you, even if you have never met face-to-face.

Sales trainer Greta Schulz, who attracts new clients using free online videos, says it's very typical for them to tell her when they meet for the first time, "'I feel like I already know you.' They wind up quoting things I've said in my videos."

Attorney Brian Mittman, who uses this type of marketing system at thedisabilityguide.com, says it helps him attract clients for his disability practice who have a deeper level of understanding about the claims process and thus make better clients: "I now have a person who didn't rush to get an attorney like everybody else. They've read the information I offer, and they're asking me whether I might be interested in their case."

That's really what the One Week Marketing Plan is about: gaining visibility in your niche market, educating people about the problems you solve, and having clients *call you* about how you can help them.

It's worked for me, it's worked for my small business clients, and it's even worked for a billion-dollar consulting firm. Now it's time to let it work for you.

Here's our agenda for the next five days:

DAY ONE: You'll determine which niche market to focus on. The key to attracting lots of new clients is to have a marketing message that speaks directly to a specific group. I'll show you precisely how to identify the most responsive niche market and how to choose if you have more than one.

DAY TWO: I'll show you how to create a compelling free offer that will motivate prospective clients to request it. This offer is the first step in the client attraction process, and I'll provide you with a comprehensive template for creating one of your own in a single day.

DAY THREE: You'll develop a simple one-page website that promotes your free offer and grabs names for your email list. Yes, I realize that technology can sometimes be a stumbling block, but I don't want you to worry about that. All you need to do on Day Three is write the copy for the web page. I'll show you exactly who to contact to get your site up and running for just a few dollars. As of this writing I have 65 websites, each one making a free offer and attracting new prospects, and I can barely spell "HTML." Trust me, if I can do this, so can you. I'll walk you through all the steps.

DAY FOUR: You will write five to seven drip-marketing messages (based on templates I provide) that will automatically be delivered to your prospects after they have requested your free offer. These messages play the dual role of building the relationship of trust and converting prospects into paying clients.

DAY FIVE: Now comes the fun part—driving traffic to your website and getting more new clients. Today you'll write ads (again using the templates I'll provide) and start running them on Google, Bing, Facebook, or LinkedIn. All you need is an advertising budget of $50–$100 and you're up and running. By the end of the day, you'll have targeted leads coming to your website.

Remember that while the goal is to have your campaign up and running in one week, if it takes a bit longer, that's not a problem. Just make sure you don't let inertia place its insidious hold on you. By the way, if you don't want to personally do any of the work I cover, I'll show you how to outsource it. Just see Appendix A for the least expensive, most reliable ways to find other people to do it for you.

I'm also going to show you how to use SEO, social media, video marketing, publicity, and joint ventures as tools to drive more people to your website and request your free offer.

One other note: Procrastination can periodically rear its ugly head, and there will be days, or at least parts of days, when you will have some resistance to the task at hand. Since everyone runs into this problem at one time or another, I've created Appendix C, "The Reluctant Marketer's Toolkit," and included some exercises that will help you move through whatever is momentarily keeping you from your goal of implementing your client attraction system.

Ready to get started? Let's begin.

Part One

THE BASIC PLAN

Chapter One

DAY ONE:
Choose Your Niche Market

MANY BUSINESSES resist niche marketing. The most common reason is that they're afraid that by focusing on a niche they'll miss out on opportunities outside of that particular area. However, the reality is that by focusing your marketing on a niche you will stand out from your competition and eliminate many of the potential objections people have about doing business with you.

Here's an example of a clever approach to niche marketing: In 2009, Matt Sonnhalter switched the focus of his Berea, Ohio, advertising and marketing agency from business-to-business (B2B) industrial manufacturing accounts to working only with companies that sell products to professional tradesmen. In other words, his clients sell to people who work with their hands, including electricians, machinists, and facility managers, among others.

He even created a new category for his business. Instead of defining Sonnhalter Advertising as a B2B company, of which they would be one among thousands, Sonnhalter now calls itself the first B2T, or "business-to-tradesmen," agency in the world.

This niche focus has had a tremendous effect. Sonnhalter has been so successful that it's been listed on *BtoB* magazine's top agency list from 2009 to 2012. Then in 2012, the company ran an ad with the tagline "Is your agency dirty?" (This is a reference to the fact his clients sell to people who get their hands dirty.) Not only has this ad accounted for 20% of the agency's new business leads, but it also won the prestigious Davey Award, a prize given for the best advertisements created by small agencies.

By focusing on this niche, Sonnhalter Advertising has attracted business from large global brands who are also targeting this niche audience. This is particularly impressive since his agency only has eight people. When they call, Matt Sonnhalter says the process of selling to them is much easier. "We don't have to respond to requests for proposals or trudge through a long qualifying process," he says. "They already know we understand this market better than anyone else."

But niching doesn't only work for services like advertising. It can be beneficial for physical products as well. Darlene Tenes' company CasaQ designs Christmas ornaments with a focus on the Latin market. The fact that her products have a specific niche audience helped her land a contract with a major department store.

One day she went to a Latina Style Business Series luncheon. The keynote speaker was from Macy's. As soon as the luncheon ended, Darlene rushed over to the speaker and gave a 30-second presentation on her products. She described them as similar to a successful competitor's brand—but with a Latino flair.

The buyer was intrigued and gave Tenes her card.

"I immediately went back to the office and packed up a sample box of items with a handwritten note," she says. "They were thrilled to discover my line of products."

What was the result of her niche marketing approach? "Eight months later," she says, "my products were on their shelves!"

Tenes' Latino niche gave her a distinct edge when it came to selling Christmas ornaments. She wasn't competing against all the other products on the market. Hers were the only ornaments with a unique aesthetic appeal to the 16% of the U.S. population that's Latino.

How a Niche Can Improve All Areas of Your Business

Matt McCormick owns JDC Repair, a company with four retail shops in Washington state and Chicago. "We used to fix a ton of different cell phones, but about nine months ago, we decided to discontinue every repair except for the three basic Apple products." They now only fix broken iPhones, iPods, and iPads.

Despite some initial concerns that he would lose business by having such a limited niche focus, McCormick's switch more than doubled his sales, from $500,000 to $1.1 million in just over a year.

Since his employees only needed to learn about fixing one product line, they became better and faster at what they were working on. "The quality of service has gone up significantly," he says. "This means happier customers and fewer problems."

The smaller niche has also had a beneficial impact on training new employees. "We can now fully train new technicians in about two to three weeks—instead of seven to eight weeks—because they only need to learn about six major repairs instead of six major repairs and twenty minor repairs."

Why You Need a Niche

Let me raise an important point about niche marketing. Focusing on a niche doesn't mean you have to give up all your other business. However, when you implement the One Week Marketing

Plan, you'll find the results will be greater if you zero in on a particular group of people. You may become so successful with this one group that you find that they're worth focusing your whole business on. Alternatively, over time, you may develop a series of niche marketing campaigns.

It's up to you.

Whatever you eventually choose for your business, for the purpose of making the One Week Marketing Plan work for you, you'll want to develop the campaign around a specific niche.

The primary reason I'm stressing selecting a niche has to do with the fact that there are two basic steps to acquiring a new client: attracting their initial attention and then motivating them to do business with you.

It may come as a bit of a surprise, but of these two, getting a prospect's initial attention is often the most challenging part of the whole process. The world is so noisy, with so many marketing messages, it's tough to break through the clutter.

The Easy Way to Create a Message That Matches Your Market

Marketing to a niche offers a simple way to overcome that problem. You are no longer addressing a general audience in the hopes that a small percentage of them are interested in your message. By focusing on a niche, you can communicate a very specific message concerning specific problems you can cure.

This instantly adds to your credibility. People assume that if you demonstrate that you understand their problems, then you also know the solution. When prospects see a reflection of themselves in your marketing materials, they're willing to stop to see what it is you have to offer.

One of the biggest objections businesses face (particularly those offering services) is "but my business is different" syndrome. When you target your marketing to a very specific group of prospects, this objection quickly goes away.

For example, let's pretend you're a Silicon Valley engineer and you just made some money from stock options with the start-up you work for. You're very nervous about your taxes because this is the first time you've ever been lucky enough to deal with this issue. Until now, you've worked for start-ups that went bust before your sweat equity was worth anything.

You're searching the Internet and you see listings for two free reports. One is called "7 Ways to Save Money on Your Taxes." The other is "The 7 Biggest Tax Mistakes You Can Make with Your Stock Option Profits."

Which of those two reports would you pay the most attention to?

Obviously, the answer is the second. It sounds like it was written just for you.

Any Business Can Find a Niche

For most businesses, finding a niche isn't too difficult. In fact, the biggest challenge people often face is deciding which niche market to focus on first. It's been my experience that *anyone* can find a great niche market that will be highly interested in what they do.

Even a comedian.

Dan Nainan is a professional stand-up who performs clean comedy around the world. "I quickly realized that comedy is a very low-paying profession for most of us," he says. "Most mainstream comedians struggle mightily, earning perhaps $25 on weeknights and $75 on weekends working comedy clubs."

But Nainan changed the economics of his profession by focusing on a niche.

"Early on, I concentrated on the Indian (South Asian) market, which has led to amazing results. I can earn literally two hundred times that in one show—up to $15,000." If a comedian can niche his market, so can you.

Kinds of Niches

Let's take a look at developing your niche market from a few different perspectives. To start, there are two large typical categories for niches:

1. **Industry**: This is pretty straightforward. You target companies in a specific type of industry. Industries are classified by either an SIC or an NAICS code. A helpful website to review industries you might want to focus on is at naics.com/search.htm. Remember that one of the first questions prospective clients typically ask is, "Who else in my field have you worked with?" Focusing on an industry niche is the most common way most people target their business. But it's not the only one.
2. **Function**: Another approach is to pick as your niche a job title, regardless of what industry they're in. For example, you could offer a training program on interviewing skills for human resources executives, whether they're in telecom, retail, or software. With this type of program, it doesn't make a difference what type of industry the HR manager works in.

Not surprisingly, niches can overlap between industry and function. If you offered an interviewing skills program, you could target HR managers in the retail industry. The trick to identifying the most hyper-responsive niche is to have it be as small as possible (so each person in the niche recognizes that you provided solutions to *their* problems), while large enough to be economically viable. This is where judgment ultimately plays a huge role. As you are working on developing your One Week Marketing Plan, especially if you have not developed one in the past, you'll find it easier to focus on as narrowly defined a niche as you can.

Dana Humphrey of Whitegate PR, a boutique PR and market-ing agency based in Astoria, Queens, found a unique industry to specialize in. When she started her company in 2007, she was a generalist, working with artists, musicians, and clients in con-sumer products, even olive oil products. After a period of self-reflection on the types of clients she most enjoyed working with, she's developed a specialization in the pet industry. "Every year we attend the big pet trade shows—Global Pet Expo in Florida in February and SuperZoo in Las Vegas in the summer," she says.

According to Humphrey, there are more than 11,000 pet product companies in the country and only six PR firms that specialize in this niche. She now has a business in which she is recognized as one of the leaders in her field and faces far less competition for new business.

Finding Your Niche

Let's turn our attention to finding a niche for you to focus on for the marketing campaign we're going to develop together. If you have an established business, the best place to start is with your current list of clients. Make a list of all your clients over the past couple of years and let's do some analysis.

- Are there any common industries, functions, or problems that jump out as you look at the list?
- Is one group of clients spending more money with you than others?
- Is one group easier to sell to?
- Who were the clients that you most enjoyed working with?

The clients that you've worked with in the past can give you great clues about where to focus. Building on your current strengths is one of the easiest ways to become the predominant expert in a particular area.

This exercise is beneficial because it may help you discover some trends that weren't apparent. I had a friend of mine who's a chiropractor do this. She immediately noticed something interesting about her patient list. Four of her favorite clients were in the same women's softball league. She didn't know if this was simply a coincidence or if there might be more to it. Working mostly on a hunch, she decided to ask the team captain if she could bring her portable chiropractic chair and offer free treatments to the players after the game. They said it would be fine.

These free treatments attracted more new clients and led her to focus her practice on women engaged in sports. She found that as an avid tennis player in her forties, she had a natural affinity to this niche group of clients. As she commented later, "In hindsight, it seems so obvious that this is who I should be focusing on. However, until I took the time to really examine my client list, I wasn't able to see that this group really stood out."

There's another set of questions that is worth thinking about as you're starting to identify a niche. Steve Harrison owns a company called Bradley Communications, which helps authors of nonfiction books get national publicity. He suggests asking yourself these questions as you analyze your list of current clients:

- Who has the strongest desire for what you do or know?
- Who could spend the most money for what you do or know?
- Who would make the most money from what you do or know?
- Who are you most passionate about serving?

- Have they demonstrated a willingness to spend money for your types of products or services?
- Are they easy to reach?

Sometimes your niche market shifts over time. According to Internet marketing guru Tom Antion, author of *The Ultimate Guide to Electronic Marketing for Small Business*, "I started out with the goal of being a great public speaker. Over time I achieved a level of success so that other speakers started asking me to help them." This led him to the niche of creating products and services for those who wanted to improve their public-speaking skills.

As Tom's business serving speakers grew, he started to focus on selling his information products on the Internet. Once again he was successful. "I got so good at it that people asked me to teach them how to sell their services on the Internet. That led to my current career of helping small businesses sell information products more effectively on the Web."

The Reason for Being in Your Niche

You'll have more success in marketing to a niche if you develop a story that explains why you're focusing on a particular group. For example, Tom Antion has a great story: He got so good at what he did that other people wanted to learn from him.

One of the most compelling stories you can tell is your track record of success in a particular niche: "I've helped others just like you achieve a goal/solve a problem because of my in-depth understanding of the unique dynamics of the industry or function." This is a very compelling marketing flag to wave, and it tends to get a lot of attention.

Another valid reason for focusing on a particular niche is that you previously worked in the field. For example, Joe Polish, who has developed a highly successful niche of teaching carpet cleaners how to get more new customers, was himself a carpet cleaner earlier in his career. Financial advisor Setu Mazumdar, who specializes in working with physicians, is himself an MD. This gives him a level of credibility that most others in his niche do not have.

In other cases, a family member or a friend in a particular niche needed help with an issue. They told you that you were such a big help that you decided to assist other people with the same issues.

An alternative story is that you are the person who takes lessons learned elsewhere and applies them to a particular niche. This approach can be pitched as: "The problem with the XYZ industry is that everyone is doing the exact same thing. I've worked in 17 different niche businesses and can apply the best practices outside your industry to make you successful." Business consultant Jay Abraham has built a highly successful practice this way. By positioning himself as having worked in dozens of different niches, Jay does a masterful job of communicating that his broad perspective is a compelling reason to engage with him.

The important point is that you need *some* reason for why you are focusing on this group. However, why you're in a niche is not as important as a thorough understanding about the current problems the niche faces. Hopefully, you already have a sense of this. If not, one day of studying the industry on the Internet will give you enough information to develop a list of the top five key problems.

A List of Factors to Consider

At this point you may have a clear sense of what niche market you want to focus on. Alternatively, especially if you're just starting your business, you may be struggling to decide between multiple options. As I mentioned previously, many people worry that by focusing on a niche, they'll miss out on potential business.

So let's be clear about what niche marketing is.

I'm not suggesting that your entire business needs to be focused on only this one niche. Rather, this is about a specific *marketing campaign*. Over time, your business may have multiple marketing campaigns, each directed at a particular niche audience. When you look at your business in its entirety, you may notice that customers and clients come from a variety of different niches. That's fine. All we are talking about here is the most effective way to attract clients to you. In order to accomplish that goal, a highly targeted niche-marketing message will beat a general message to a broad market every time.

As I've been sharing, there are a number of factors to consider when selecting a niche market. In this next section, I've compiled 14 additional items to consider. Some may be more important to you than others, but they're all worth thinking about.

1. **The Size of the Market:** There are trade-offs that are worth considering. My former boss at Kraft Foods used to refer to this as the "fisherman's dilemma." You can choose a pond in which there are a lot of fish, but the banks will be filled with fishermen, or you can choose a pond in which there are few fish, but fewer anglers crowding the bank.

   The key point is to make sure you know the size of the market before you jump in. You don't want to look back a year down the road and realize that the market isn't as big as you assumed. Market size should factor into your decision, but it shouldn't be the only point you consider. The truth is that you can still make a lot of money by focusing on a very small niche. Conversely, you can have great difficulty gaining entry into a large niche,

especially if there are a number of large established
players.

2. **Growth:** Is the marketplace you're thinking about
   growing or shrinking? How many new people are
   entering the niche who may need your products or
   services? For example, one of the reasons sales training
   is such an attractive business is that there is a continual
   stream of new people entering the field who need
   training on the fundamentals of selling.

   Alternatively, I had a client who was in the CD
   manufacturing business. With digital downloads, that's
   a business that is shrinking fast. Will there be a market
   for CDs in the future? Sure—but it won't be huge, and it
   won't support a lot of players. As common sense would
   dictate, you want to focus on a business that's growing.

3. **Reachability:** This is a huge factor. You want to focus
   on niches where you can easily reach the key decision
   makers. Are there magazines just for the market you are
   targeting? Associations? Are there other people selling
   products or services to this group that you can joint-
   venture with or rent a mailing list from?

   This can trip up people who define their niche
   through attitudes or behaviors such as "I market to
   people who are seeking greater fulfillment in their lives."
   It's tough to find those people.

4. **Geography:** Sometimes this is important; sometimes
   it's not. One question you need to answer is if meeting
   people face-to-face is crucial for your business. Would
   you be happier doing business with people you could
   sit across from? Or would you be just as comfortable
   communicating with them by phone and email? Some
   businesses (such as Realtors, dry cleaners, dentists) have
   a natural geographic focus. Other times the geography

issue is more a matter of preference. However, it's important that you check your assumptions. You may think you need to interface with clients face-to-face when in fact you don't.

When I began my career as a marketing consultant, I assumed that I would need to physically see my clients. The reality turned out to be that phone, email, and eventually Skype sufficed just fine. In fact, of the 30+ clients I'm working with currently, I've only actually met one of them face-to-face. This is not to say you shouldn't focus your marketing on a particular geography, just make sure you're making that decision for the right reasons.

5. **Men vs. Women:** One way of super-focusing your niche is to target a single gender. I work with a female financial advisor who originally focused on retirees. That's a tough market with lots of competition. She changed her niche to widows, because as a widow herself, she has a natural empathy for this audience, as well as a story to tell that lets them know that she understands them better than any of her competition.

6. **How Passionate Are They?** There are certain markets where people will buy practically anything you offer. Golf and fishing are two great examples. Why else would I have a dozen drivers in my garage? My cousin Stan has boxes of fishing lures stacked up in a shed. He can't seem to resist the latest infomercial that promises that this next lure will enable him to catch a fish the size of Jaws. Personally, I don't get it. Then again, he doesn't understand my ever-expanding collection of golf clubs.

One of the things that makes passionate markets very attractive is that people are likely to simultaneously buy products or services from competing companies. When

I hire an accountant, it's unlikely I'll hire another one.
That's not the case in passionate markets. It's likely I'll
buy from you *and* your competitors. The downside to
passionate markets are that they tend to be very crowded
and the competition is usually first rate. The reality is
that we all can't market to a highly passionate niche, but
if you can, you have an immediate advantage. That said,
if we can make what we do the least bit "sexy," we can tap
into this passionate hook. This is where the automated
messages we send out can play an important role.

7. **How Passionate Are You?** You can sell anything better
   if you care about what you're selling. The woman who
   markets financial planning to widows really cares
   about what happens to them. This comes through in
   everything she communicates, and her prospects pick up
   on it. I'm a marketing geek and can spend hours talking
   passionately with similarly minded geeks. Even if my
   clients don't have that much interest in the topic (aside
   from the end result of getting more or better clients),
   my passion for what I do increases their level of comfort
   in hiring me. My dentist goes on endlessly about the
   newest advances in fighting gum disease. Although
   it bores me to tears, her passion does make me more
   willing to follow the suggestions she makes. Prospective
   clients will pick up on your passion, so the more your
   work reflects what you're a "geek" about, the better.

8. **Is There a Need?** Unfortunately, simply having a lot of
   passion isn't enough. The people you market to have to
   understand they need what you have to offer. Missing
   this point has caused many computer and Internet start-
   ups to go bust. The founders thought they had a great
   idea for a product, but there wasn't anybody else who
   cared about it. Just because you want to open a vegan

raw food restaurant doesn't mean there are enough people in your town who actually want to eat that way.

On the other hand, if the commercial district in your town is only serviced by food trucks, your sit-down sandwich shop should be a sure winner. It's important to remember that just because you think there's a need, it doesn't mean one actually exists. Why more people don't talk with prospective clients about whether they'd be willing to invest in a service before jumping whole-hog into a business remains a mystery to me.

9. **Price Sensitivity:** How much money is your niche able or willing to spend? Are you selling to bigger corporations or smaller ones? To the affluent or the almost broke?

You can accept as gospel that some of your prospects will think your prices are too high. In reality that has more to do with how well you communicate the benefits, but the market you choose to sell to will also influence how much you can charge. You can charge more money for a tailored product to a specific niche than you can for its generic version.

For example, let's suppose you offer a time-management training program. As a generic one-day program, you'll hit the price ceiling at around $99 per head to attend. But suppose we offer time management for sales representatives? Now we're in the $200 per person range. Time management for pharmaceutical reps? More money. Time management for pharmaceutical territory managers? Even more.

You get the idea. The more that you can position your product or service as meeting the needs of a specific niche, the more that niche will be willing to pay for it. The reality is that there's usually not a huge amount of difference between the generic Time Management for Everyone program and the others, but the perception is that "this is something that meets my unique needs."

It would seem self-evident that you're far better off selling to people who have money rather than those that don't, but unfortunately many budding business owners don't fully think this through when they're selecting a niche. For example, many entrepreneurs target the very small business community as their niche. The reality is that micro-small-businesses usually have very little money. They may have a *need* for what you sell, but their ability to pay for it is likely to be another thing entirely.

Sometimes you need to be a bit creative with finding the right niche that can afford your services. This is certainly the case for those who offer job search services to the laid-off or unemployed. Not surprisingly, this group has little money and is extremely frugal about spending what little they do have. However, the "outplacement" industry, which basically sells job-search assistance, owes its success to targeting a different niche than the out-of-work individual. With a bit of research, the industry discovered that they could sell outplacement services to the corporate human resources department. Thus a service that was a bust in one niche (unemployed workers) became a huge success when marketed to a different one (the corporations laying off employees).

In a similar fashion, selling expensive products to students doesn't make sense, but selling to their parents does. An example of this is a company called Creative Circus. Their niche market is creative types who haven't settled on a career but don't want a typical job.

Creative Circus offers a $45,000, two-year training program for people who want to be copywriters and graphic artists, which is well beyond the reach of these young adults. However, their parents are often able and willing to foot the bill, so the marketing is directed at them.

You also want to consider whether you want to sell to corporations or to individuals. Generally speaking, you can charge corporations more money; however, it usually takes longer to get paid. There's also more bureaucracy to deal with, and the sales cycle is longer. However, once you secure a large corporation as a client, they may remain with you for many years.

10. **Is Seasonality a Factor?** There are some businesses where seasons matter. If you're selling to teachers or accountants, this can be extremely important. You can't sell accountants anything during the first five months of the year.

I have a client who sells custom software to accountants. He hangs out on a tropical island from January to May, then works really hard from June to December.

11. **Competition:** How much competition is there in your niche? Ironically, having no competition is a big red flag about the viability of the niche. None of us are so smart that we're the first ones to think about selling something to a particular group of people. It's very rare that what you're offering hasn't been offered before. A lack of competition may mean that there's not much hunger for it or that it's available for free on the Internet.

Instructional videos are an example of this. Ten years ago you could command significant money for all sorts of videos that would teach various things. YouTube significantly changed the economics of that business. If you're thinking about producing "How To" information, it's a wise move to find out how much of it is currently available on the Internet for free. However, just because the generic version of your topic is available for free, that doesn't mean that you can't earn good money with a niche product. There are lots of free videos about how to hit your driver longer. It's doubtful that I would pay money for another generic video, unless it was done by a celebrated golf pro. However, I probably would invest money on a video that targeted the over-50 male golfer who suffers from lower-back issues.

Ideally what you want is bad competition. There are enough competitors to make you feel good about the viability of the niche, but they're doing a lousy job at marketing their products or services. By following the strategies I discuss in this book, you should be able to capture a nice share of the market. Very few people in any niche implement the type of marketing program I'm going to have you develop, so you'll have a significant competitive advantage.

If there's intense competition in a niche and they seem to be doing a good job of marketing, you'll need to ask, "What can I offer that others can't?" "Is there some way I can position my products or services that is different from the competition?" If you can't come up with a reasonable answer, you might want to think about a different niche.

This was a challenge I faced when I decided to focus on developing a marketing consultancy with a niche market of consultants, advisors, and experts. It quickly became apparent that this niche was crowded with marketing consultants, many of whom were quite good.

As I analyzed the competition what I noticed was that most of them focused on one or two aspects of marketing. There was an Internet expert. A social media advisor. A person who would teach you how to write a sales letter. Lots and lots of consultants who had expertise in a particular component of the overall marketing strategy.

But there wasn't anyone who was focusing on the marketing system as a whole. No one was working on the question of how do you attract the initial attention, build a relationship with the prospect, and eventually turn them into a paying client? I decided that there was an opportunity to position myself as the "marketing system" expert. It turned out that this was an untapped area within my niche, and my business blossomed as a result. Just because there is a lot of good competition in a niche doesn't mean there isn't room for you, if you can offer something that the others aren't.

12. **Can You Use Pain & Gain?** The classic twin levers in motivating people to buy something are "Pain & Gain." Either people want to avoid pain (or get out of the pain they're currently experiencing) or they want to achieve some sort of gain. Both of these levers are important, and you'll notice as we dive into the implementation of the One Week Marketing Plan that we will use both of them. However, they each have their own unique benefits, and we will use them at different stages of the client-attraction process. Pain tends to be more effective for getting people's initial attention. Of course, we will need to show our prospects that they can achieve the desired outcome (Gain) before they'll give us money, but Pain is what will tend to hook them initially.

Closely related to Pain is Fear. If we can communicate a message that focuses on the Fear of Some Pain That May Occur, it's likely we'll get a lot of people interested in what we have to offer. As one of my marketing professors said, "It's easier to sell fear than it is prevention."

For example, if you're selling water heaters, you'll get more attention when you say, "You have an 85% chance that your water heater will explode all over your house if it's more than five years old," than you will if you say, "Buy my heater because it will save you money over the next five years."

13. **Your Advantage:** You've probably heard of the term "unique selling point," or USP. The term was developed in the 1940s by advertising executive Rosser Reeves of Ted Bates Inc. Many business owners feel pressure to develop their USP, which usually becomes little more than an exercise in frustration. After all, for most of us, there isn't anything truly unique about what we do.

However, you may be able to combine elements of what you do and create a service that others in your niche are not offering. For example, I discovered that while the advice I was providing was helpful, the real need was in implementing a marketing program for my clients. As I analyzed this, it made perfect sense. My clients tend to spend most of their day delivering their services. They simply don't have the additional time or energy that's necessary to implement a marketing program. Eventually, the proverbial light bulb went on and led me to offer Done For You Marketing programs. Now I had two advantages: 1) focusing on a marketing system rather than just a single activity, and 2) offering a service in which we actually do the work.

Now, is this truly unique? No, not really. Many other marketing consultants offer the same scope and services, but none of them were playing in my niche.

This is one of the reasons why you want to subscribe to all of your competitors' newsletters and mailing lists, even if they serve a different niche than you. There may be something they're doing that you can transplant into your niche, which gives you a unique advantage.

14. **Is There Potential for Additional Business?** Although by implementing the One Week Marketing Plan you'll have consistent streams of brand-new prospects, the reality is that it's easier to sell something additional to an existing customer than it is to acquire a new customer.

Not surprisingly, a niche that will purchase goods or services from you repeatedly is far more attractive than one that only buys from you once. The type of business you're in dictates some of this, but it can also be influenced by how you structure your services. Accounting services are rather straightforward. If the service is good and I don't get audited, I'll most likely return next year.

A dry-cleaning business has a similar built-in advantage. As long as they don't lose or destroy your clothes, you'll keep returning. This is why dry cleaners offer lots and lots of coupons to first-time customers. Studies indicate that once you've made three visits to the same dry-cleaning establishment, it's their business to lose. That's what they're betting on when they initially offer you a great deal to clean six shirts for the price of one. They know they'll make a lot of profit off you if they can get you in the habit of using their services.

For other types of businesses, you may have to be more creative. A web designer who also offers SEO, mobile apps, social media development, and even ghostwrites your blog will have an opportunity to sell multiple services to a single client. Thus, as you're considering what niche to focus on, this is also a great time to think about what you offer clients and if there are additional services that could make you stand out from the competition. I'll talk in more detail later about how to develop joint-venture relationships in which you partner with others who can deliver complementary services.

One Important Note: You need to be aware of any legal or regulatory issues that govern your services or niche market. For example, financial advisors have compliance issues that limit what they can communicate on websites and in their marketing materials. Lawyers have restrictions, as do physicians.

If you are working in a niche that has restrictions and you can figure out how to handle the regulatory hurdles, that gives you an advantage. You'll have a barrier to entry that other people need to overcome if they want to enter that business. I do a lot of work with financial advisors and have a thorough understanding about what they can and cannot do to attract new clients. That gives my firm an advantage that many of my competitors don't have. In some cases it may make sense for you to enter a highly regulated niche simply because once you master the learning curve, you'll face a limited number of competitors.

Your Task for Day One

Your task for today is simple: Pick your niche and assess it against the criteria points I've been discussing. Once you've decided on the niche, head over to Google and find out who else is offering similar products or services. Get on everyone's mailing list and subscribe to their newsletters. I'm always surprised when people tell me they haven't taken this step.

To further help you decide on a niche, here's a sequence of activities to follow:

1. Start with the clients you already have and answer these questions:

   - Do you have a pattern of success with a particular group of clients?
   - Is one group of clients spending more money with you than others?
   - Is one group easier to sell to?
   - Is there a group that you have a natural affinity with?

If you have more than one niche market and you're having difficulty deciding between them, that's fine. What we're going to be doing over the next week is implementing your *first* marketing plan. Next week you can come right back and do the same thing for the second niche on your list. When I have a real hard time choosing between two options, I usually trust my gut, and it works out fine.

If your current client base doesn't point you toward a niche, you'll want to think about what types of businesses or people are likely to have the most pressing need for your product or service. What group is experiencing the greatest amount of pain that you can alleviate?

continued on next page

continued from previous page

2. Next, I'd like for you to create a bullet point list of
    precisely why you can serve this niche. What skills,
    experience, and knowledge make you well suited to
    serve this niche? This is also going to be handy to have
    for some of the later work we'll be doing together.

Today's goal is to plant the flag and select a niche to focus
on. Try to do as much research on your niche as time allows.
What you'll discover is that we will be taking a building-block
approach with the One Week Marketing Plan. Everything you
do today will help you with tomorrow's assignment, which is
creating a "bait piece" that will motivate prospective clients
to raise their hands and express their initial interest in learning more about you and the products or services you offer.

I'll explain it all in detail tomorrow.

Chapter Two

DAY TWO:
Create Your Free Offer

A FEW YEARS AGO, life didn't smell too sweet to Sonny Ahuja. The recession and competition on the Internet had created the perfect storm, driving five of his seven mall-based retail perfumeries out of business. Plus he owed more than $100,000 to his suppliers.

His only hope was to compete on the Internet. But how would he attract new customers?

Ahuja decided that the best strategy was to give something away for free. But what?

In person, he was able to share tiny vials filled with samples of new perfumes, or at the very least, *spritzes* from the bottles he kept as samples. But you can't download digital scents in a PDF.

So Ahuja decided to create a downloadable free report.

Most marketers would be hard-pressed to come up with an information product that makes sense for perfume buyers.

But Ahuja knows his customers. And he knows there is one fear most online buyers have when they buy fragrances from a new company on the Internet: paying for an expensive perfume but being sent a cheap imitation.

Frankly, consumers should be worried. These counterfeits often have ingredients like urine, bacteria, and antifreeze.

So Ahuja wrote a free report that takes aim at that very issue: "20 Ways to Spot a Fake Perfume." It's available at GrandPerfumes.com.

Offering a free report that focuses on one of the major concerns his niche market has about his products has changed his business. He now has an email list with 18,000 subscribers, 5,000 friends on Facebook, and more than 100,000 Twitter followers.

Ahuja says his report does more for his company than simply generating leads. "If we're telling them twenty ways to spot fake perfumes, then they know we're not going to send them a fake perfume."

The result is a relationship with his customers that gets them to buy again and again. In an Internet world dominated by the lowest prices, Ahuja has an advantage. "We are not the cheapest company for perfumes on the Internet," he says. "We have built a business on credibility from the report and from the relationships we build through our newsletter."

Ahuja has achieved great results by driving traffic to his website. But Raleigh Regan found quick success in a simpler way. Regan, who creates employee newsletters for companies, gained a client worth $36,000 by simply responding to a LinkedIn posting.

"They had a question about starting an employee newsletter. I answered the question and posted a link to my free report (available at StartingAnEmployeeNewsletter.com)," he says. "Two days later someone read the answer, called me up, and literally with no vetting said, 'Can I get a quote for a newsletter?'"

Because the report established Regan's credibility, the company didn't even bother seeking other quotes. "They've been a client for more than two years," says Regan, "and they're worth more than $18,000 a year to us with the four big newsletters they do a year."

The free report strategy helped disability lawyer Brian Mittman (mentioned in the introduction) make a big lifestyle change. A little over five years ago he moved his entire office from Lower Manhattan to the suburbs, which allowed him to reduce a three-hour round-trip commute to a mere ten minutes. "Everyone told me I was out of my mind," he says. "Yet in the last five years I have continued to dramatically increase the number and quality of new cases I take on."

He credits the educational marketing benefit of using a free offer for making the difference. "Even though we've been in somewhat of an economic recession, my gross and my net have continued to increase dramatically, and it's not because of one huge case I picked up."

Your Day Two Task

Your job on Day Two is to come up with a free offer that is as meaningful to your target market as the report on spotting fake perfumes is to Sonny Ahuja's customers.

No matter what business you are in, there's some kind of information your customers want. Your goal is to uncover what will be the most intriguing to your prospective clients. Sometimes the answer to that is readily apparent. Other times it takes a bit of reflection and thought. The more you can put yourself into the mindset of your prospect and answer the questions, "What would I be most interested in learning? What am I most worried about?" the greater the likelihood that your free offer will be eagerly requested.

Your goal is to have this finished by the end of the day.

Step One: Choose Your Format

There are a number of choices, but the reality is that *how* you deliver the information is far less important to your audience than the content. You may decide to offer a free video, audio program, software, or diagnostic tool. These are all fine options, but you're going to be hard-pressed to get them done today, unless you already have them developed.

For the purpose of getting your marketing program up and running quickly, we're going to focus on creating a free report. However, since video is increasingly becoming an important marketing tool, I've included information on how to incorporate it into your system in Chapter 8.

Remember, the key with developing this free report is to zero in on providing information your niche market really wants to have. Although I'm calling this a "report," don't let that scare you off. Some of the most effective free offers have been simple lists. For example, Guy Giuffre, a Realtor, offers a list of foreclosures in his area at santacruzbankrepos.com. Investors who are interested in this particular niche segment of the real estate market repeatedly come to his site to download the most current list.

It is interesting that Guy doesn't have to do the work to compile the list. It's offered to Realtors via ForeclosureRadar.com. He simply reformats the information and then promotes its availability to his particular niche market. Giuffre says that foreclosure list is worth $50,000 per year to him in new business.

Although Guy periodically updates his free offer, you may find that your report can exist for years without revisions. The more you focus on "evergreen" topics or advice, the longer its shelf life. My "how to write a sales letter" offer (GentleRainSalesLetters. com) has been up and running for the past eight years without my doing a single thing to it. The mechanics of how to write a compelling sales letter haven't changed much in the past ten years. As long as the free offer works and continues to bring in new prospects, there's no point in fiddling with it. Thus, if you have a choice and want to make your life simpler, I recommend trying to find a topic that will have a high "curiosity index" for years to come.

Step Two—Picking a Hooky Subject

Since the success of the free offer will depend on what we choose for the subject, this is worth spending some time thinking about. There are three questions that I think are particularly helpful for selecting a topic:

- What's the biggest area of pain to your target audience?
- What are they most afraid of?
- What are they most curious about knowing?

All we need is one topic for what you're going to do today. Although I said that this is a very important step, I don't want you to think that if you get this wrong, disaster ensues. The reality is that in the months and years ahead, I want you to create lots of free offers. Some will be home runs and a few may be whiffs. That's just the nature of the game. Over time you'll become increasingly adept at knowing precisely what your niche market is most insecure, curious, and fearful about. That knowledge will enable you to create numerous reports and a virtual tsunami of new prospects opting in. I currently have more than 60 websites, each offering some sort of free information. But it all started with a single report.

Here are some additional ideas for your topic:

- Your target audience's biggest ongoing frustration
- A new trend or strategy they're aware of—but haven't figured out how to use

- A myth you can debunk (For example, this book debunks the myth that marketing is too complicated and too expensive and takes too long.)

Another good idea is to ask current clients in your chosen niche market what's keeping them up at night. The answer is likely to make a great subject for this report. I'd like you to develop a list of *all* the potential topics for your free report, and then you'll narrow it down to just one for today's assignment.

I'm sometimes surprised that more companies don't use free reports to attract more prospects. In fact, when I speak to groups, it's not uncommon for people to come up to me at a break and say what a "great idea" free offers are. I guess this surprises me since this approach has been around for decades. I distinctly remember my first experience with this type of marketing. I was eleven years old when I saw an ad in the back of a comic book with the headline, "The Insult That Made a Man out of Mac."

The five-panel cartoon that followed was the Charles Atlas classic where a bully kicks sand on scrawny Mac and his date, getting Mac so mad that he is willing to "gamble a stamp" so he can get a free report that will help him get a "real body." In the final panel, Mac has successfully transformed from skinny wimp to muscular dude and (completely politically incorrect by today's standards) socks the bully in the jaw.

At the bottom of the ad was a reply form to receive the free report about the "Secrets of Dynamic Tension." It asked me to check the boxes for what I wanted. Bulging biceps? Abs of steel? I remember thinking, "Is it possible to have both?"

A couple of weeks later I received my free report about Dynamic Tension, the Charles Atlas exercise system that helps you "get fit fast ... no gadgets, just results." Not surprisingly, a few days after that, I received a letter from Charles (call me Chuck) Atlas, who told me that while the information in the report was good, investing in the Charles Atlas Muscle Building System would get me the results I wanted quicker.

A few days later another letter arrived and then another (for all I know they may still be coming to my parents' house), each one encouraging me to continue the exercises in the free report and gently pushing me to take the next step in the sales cycle.

What made this marketing campaign so successful was that Charles Atlas understood exactly what was going on in the heads of scrawny prepubescent boys who read comic books. Because they were targeting a very specific niche audience, the copywriters were able to speak to the insecurities and desires of their very specific market. This is important. In order to create marketing materials that will motivate your prospects to engage with you and to take action, you need to have a very clear vision of who they are, of their fears, hopes, and aspirations. This is true regardless of whether you are selling products to consumers or services to businesses. So let's do a quick exercise that I first learned from marketer Frank Kern that will help you get into the mindset of your niche audience.

Answer the questions below, to create a *"perfect prospect"* for what you are marketing. (Tip: Write down what immediately comes to mind.)

- John (or Jane) is my ideal client. He/She is __ years old. His/Her three biggest frustrations are ___, ___, and ___. Sometimes he/she even wakes up in the middle of the night worrying about___.
- If he/she could wave a magic wand, he/she would want these three things to occur:
  1.
  2.
  3.

- When he/she goes online to find a potential answer to this
  problem, he/she may enter keywords into Google such as
  ___, ___, and ___.
- If he/she is going to do business with me, he/she needs to
  believe I can ___, ___, and ___.
- The myth he/she believes (which I will shatter) is ___.
- He/she might not invest in my products or services
  because ___, ___, and ___.
- The biggest obstacle he/she faces when trying to solve this
  problem is___.

This exercise is important not only for writing your free report
but also for positioning your products and services in such a way
that they become irresistible.

Based on what I've covered thus far, I want you to write down
what the topic of your report will be. If you have a number of
potential subjects, go with your gut and select one. Remember,
over time, it's likely you'll create multiple free offers that cover all
the topics on your list.

Step 3—Create Your Title

Now that you have a topic picked, it's time to come up with a title.

A good title is crucial since it's what will initially motivate prospects to request it. While the content is important, if we don't hook
people with the title, our marketing effort stalls out. That's unfortunately what happened to a financial advisor I'll call Steve.

To his credit, Steve believed in the marketing system I've been
discussing, and he certainly was passionate about his topic. Perhaps that's why he decided to title his free report "Indexed Solutions Simply Explained." Not surprisingly, after a month of making
the report available on his website and spending a good amount of
money promoting it, not a single person downloaded it.

So our first step was to come up with a new title for the report. I asked Steve what his clients' biggest fear was. He said, "That's easy. They're afraid they'll outlive their savings." We put those words right into his new title: "A Simple Solution to Make Sure You Won't Outlive Your Retirement Savings."

And even though the information in the report was still about indexed solutions, the new title was a huge improvement. He went from zero requests during the first 30 days to over a hundred per month.

Another of my clients, Alan, is a roofing contractor. He tried to offer a free report that was just a brochure about his company. "I thought that if people saw my company as trustworthy," he says, "they would decide to hire me."

We replaced his brochure with a giveaway called "7 Warning Signs Your Roof Is About to Leak Even When It's Sunny and Dry Outside." Alan went from no response to 300 requests in two months. Those reports converted into five new roofing customers, or a total of $50,000 in new business. Annualize that and you've got an additional $300,000 worth of business.

Not bad for a marketing program that only takes you one week to implement.

The secret to a good title is to focus on your market's challenges, frustrations, and aspirations, just as you did when you picked your topic. Choose the biggest one they face. Your report should convey that you have a solution to their problem, using "fear of pain," as in the roof report above.

If coming up with a good title sounds hard to you, don't worry. In a minute I'm going to share some fill-in-the-blank templates to make it easy.

It's important that your report focuses on the benefits your product or service offers, not just the features. Although most of us have heard about features vs. benefits, it still is sometimes confusing. An easy way to define a benefit is that it answers the question, "Why do I care about that?"

Let's say you're talking about a Tempur-Pedic® mattress: A feature is that it's made of space-age foam. Another is that it has a higher density of cells than any other mattress. And even the fact that it contours to your body is a feature.

So let's add benefits and make our reader really care about these. For example, space-age foam gives you a more relaxing night's sleep. A mattress manufactured with a high-density cell structure keeps you from waking up in pain. The unique design that contours the mattress to your body ensures you feel energized when you wake up in the morning. So whenever you are struggling to create a benefit, remember the question, "Why do I care about that?"

Benefits are a critical component in creating the title of your free offer. Here are some classic report titles you might have seen before:

- "Do You Recognize the 7 Early Warning Signs of High Blood Pressure?"
- "How to Ensure You'll Live Long Enough to Celebrate Your Granddaughter's 25th Birthday"
- "The Lazy Man's Easy Way to Riches"
- "The Most Useful Time-Saving Tips You've Ever Seen for Harried Housewives"
- "How to Have Your Home Beautifully Remodeled on a Shoestring Budget"
- "What the IRS Doesn't Want You to Know That Can Save You Thousands of Dollars"

You might be able to just adapt these templates for your report. Change a few words and you've got a brand-new title of your own. For example, number 4 could easily be changed to "How to Optimize Your Tax Return on a Shoestring Budget."

Here are some more fill-in-the-blank formulas:

1. "7 Secrets Every _____ Needs to _____" (The first blank should be the name of your target audience, e.g., CPA, hospital, etc. The second blank should be the benefit your prospects want the most—e.g., "attract hordes of customers" for CPAs, or "avoid lawsuits" for hospitals.)
2. "10 _____ You Should Never _____ if You Want to_____" (Start with a noun like "foods" or "deductions," next blank is a verb—eat or ignore, third blank is a benefit—lose weight or lower your taxes.)
3. "Is Your Competition Getting More_____ Than You? What _____ Never Taught You About _____" (This one's a little different. The first blank is a benefit or an opportunity: I.T. work, customers. The second blank would be an authority, e.g., your marketing professor. The third blank is a benefit related to the first benefit—such as more customers.)
4. "Secrets Revealed: What _____ Say When You're Not in the Room" (Fill in the blank with a group your target market values—"your customers," "your employees," etc.)

One style of report that generates a lot of curiosity is a myth that people believe but that's not true. The "debunking a myth" model works quite well in many different businesses. An example of a successful report in the insurance industry that uses the myth model is "The #1 Health Insurance Myth: The More You Pay, the Better Your Coverage."

One of my personal favorite formulas is the "Steps" model. "7 Steps for Developing Leaders to Take Your Company to the Next Level." "5 Steps for Hiring Great Assistants That Work Independently." "10 Steps for On-boarding New Employees to Reduce Turnover." The reason I particularly like this model is that one of the biggest problems you face when marketing your services is that people just don't understand what you do. By breaking your process down into a series of steps, these reports are both easy to write and easily understood by your prospective clients.

How Much Should Your Report Cover?

One of the challenges of writing your free report is deciding how much information to include. If you don't include anything of value, the reader will feel tricked and be unlikely to convert into a paying client. Conversely, if you provide too much information, they may decide that they know everything they need to know and, again, don't need to engage your services. So it's a bit of a balancing act. As marketing expert Jimmy D. Brown says, "We want them to feel satisfied, but incomplete."

The way we accomplish this is to focus on telling our readers what to do and what not to do, but not precisely *how* to do it. That's what leaves them incomplete.

Here's an example that will illustrate this point. Suppose you were writing a free report for foreigners who were unfamiliar with cooking a Thanksgiving dinner. Using this model, your report would tell them not to cook lobster or Quiche Lorraine on Thanksgiving. Then it would explain that the perfect meal for Thanksgiving is turkey with stuffing, cranberry compote, and sweet potato casserole. You could go on in great detail describing what a Thanksgiving dinner looks and smells like. You might tell the reader about the history of the holiday and how the traditional meal evolved over the years. However, you wouldn't give them recipes or tell them *how* to cook those items. That's the information that you charge for.

Will people who download your free report be satisfied even though you aren't giving them all the information they want? Most likely the answer would be yes. They would have learned about the history of the holiday, what they need to prepare, how many courses, why Detroit always plays football on Thanksgiving Day, and lots of helpful information. In fact, if we wrote the report in an engaging style, it would be likely that the reader would be very enthusiastic and motivated about preparing their first Thanksgiving dinner. If we followed up the report with an offer of recipes or a video with step-by-step instructions, we'd have a lot of buyers.

The Development of Your Report

One of the easiest reports to create is one that follows this six-part structure:

1. *What is the biggest problem your target market is facing?* (By this time you should have this one down cold.)
2. *What are the consequences if they ignore the problem?*
3. *What are the other options they might consider to solve this problem?*
4. *What is your solution?* (Think about the steps you take to solve the client's problem or deliver your services.)
5. *What results do you get?* (To the extent you can quantify your results, the better. If you have testimonials about the results you get, include them in this section.)
6. *What do you want the reader to do once they've finished?*

As I go through each of these in detail, make notes about what you would like to include in each section. It will then be a simple task at the end to compile your notes into the final report.

Problems and Consequences

I've covered identifying the big problems your clients face, so you should have those pretty clear in your mind. However, simply stating the problem usually isn't enough. It's too easy for the prospect to shrug and say, "I'll worry about that later." We want them to worry about it now, and that's where consequences are helpful.

The goal of consequences is to convince the reader that their problem will cause them a major headache if they don't address it ASAP. Consequences are a powerful tool and easy to develop. Simply bullet-point out a list of what might happen if the problem is ignored. In workshops I called this exercise, "How many steps till bankruptcy/death/divorce?"

For example, in my world, the problem my prospects face is a lack of new clients. So what are the consequences?

- You'll have to rely on referrals that may not come when you need them.
- Which causes the "famine" business cycle . . .
- So you dig farther into your savings . . .
- And you no longer can go on vacation . . .
- Which causes stress in your marriage . . .
- And eventually divorce . . .
- Which causes you to start drinking . . .
- And your current clients all leave you . . .
- Forcing you into bankruptcy . . .

In reality you're not going to put this into your actual report, but the exercise is helpful nonetheless. What I find is that it frees up the imagination, which then enables you to scale back the "bankruptcy/divorce/death" scenario but still communicate real consequences that may occur. Remember, it's simply not enough to just communicate a problem. You need to put the salt of con-sequences in the proverbial wound if you're going to make peo-ple care enough to take action.

The Other Options

Our solution to the problem is not the only option available. Your competition probably offers some alternative ideas, and we all have to deal with the option that a prospective client may just decide to do nothing. Excellent marketing is all about proactively addressing concerns and objections. By including this options section in your free report, you may be able to minimize or even eliminate your competition.

Think about what you offer. Then compare your solution to others that are:

- More costly
- More time-consuming
- More complicated
- Less effective
- Less proven
- Less pleasant

Obviously, not every business will have competitors with each of these characteristics, but you get the basic idea.

Let me give you an example.

By now you have a good sense for the marketing system I champion. It focuses on making compelling free offers, which are then followed up with a drip-marketing sequence that builds trust and eventually converts prospects into paying clients. It's a highly effective system, but it's only one of many differ-ent approaches for getting more new clients. Thus, in my free report, it's advantageous for me to try to paint other options in a less-than-favorable light. Here's how I handle one option, which is cold calling for new business.

> *And then, there are those methods that may be productive (although I have my doubts), and certainly don't cost much money, but aren't any fun at all.*
>
> *This category is dominated by—you guessed it—cold calling. I equate cold calling to plowing a field with a mule. I suppose it's possible to accomplish the task, but with all the other options available to you, why would you want to?*
>
> *Personally I think cold calling is unpleasant, boring, repetitive work that's best left to those who can mindlessly "smile & dial" rather than use their brains to develop labor-free marketing systems.*
>
> *But again, that's just my opinion. You may feel differently.*

Granted, there's nothing terribly subtle about what I'm communicating, but I've found that many of my prospects think that cold calling is the only option available to them. This section disabuses them of that belief and reinforces the unpleasantness of going down that road. Those who love to cold call are unlikely to ever adopt my type of marketing, so the fact I'm calling them "mindless" probably doesn't hurt me in the long run. Remember, not everyone is going to become your customer, and it becomes a Herculean task to try to convince those who are not slightly predisposed to your approach to pay attention to you. I'd much rather cast my net wide and communicate who my approach is right for and who it isn't. That way when it comes time to actually talk with prospects, you're spending most of your time with those who are inclined to be positive toward you.

Your Solution

Now that you've addressed the options they shouldn't take, this next section focuses on your solution. As I mentioned before, in this stage we're going to share what the solution is but go very light on the specifics about *how* to actually accomplish it.

There are a couple of items to keep in mind:

Focus on benefits rather than features. Just to reiterate, the feature is the grass seed. The benefit is the lawn that will be the envy of your neighborhood. When you talk about benefits, you appeal to your prospects' emotions. As the old marketing saying goes, people make their buying decisions based on emotions and justify them with facts.

(There's one caveat here: If your market is made up of engineers, load up on features. Engineers make buying decisions mostly based on logic.)

Here's one additional item to think about as you are communicating the benefits of your products or services: As long as it's accurate, you want to position what you offer as the opposite of what you said about your competition. If they're expensive, you're less so or a better value. If they're complex, you're simpler. And remember to reiterate that you specialize in people just like your audience. Simply by emphasizing the niche focus of your business, you'll eliminate a large percentage of your competition.

Mention benefits even if they seem obvious. Don't assume that your reader knows what the obvious benefits are. Even if all of your competitors could make the same claim, there is absolutely no downside to reiterating what might appear on the surface to be obvious. It is extremely hard to overdo benefits.

Explain Your Solution as a Series of Steps

Prospective clients will more readily understand what you do if you explain it as a process or series of steps. The number of steps doesn't need to be seven. Ideally, you should have at least five and no more than ten.

The easiest way to come up with your steps is to describe the process you go through with clients. What do you do first? Then what? And then?

For example, an organization offering change-management consulting might describe their solution in the following way:

1. We identify the gaps between where you are now and where you want to be. This enables us to establish metrics by which we can measure the success of the project.
2. We obtain organization-wide buy-in. The reason most change initiatives fail is because of a lack of senior management support. We will work with you to ensure that your program has the necessary levels of support to achieve the long-term results you desire.
3. We provide customized skills and knowledge training for management and sales teams, which are delivered in both classroom and online formats. We structure the implementation schedule so that it best serves the needs of your sales team.
4. We capture and publicize success stories to reinforce the value of the initiative through internal publications, Web success stories, a catalog of success cases, and other means.

The Results You Get

This is often overlooked, but it's an important section. If you want people to buy from you, show them that you get results. There are three ways to do this:

- Big-Picture Totals
- Mini Case Studies
- Testimonials

With *big-picture totals*, you make a sweeping statement about how many companies you've worked with in total and what you've accomplished overall on average. For example, you might say, "We've worked with more than one hundred manufacturing companies and lowered their power consumption a minimum of 10%, saving them a total of $1.5 million a year on average."

The more specific you can be, the more power these statements will have. If you are able to mention a particular industry and a total amount that you either saved or earned, that's impressive.

Big-picture totals are helpful, but if you can't come up with the numbers, don't worry. There are other ways to communicate the results you achieve for clients.

Mini case studies are simply one or two paragraphs that describe what you did for a company. You are telling a story in three steps:

- Here was the problem.
- Here's what we did.
- These were the results.

We assisted a national franchising organization facing signifi-cant growth challenges in creating a vivid picture of the future that aligned their leadership and enabled them to implement a strategy for growth resulting in 18 new franchisees in 6 months.

If you have permission from the company, you can use their name and provide details. If not, you can create an anonymous company or a combination of companies and talk about your results with them.

Finally, make sure you don't forget to include *testimonials*.

Ideally, you already have some. Use them. Especially if you can combine a testimonial with a great mini case study.

But if you don't have testimonials yet, or you don't have the right testimonials, try to get some in the next few days. I'd like you to have them before we launch the website that gives out this free report. Keep in mind that testimonials provide the social proof that you can do what you say you can do, so they're extremely important. Although written testimonials are the quickest and easiest to get, if circumstances allow, try to get video testimonials as well. Posting these on your website will play a huge role in building credibility for the services you offer.

The best testimonials are ones that communicate the benefits you offer or address concerns or reasons why someone wouldn't do business with you: "I thought implementing a new software system would be too complex, too time-consuming, and cost a fortune, but . . ."

Tip: The best way to get your clients to give you the kind of testimonials you want is to write them yourself.

Don't worry, this isn't unethical. Here's what you do:

1. Write to your customers or clients and tell them that you are looking for testimonials for a new marketing campaign you're launching. Tell them that if they provide one, you'll gladly link the testimonial to their website, which will increase their visibility on the Internet. (It's

always good to get in the habit of including benefits when
you're asking someone for a favor.)

2. Tell them you've provided a sample testimonial that
   covers the points you'd love for them to make but that
   they can edit it as much as they wish.
3. Include the sample testimonial.
4. Tell them when you need a response. (Keep the deadline
   short so that they don't procrastinate and put it into the
   pile of "things to do later.")

Most of the time they'll tell you to use what you sent, exactly
the way you wrote it.

The All-Important "Call to Action"

Remember, marketing is a series of steps. At each one we want
to motivate the prospect to advance to the next level. Thus, we
want to make sure we wrap up with what we want the reader to
do once they've finished the report. This is your *Call to Action*.
In most cases, we want people to pick up the phone and speak
with you. You may call this your "free consultation" or "compli-
mentary strategy session," but the goal is to get the phone
ringing.

It's important in this section to outline the benefits of what
goes on during this call. Unfortunately, simply asking people to
call for the free session isn't enough. One trick that I've found
effective is to list the types of questions people typically ask.
Don't give the answers, just the questions. This feeds the desire
for them to learn the answers by calling you. I sometimes also
use language such as, "I guarantee (you'll leave the meeting/
put down the phone) with new information that will help you
address (the particular problem you solve)."

Starting to Write Your Report

Now that you have notes for the sections of your report, it's time to get started actually writing it.

The easiest way to start your opening paragraph is to focus on the problem your prospective clients face. Here's a simple sentence you can use to begin your free report (this also works great for sales letters): "I know from speaking to other individuals like yourself that many of them are worried about_____."

Another approach is to open with a story. It could be a case study that starts off as simply as this: "Allen Jones had a problem."

A good story can have an impact on your readers and what they remember about your report.

My company once did a follow-up survey on two different free reports. The companies offering these reports were in the human resources consulting field, though each offered different services. Our goal was to see how many of the reports actually were read and what people remembered after reading them.

The first report was about seven mistakes executives commonly make in performance reviews. We talked to 195 people. Of those, 23 read the report cover to cover, and another 60% started, but never finished.

Then we tried to ascertain how much of the information readers of the full report retained. We hoped that a majority of readers would have remembered at least four items. Seventy-five percent of the readers remembered one item, but no one remembered more than that. (That one item was highly guessable, so those results are a bit dubious.)

Next we reached out to the people who downloaded the second report. The report's message focused on mistakes executives made training and acclimating new employees. We managed to speak to 101 people. When we asked a series of similar "recall" questions, an impressive 65% could name three or more of the correct answers.

Obviously the second report resonated to a far greater extent than the first one. And what's more, the message from the second report was remembered and retained.

Although both reports were written for an audience of human resources directors, there was one significant difference between the two reports. The first only conveyed facts. The other told a story. So there's a strong argument to be made to start your report with a story.

Here are some examples:

- Marshall Coltrain gazed at the shattered window from which protruded a branch that had, until recently, housed his eight-year-old daughter's swing. With a sigh of frustration and fear, he contemplated the wreckage and mused, "Damn, I hope this is covered." (Insurance free report)
- Although the casual observer would never guess, Vice President of Operations Dan Townsend emerged from his staff meeting in a rage. "What is wrong with these people? They can't get along for two minutes without adult supervision. There's no way I'll get the process control system implemented by July if this back-biting and petty sniping doesn't come to a halt. I wish I could just fire the lot of them." (Leadership free report)
- Fran Sullivan wondered why, with the economy so poor, was it so difficult to recruit a top-flight sales rep? When she started the search nine weeks ago, she felt confident that she would have it wrapped up by now. Unfortunately, nothing could be further from the truth. (Recruitment firm free report)

Add Content to Each Component

Now that you've started, fill out each section from the notes you've been making. Write anywhere from a paragraph to a page about each step. After you've completed the first draft, take a one-hour break (no more, no less). Then come back and read what you've written. Add examples where you think they might be helpful. Finally, read the report out loud. Does it sound like you speaking? If so, it's probably pretty good. If it bogs you down as you're reading or you find yourself wondering "What's the point?" that's a heads-up that you need a bit more editing.

Visual Impact

I've had reports that were simply Word documents that I saved as a PDF, and they've worked fine. In the interest of getting your campaign completed in five days, this may be all you have time for. Remember, your prospects are primarily interested in the content, not the packaging. However, if you have time (or at a later date), you'll want to make your report look even more professional by adding pictures or graphics or having it designed professionally.

My favorite place to get photos, because they offer a great selection at an inexpensive price, is 123rf.com. You can also use istockphoto.com.

If you'd like a little help from a graphic designer to really spruce up your report, you can hire one inexpensively at Guru .com or Elance.com. You might even be able to find someone who will quickly put your report together with images at Fiverr. com, where everyone works for five dollars. I'll talk in more detail later about how to effectively outsource various components of the marketing system, including adding these professional touches to your free report.

But remember, your goal for today is to get your report written. You can add professional flourishes later, after this week is up.

Okay, now it's time for you to get to work. This is probably the most challenging day since it involves the greatest amount of writing. However, if you follow the structure and outline I've provided, I have every confidence in you that you can complete this today.

Tomorrow, we're going to develop the content for a simple website that will motivate your visitors to give you their email address and download the report you just wrote. I promise to make it easy—with examples, templates, and ways to hire someone inexpensively to do the technical stuff. See you tomorrow.

Chapter Three

DAY THREE:
Create a Website for Your Free Offer

NOW THAT YOU'VE GOT your free report done, you need a place where people can go to get it. That's a page on your website, and today you're going to write everything that goes on it. Whether you already have an existing website or not, I'm going to walk you through all the steps. Once you've completed this, then it's simply a matter of sending it to a web page designer (I'll show you how to find an excellent one) who will make it look great and make it live on the Internet for around $75–$100.

You have a couple of options for where this page appears on your website, so let's quickly review your choices.

The page that promotes your free offer could be the landing page, otherwise known as the home page, on your existing website. Alternatively, it might be a dedicated page that resides within your site. If you don't have a website, what we're going to develop today can serve as the home page for your new site.

Since the primary purpose of this page is to encourage visitors to opt in for the free report, the focus needs to be on the specific issues or problems your report covers. Over time you may create separate pages, each focusing on a specific problem and each one offering a unique free report. For example, a cosmetic surgeon might have individual pages about the top issues his potential clients search for. One for Botox, another for face-lifts, a page for eye surgery, and one dedicated to cosmetic fillers. This laser-focused approach ensures that visitors feel they have come to the right place regarding their specific needs.

My personal recommendation is that your free offer be promoted heavily on your website's main landing page. This is the model I follow. If you visit GentleRainMarketing.com you'll notice that the call to action in my video is to download the free report. This is different from a more traditional approach in which the landing page focuses primarily on communicating what the company does. My personal belief is that if we do not get our visitors to opt in when they come to the site, we lose control of our ability to follow up with them. (It's a wee bit hard to send ongoing messages to people if they don't tell us who they are.) That's the reason why I have an offer on my landing page and then additional free offers on most of the pages that are deeper in the site. We'll discuss later how to create a blog so that it too can play a key role in adding subscribers to your list.

Remember, the overwhelming percentage of paying clients will come from your subscriber list rather than first-time visitors to your site. The more you sell high-value products or services, the more this is true. A relationship needs to be in place *before* prospects are likely to become paying clients. Thus, always keep in mind that mission #1 is to get visitors to tell us who they are so we can stay in contact with them.

As you are creating the page to promote your free offer, a reality we have to deal with is that new visitors have a very short attention span. If the copy on the page doesn't immediately convey the message that you focus on their problems, they'll leave. What we're going to work on today is designed to get your visitors interested, keep them engaged, and motivate them to sign up for your free offer.

Some people worry that designing web pages where the primary motivation is to get people to opt in lacks a certain level of professionalism. Rest assured that all sorts of businesses and people, including the President of the United States, use this approach. (You can opt in for his list if you're so inclined at whitehouse.gov.) Assertively asking someone to give us their contact information in exchange for interesting free information isn't inconsistent with a professional image. The key is to have a very specific focus so that your copy reads as if you are speaking directly to your visitor. That's how we build credibility and trust.

Before I share some examples of pages that you can use as templates, let me take a moment to discuss the advantages and disadvantages of having this page be the *only* page on your website.

One-page websites that have the sole purpose of getting people to opt in for free information are often referred to as "squeeze pages." The idea is that since these sites have no links to other pages, they "squeeze" the visitor to make one decision: either opt in for the free information, or leave. They are still popular and can be very effective if you already have a list of people that you are trying to promote an offer to. An example from GentleRain-SalesCloses.com appears on page 66.

However, there are disadvantages. Google hates one-page websites and it's virtually impossible to get one to appear on the first page of search results. Moreover, Google AdWords (their advertising program, which I'll cover in great detail later on) may permanently bar you from advertising if you try to direct your ads to a squeeze page.

However, the design and layout of squeeze pages offer some valuable lessons that you may want to incorporate into the look and feel of your own page. So my recommendation is this:

- If you already have a website, develop the page to promote your free offer as either a new home page for your current site or as an additional page within your site.
- If you don't have a website, create your site using the WordPress platform. I'll explain more about WordPress shortly, but one of its biggest advantages is that it has a built-in blog feature. Why is that important? Each time you write a blog post, your site will grow by an additional page. Thus, even if your site only consists of the one page you're doing today, it will quickly grow as you add blog posts. By following this advice you shouldn't run into any problems with Google.

Examples of Lead Capture Pages

Let's look at some examples of these:

The site at http://bit.ly/11YM20c is aimed at individuals who want to get more publicity for their business. In this case, instead of a free report, the site promotes a free teleseminar, which is designed to attract authors and entrepreneurs to a one-year training program called Quantum Leap.

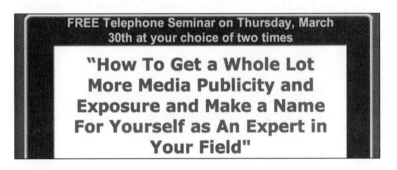

Here's what is interesting about it:

1. The headline is "How To Get a Whole Lot More Media Publicity and Exposure and Make a Name For Yourself as an Expert in Your Field."

    Those quotation marks are actually part of the headline. Many people say that adding quotation marks to a headline increases your opt-ins.

    The headline is also written in a very conversational manner. Notice the use of the phrase "A Whole Lot More." It's simple and it's the way people talk.

    You don't have to use over-the-top terms such as "skyrocket" or "geometrically increase" to convince people to sign up for your free offer. My general rule is that if you would be uncomfortable saying the sentence to someone, it's probably pushing the boundaries of hyperbole.

2. Notice that the copy is written in letter format. If you look at the screenshot below, you'll notice that it only takes seven lines to get to the bullet points. This is important. You want to draw your visitor into the site quickly, and this is a great example of doing just that.

3. The bullet points arouse curiosity. There are lots of teasers that talk about "five proven ways," "what to send instead," and "some tricks" that make you want to know what the tricks and the proven ways are.

4. The bullet points also leverage a potential concern: "What you should never wear on a TV show." Remember the levers of motivation: pain, fear, and gain. This bullet point plays to the fear that you might embarrass yourself by wearing the wrong outfit on TV. It's always good to have your bullet points be a mix of appeals to the different levers.

5. Notice that one bullet point is done in boldface type, so it stands out. The name in boldface is *Good Morning America*, which is a show this audience would love to be on. This bullet point, about dramatically increasing your chances to get on the show, is arguably the most important one in the series. The eye will naturally gravitate to a bullet point in bold. This is a very effective trick, but be careful not to overuse it.

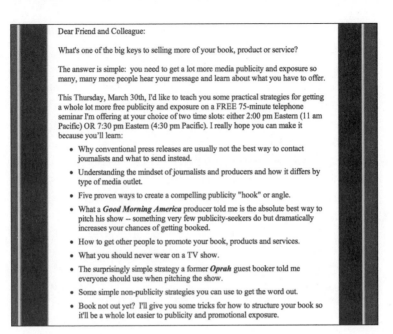

Dear Friend and Colleague:

What's one of the big keys to selling more of your book, product or service?

The answer is simple: you need to get a lot more media publicity and exposure so many, many more people hear your message and learn about what you have to offer.

This Thursday, March 30th, I'd like to teach you some practical strategies for getting a whole lot more free publicity and exposure on a FREE 75-minute telephone seminar I'm offering at your choice of two time slots: either 2:00 pm Eastern (11 am Pacific) OR 7:30 pm Eastern (4:30 pm Pacific). I really hope you can make it because you'll learn:

- Why conventional press releases are usually not the best way to contact journalists and what to send instead.
- Understanding the mindset of journalists and producers and how it differs by type of media outlet.
- Five proven ways to create a compelling publicity "hook" or angle.
- What a *Good Morning America* producer told me is the absolute best way to pitch his show -- something very few publicity-seekers do but dramatically increases your chances of getting booked.
- How to get other people to promote your book, products and services.
- What you should never wear on a TV show.
- The surprisingly simple strategy a former *Oprah* guest booker told me everyone should use when pitching the show.
- Some simple non-publicity strategies you can use to get the word out.
- Book not out yet? I'll give you some tricks for how to structure your book so it'll be a whole lot easier to publicity and promotional exposure.

The bullet points on this page are a lesson in good sales copy. In fact, several would make great fill-in-the-blanks that could apply to most any business.

- Why _____ (is/are) not always the best way to _____ and what to _____ instead. (*Why sending résumés is not always the best way to get a job, and what to do instead/Why chiropractors are not always the best way to deal with your back problems, and what to do instead/Why listing your house with a Realtor is not always the best way to sell a house, and what to do instead.*)
- Five proven ways to _____ (*get a raise even within your first six months on the job/earn enough to retire on by 55/speed up your computer*).

- What you should never _____ (*say on a job interview/invest in during a bad economy/do during a negotiation*).
- Three keys to _____ (*a pain-free back/marketing to the affluent/selling more lifetime memberships*).

Another site that's worth looking at is doubleyourdating.com. This site has led to millions of dollars' worth of business for Eben Pagan and catapulted him to fame within the Internet community. (Pagan writes under the pseudonym David DeAngelo for this site.)

Here are some things worth noticing about this site:

1. The banner includes the tagline "Attraction isn't a choice." This pairs well with the actual headline, whether you read it before the headline or after it.
2. The headline, "Learn Secrets Most Men Will Never Know About Women and Dating," is perfect for the niche market he is after: men who are either not getting

enough dates or not getting to date the types of women they'd like to.

This headline formula has been successfully used by a wide variety of companies in many different fields.

"Learn Secrets Most _____ Will Never Know About _____" (*Learn Secrets Most **Employees** Will Never Know About **Getting a Promotion**/Learn Secrets Most **Investors** Will Never Know About **Short Sales**/ Learn Secrets Most **Homeowners** Will Never Know About **Increasing the Value of Their Home by Spending Less than $1000**).

A highly effective variation on this headline is: "Learn Secrets Most _____ Will Never *Tell You* About _____."

3. There's both a video and a set of bullet points on the site. Some visitors are more likely to watch, others are more likely to read. This site serves both types. The video discusses the bullet points and reiterates their benefits. By the way, if you want to add a video to your site, I've got a script you can use as a model later on when we dive deeper into using video to promote your business.

4. There's a big red arrow that points to the attractively designed opt-in box. You will want to use arrows for your site to accomplish the same task. This big, curvy arrow shown here is just right for a dating site. This is something you may want to outsource to a website designer if you're like me and have zero technical skills. You won't have to pay more than $25–$50 for a great visual effect.

Take a closer look at the opt-in box. It has some of the most compelling copy on the page. First of all, the report has a great title: "Exclusive Report: The 10 Most Dangerous Mistakes Men Make With Women." I particularly like the last bullet point in the box: "Articles and newsletters to help you date the kind of women you've always wanted." This final phrase, "date the kind of woman you've always wanted," is the most powerful hook in the series, and he places it just above the box where he asks for your name. This is the point at which a lot of people might feel reluctant to give their contact information, so this powerful bullet point is placed there to move them over the edge.

There's a lot for you to consider modeling from just these two sites. If you want to see lots of examples of highly effective squeeze pages, head over to ClickBank.com. This is the hub from which many information marketers launch their products. While some of the sites are admittedly cheesy, there are a lot of extremely good examples as well. As an exercise I suggest that you spend 15 minutes perusing the various pages. When your eye catches a particular headline or bullet point, make a note to yourself. Many of us market to clients who are not terribly dissimilar from us. What engages you is likely to also intrigue your niche market.

Now it's your turn to create the text that goes on your web page. You'll be pleasantly surprised at how easy this will be.

Your Headline

Let's start at the top—with your headline.

The overarching mission is to get visitors to opt in, so you want to keep your message simple, yet highly engaging.

Remember, the headline is where you tell your prospects, "Here's the pain I can solve for you or the benefit I can give you." It's arguably the most important part of the page because if we don't hook them with the headline it's unlikely that they'll read the rest of the copy, and our chances of getting them to opt in are significantly reduced. (In some cases, if you create a really great headline, you may get lots of new subscribers who sign up just based on that.)

If your free report has a great title, you may be able to simply use that. For example, let's say your free offer is called "7 Secrets to Buying Great Homes for Bargain Prices in Any Real Estate Market." That would also make a great headline for the top of the page.

You could add one additional word and create a slightly more powerful headline by saying: "**FREE:** 7 Secrets to Buying Great Homes for Bargain Prices in Any Real Estate Market."

Alternatively, you may want to look at some of the other headline templates we covered in the last chapter and create something new. Sometimes I come up with a few different headlines during the process of writing a free report. The ones I don't use are often repurposed on the website or as bullet points.

Bullet Points That Sell

After your headline, you will need a transition sentence to lead to your bullet points. Here, simple often works best. Just say "In this free report you'll discover," and follow that with a colon.

Easy.

Next come your bullet points. You will want between 4 and 12 of them. Obviously, as with any list of items, some will be more important or compelling than others. Here's a trick to help you decide what order to list them in: Your two strongest points should come first, but your third-strongest bullet should be the last one. Research shows that the eye tends to read the top two bullets and then jumps down to the last one.

There are two things you want to accomplish with each bullet point:

1. Arouse the reader's curiosity about what it is you are going to share with them. For example, the real estate report we mentioned could have a bullet point about "3 secrets to finding undervalued properties that have the

best chance of doubling or tripling their value." It makes you wonder what the secrets are.

2. Convey the benefit they are going to receive or the pain they will avoid by knowing this: "How to avoid paying thousands of dollars in real estate commissions with this simple technique."

Curiosity plus Fear, Pain, or Gain is the winning formula for writing bullet points.

Writing Down the Benefits

Before you work on your bullet points, I suggest that you write down a list of the main benefits people will get from reading your free report. These may be the same benefits you wrote down yesterday, or they may be slightly different because you're talking about your report and not your complete service or product.

Some of the benefits might include:

- Save money
- Make money
- Save time
- Avoid difficulties or confusion
- Accomplish a goal
- Be more effective
- Get more done
- Improve the quality or value of their experience

Next, write down the pain or fears they will avoid by learning the information you are conveying. These might include:

- Wasting money
- Wasting an opportunity

- Wasting time
- Making bad decisions
- Experiencing something as more frustrating than it needs to be
- Getting ripped off
- Being embarrassed

Creating Your Bullet Points

Now that you've written down the basic pains, fears, and gains your free report focuses on, it's time to create your bullet points. Here are some more fill-in-the-blank templates with examples:

- How to (**your top benefit**) in as little as (**number of minutes, hours, days, or months**), even if (**whatever they fear will stand in their way—this can be a verb or a noun**). EXAMPLES: *How to **get a sales job** in as little as **60 days** even if **you have no sales experience**; How to **get on national television** in as little as **five days** even if **no one's ever heard of you**; How to **get three new clients** in as little as **30 days** even if **you hate selling**.*
- The one _____ mistake 90% of (**your niche audience**) make that will lead to (**their biggest fear**) and how to avoid it. EXAMPLES: *The one **warm-up** mistake 90% of **amateur athletes** make that will **lead to injuries** and how to avoid it; The one **investing mistake** that 90% of **seniors** make that will lead to **higher taxes for their heirs** and how to avoid it; The one **mental** mistake 90% of **professional sales people** make that will **keep them from closing really big sales** and how to avoid it.*
- The little-known tactic that will (**benefit**) that most (**experts in your field or your competition**) haven't even heard of. EXAMPLES: *The little-known tactic that will **get***

you a book deal for $100,000 that most literary agents haven't even heard of; *The little-known tactic that will save you an extra 8% on your taxes* that most **accountants** haven't even heard of; *The little-known tactic that will increase your salary by 11%* that most **career coaches** haven't even heard of.

- How to make sure you won't get ripped off by (**fake, lousy, or immoral experts or products**) and (**big fear**). EXAMPLES: *How to make sure you won't be ripped off by **a dishonest website that sells fake perfumes as name brands**; How to make sure you won't be ripped off by **a defense attorney who is more interested in taking your money than winning your case**; How to make sure you're not ripped off by **a financial planner who is more interested in big commissions than in making the most money for you.***

Here are the bullet points I use for my copywriting course:

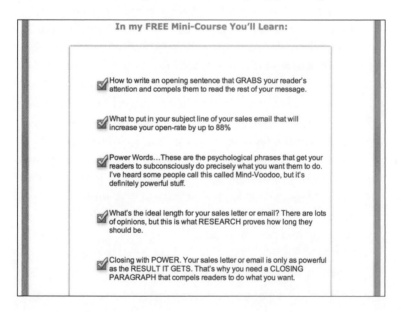

In my FREE Mini-Course You'll Learn:

☑ How to write an opening sentence that GRABS your reader's attention and compels them to read the rest of your message.

☑ What to put in your subject line of your sales email that will increase your open-rate by up to 88%

☑ Power Words...These are the psychological phrases that get your readers to subconsciously do precisely what you want them to do. I've heard some people call this called Mind-Voodoo, but it's definitely powerful stuff.

☑ What's the ideal length for your sales letter or email? There are lots of opinions, but this is what RESEARCH proves how long they should be.

☑ Closing with POWER. Your sales letter or email is only as powerful as the RESULT IT GETS. That's why you need a CLOSING PARAGRAPH that compels readers to do what you want.

Now it's your turn. Write down 4–12 bullet points that will make the prospects who come to your microsite ready to sign up for your free offer. Feel free to adapt any of the bullet points in the templates and the examples.

The Opt-In Box

Your next step is to create the box where your prospects give you their email address and other contact information.

Here are some factors to consider when creating your opt-in box. As common sense would dictate, the less information you ask for, the greater the percentage of people who will sign up for your offer. If you ask for just an email address, you will have the greatest number of people opting in.

So you should just ask for their email address, right?

Not necessarily.

The more information you require, the higher the quality of the prospect, but smaller the number of opt-ins. Also, the more information you have, the more you can do with it. If you ask for their name, you can personalize their emails. Their address lets you send them direct mail, and their phone number enables you to call them. However, the numbers of people willing to opt in will dwindle with each piece of data you request.

So how do you decide on how much information to ask for? One solution is to use a two-step process. First, ask people to simply give you their name and email. When they hit the "Submit" button, you can send them to a second page that shows your version of this screenshot:

Thank You for Requesting My Free Report,
I am sure you will find it of interest. Watch your inbox for an email from me which will contain a link to immediately download it.

I also have some additional information that I would like to send you by MAIL. Quite frankly this information will only be of interest to the 5% of my readers who sincerely want to IMPLEMENT a highly effective marketing system that will bring them as many new clients as their business can handle. If that's you please fill out the information below and I'll rush the information out to you in today's mail. Thank you.

Name*   Title*

Daytime Telephone*   Company*

Address*   Suite/Building/Apartment

City*   State   Zip*
                         choose ▲▼

Country

To be perfectly honest, the information I send them in the mail is little more than a sales letter for our services, but the conversion percentage on those who complete the second form is considerably higher than for those who only provide their name and email address.

Another option is to just ask for name and email when they initially sign up, and then in a subsequent follow-up message tell them that you have additional information you would like to send them by mail.

Some of you may wonder, *Why are you asking for their phone number if you're sending them information in the mail?* It's a valid question, and the truthful answer is that technically I don't need it, but I might want to follow up with them on the phone at some point in the future. What I find interesting is that hardly anyone catches on to this when they're filling out the form. I suggest you give it a try, especially if you want to call prospects as a part of your sales process.

Your website developer can easily set up your opt-in box. (If you don't have one and need great inexpensive talent, go to Appendix A to learn how to hire someone today.) I like arrows that point to the box and find that opt-in percentages increase on pages that use them.

It's good etiquette (and somewhat noticeable by omission) to include a simple statement saying you respect their privacy and will not sell or rent their contact information. This makes prospects feel safe and helps slightly with your opt-in percentages.

An often-overlooked feature is the button they need to click to submit their information. Studies have shown that if you make the words on the button convey an action such as, "Send It to Me" or "Send My Report," there is a higher response rate than if you just use the word "Submit." I find that having my button in a bright contrasting color also helps increase the number of people who take me up on my offers.

Your Thank-You Page

After your prospects click the button to submit their information, you want them to be taken to a thank-you page. As the name would imply, this is where you thank them for opting in to get your report, reiterate that they have made a good decision to do so, and let them know how the information will be coming to them.

For example, you might say:

*Thank you very much for requesting your copy of (**name of report**). I've sent you an email that contains a link to download it. Since Internet traffic can vary, it may take up to 30 minutes for you to receive it, but it's likely already in your inbox as you're* *reading this. One thing that I need for you to do is to make sure my email address, (**your email**), is white-listed, added to your address book, or however you make sure that important emails don't wind up in your spam folder. If for some reason you don't get the email with the link in the next 30 minutes, let me know and I'll send it to you again.*

*Once again, thanks very much for requesting (**name of report**). I truly believe you'll find it extremely valuable.*

The tone of the copy on this thank-you page needs to be sincere, friendly, and conversational. It should convey the message that you are interested in beginning what will hopefully be a mutually rewarding relationship.

I suggest that you send your report via a link in an email rather than letting prospects download it from your thank-you page. The reason is that you'll eliminate someone putting in a bogus email address since he or she has to give you a valid one in order to receive the link.

Other Options for This Web Page

There are two other content options you can use for this page. If you're comfortable with video, it can be extremely effective in bringing in leads for you.

There's also a technique where you share part of your free report before you ask visitors for their email addresses. Let's look at both of these methods in greater detail.

Video Opt-In Page

I've found that video can increase conversion rates significantly. I had one page that did almost 40% better when I changed it from print to video. It also builds trust and credibility faster.

If you want to try video, here's a script you can use.

- *Welcome . . . I'm glad that you're here.*
- *If you're similar to most of my visitors, it's likely that you're frustrated by _____ (a particular challenge or problem).*
- *That's why I created _____(Your Report's Title).*
- *In this report you'll discover _____(your top two or three benefits).*
- *So what I'd like you to do is fill in your name and email address and click on the button below. You'll immediately receive an email that will let you instantly download your free report.*
- *Again, thanks very much for visiting my site. I'm sure you'll find (name of report) a good investment of your time.*

I suggest also paraphrasing your welcoming message in text and putting it below the video. The reason for doing this is that some people have slow Internet connections and they may have to wait a while before the video starts to play. Unfortunately, people are impatient and may leave your page if that happens. By also having the copy available for them to read, you increase the likelihood that these people will stick around and become subscribers.

Reverse Squeeze Pages

Another way to offer your free report is in a format that is referred to as a "reverse squeeze page." Instead of asking people to opt in before they get to see your report, you start off by showing them a few pages before asking for their contact information. This gets them engaged in the story and can be quite effective with certain niche markets.

There are several benefits to this approach:

1. Unlike traditional squeeze page websites, it's Google-friendly, since it immediately has multiple content pages.
2. It has the potential to get higher search engine optimization rankings on Google since it's keyword and content heavy.
3. The total number of opt-ins tends to be lower than with more traditional squeeze page designs, but the conversion-into-client percentages are often higher.
4. You can tweet about it and post it on Facebook with good results. Since the page is mostly copy and therefore seen as educational, it plays well with the mindset of those who are active on social media sites.
5. Creating a reverse squeeze page isn't particularly difficult. If you've got seven secrets to help your niche market solve their problem, provide the first three, then make readers opt in to see the last four. You want the order to be similar to David Letterman's top ten lists; save your best for last.

You can also use this approach even if your report isn't of the "7 Ways to…" variety. Here's how you could approach a report on insurance:

- Page 1: You start to read about little-known gaps in a typical homeowner's insurance coverage that can potentially cost them lots of money.
- Page 2: You learn how this cost John Smith thousands of dollars.
- Page 3: You discover there is hope for you to avoid this mistake by asking three key questions to ensure you have the coverage you need.

- Page 4: This is the opt-in page: "To read the rest of the article and receive future helpful information on this topic, just provide your name and email address."
- Page 5: You continue to read the article and learn that you can make sure there are no gaps in your insurance coverage and actually wind up paying less for insurance than you are paying now.

Making Your Web Page Google-Friendly

As we discussed in the beginning, you want to do what it takes to make sure Google is happy with your website. My recommendation is that if you are starting from scratch, you build your site using WordPress so you can add additional pages with the blog feature. Although the basic HTML one-page sites we reviewed are great from a design standpoint, I would have serious reservations about launching them as a standalone site, unless you are only going to use them as a place you send existing subscribers to.

For example, I have a site, GentleRainSalesLetters.com. It offers a free tutorial about how to write a sales letter, but its real purpose is sell my directory of sales and marketing letters.

This page works extremely well as a place to send subscribers *after* they are on my list. However, because it's a single page and is obviously only designed to capture leads, it doesn't show up in the search listings. Even worse, one time I tried to advertise this site on Google and had my account banned. If I was going to do this site again, I would create it using WordPress so I could add some blog posts and quickly have it become a multipage website. Please don't make the same mistake I did, and remember to create your site using the recommended methods.

Reserving Your URL

One final task for creating your website is to reserve your URL or domain name (that's www.yourwebsiteaddress.com. The terms URL and domain name tend to be used interchangeably). One of the easiest places to get your URL is at GoDaddy.com. They have a very user-friendly process for researching which names are available and for getting you set up. Their customer service is top-notch, so if you need some help, just call the number at the top of the page. Although I'm listing this task last, from a practical perspective you can reserve your URL at any time.

You'll want to consider whether to name your website after your company (BulbrookDrislane.com) or have it be more descriptive of the services you offer. For example, one Australian real estate company offers a relatively new method for retirees to invest in real estate and decided on RetirementOptionsToConsider.com as their website address. Since they also plan on advertising their services on radio, they needed a URL that would be remembered by listeners. Having a descriptive website address is helpful if you plan on promoting your website through methods that are outside the Internet, such as print advertising, radio, or television. Conversely, putting your company name in the address assists with your overall branding efforts.

If at some point you decide that you want to change the URL for your website, it's easy to do so. Simply choose a new address and then "forward" your old URL to the new one. One of the reasons I recommend GoDaddy for registering your website name is that they make this process extremely simple, and if you get lost, their customer service team will walk you through the steps.

You Know What to Do, Now Do It

You now know everything you need to create a page that will get prospects to opt in. Now it's time to create yours. You've got about eight hours to complete this assignment, but if you follow the guidelines as I've discussed them in this chapter, you should be able to get this up and running. (Go to Appendix A on outsourcing to find someone who will take the copy you write today and make it a live website. If you tell them you're on a deadline, it is very likely they'll have your site ready for you when we launch this marketing campaign in two more days.)

What we have accomplished today is setting up a place where prospective clients will come and indicate they have an interest in what you do by requesting your free report. The next step is to put in place an automated drip-marketing messaging system so that we can convert these prospects into paying clients.

Tomorrow we'll create the first seven follow-up messages, and I'll introduce you to the system that will send them out automatically.

See you back here then.

Chapter Four

DAY FOUR:
Develop a Series
of Drip-Marketing Messages

WHILE CREATING YOUR FREE OFFER that motivates prospects to "raise their hands" and express their initial interest is important, keep in mind that it's just the first step. Now it's time to develop your drip-marketing messages that will convert these prospects into paying clients.

These ongoing messages will build trust and credibility and play a significant role in getting you more new clients.

Today you're going to write seven emails that will go out to your prospects during the first eleven days after they sign up for your giveaway. The reason we send a large number of messages over a short period of time is twofold: First, we want to cement the name of your company and the services you offer in their minds. Second, since the prospects have just requested the free information, we know that they have a strong interest in solving a particular problem. Sending a rapid series of messages enables us to strike while the proverbial iron is hot.

I'll show you exactly what to do and say. I'll also give you ideas for how to continue your correspondence with your prospects in the weeks and months ahead. The reality of attracting new clients is that it often takes a long time to overcome skepticism and resistance. Thus, the more you stay in ongoing contact with your prospects, the greater the likelihood of success.

However, just staying in touch for the sake of staying in touch doesn't provide a huge benefit. Our goal with these messages is to give our readers a sense of both our expertise and our personality. We want them to believe that we know what we are talking about *and* that we would be a pleasure to work with. That's why both content and tone are important when preparing these messages. You'll get a sense for this in greater detail as I walk you through the development of your customized stay-in-touch emails.

One overarching goal with our messages is to be helpful whenever possible. Andre Chaperon of AutoResponderMadness.com says the more you can be helpful to prospective clients, the greater the likelihood that they will become real paying customers. Much the same way as we did with the development of the free report, we want to convey helpful information with the underlying message being, "You really should call me to assist you in solving this problem. I've worked with lots of people like you, and I'm sure I would be helpful." The beauty of the continual drip-marketing sequence is that it conveys this theme without you repetitively having to come out and say it.

This marketing strategy has been effective for Andre. "The end result," he says, "is that I create a crowd of followers that will buy my materials over and over again, because I have already earned their trust."

How to Use Autoresponders

The system you will use for actually sending out these messages is called an autoresponder. For those of you who are new to autoresponders, let's take a minute to explain what they are and how you'll use them.

An autoresponder system is primarily a database of contact information. When people fill out the form to get your free report, that information goes into a database. An autoresponder system creates the forms, collects the information, and enables you to send out sequences of email messages. There are a lot of companies that provide this service (I'll give you my personal recommendations in a moment), and they are very inexpensive.

There are a few rules about autoresponder services that you should be aware of. In a somewhat futile attempt to reduce unsolicited spam emails, the CAN-SPAM law was enacted. All of the large autoresponder services strictly follow this law. How this impacts us is that in order to send out our email messages, people have to first opt in by signing up for your free report. Thus, if you have a list of email addresses that you either bought or have been collecting over the years, you first have to send them an email requesting that they sign up for your free offer. Only then can you send them the automated drip-marketing messages I'm going to be discussing in this chapter. (There is a bit of leeway to this rule; if you have a handful of names that you want to manually enter into your autoresponder service, that is usually fine. However, as a general rule, remember that everyone needs to give you permission before you send them emails. That "permission" is granted when they opt in for your free report.)

Let's talk about the two types of messages you can send out from your autoresponder service: timed and broadcast.

Timed messages are emails that are sent out based on the number of days that have elapsed since a person initially signed up for your free report. You might set up a schedule so that immediately after your report is requested, your readers get "thank you" emails. Then one day later, email message #2 goes out asking them if they have any questions. Two days after that, they get email #3, then another email every two days after that, and so on. Just keep in mind that the sequence starts with the day prospects initially sign up for the free report. Thus, if I sign up for the report on Monday, I'll get email message #1 that day and email message #2 on Tuesday. If you sign up for the free report on Wednesday, you'll get email message #1 the same day and email message #2 on Thursday.

After the initial sequence you'll develop today is completed, you can add emails that go out whenever you want for a year or even longer. That's obviously more than you can accomplish today, but it's a goal to have in mind.

My wife, Marian, is a clinical hypnotherapist and success coach (MarianMassie.com). When I set up her autoresponder sequence, we bit the proverbial bullet and created two years of timed messages that go out approximately every ten days. At the end of two years, we just reschedule the person back to day #1 on the assumption that no one remembers an email they got two years ago. Talk about a "set it and forget it" approach to staying in touch!

You can choose any frequency you desire for your timed email sequence. I like a schedule in which we send out the initial messages rather frequently and then segue into longer intervals between messages. Personally, I'm in touch with my list of subscribers every week, and I wouldn't recommend that you let more than two weeks go by without connecting.

Not surprisingly, you'll need to make sure that the messages in a timed series address issues that are "evergreen" or "timeless." By this I mean you want to focus on client problems that were problems yesterday, are problems today, and are likely to be problems for the foreseeable future.

If you're a financial planner, an evergreen topic might be the fear of running out of money during retirement. That's a concern that people have had (and will have) forever. Conversely, you wouldn't want to mention the Dow Jones Industrial Average hitting a new high since that reference will quickly become dated.

Although timed messages are what you will be working on today, I want to spend just a minute talking about broadcast messages since these will become important once you have a number of people who have opted in for your free offer.

As the name "broadcast message" would imply, these are messages that are sent to everyone in your database at the same time. The advantage of a broadcast message is that it can be timely. This is where you can mention the Dow Jones reaching a new high or something else that is currently in the news. The immediacy of broadcast messages makes them stand out amid all the emails your prospective client receives on a typical day. They're a powerful tool, but they're something that will only be worth doing after your list of opt-in subscribers is greater than 100.

Your Seven Email Messages

I'm about to give you templates for each of the seven emails you will be sending out. Feel free to adapt them to your personal voice. Try, though, to keep the topic of each email similar to what I'm suggesting.

One of the advantages of using an autoresponder is that the software lets you address each of your prospects by name. (I'm going to walk you through the steps for how to load these messages into your autoresponder service shortly. For the purposes of developing these messages, you can just do them in a Word document and then cut and paste them into the system.) When we send out the messages using the autoresponder, each message will be personalized to the recipient. For example, if you're a Realtor, instead of writing "Hi Homeowner," the code in the system will automatically input the first names of all your prospects. Thus, Ron gets a message that says, "Hi Ron."

Your Seven-Letter Sequence

Here's the sequence I recommend you use. This will immediately put you on the path to building a strong relationship with your reader. The themes for the seven emails are as follows:

Message 1: Send the link so the recipient can download your free report.

Message 2: A quick follow-up message to make sure they received email #1. Make sure you include the link to access the free information again.

Message 3: Ask them if they found a specific piece of information in your free offer helpful. This is a highly effective way to motivate those who have not yet read the report to do so. This is also a great opportunity to ask for some feedback.

Message 4: Tell a story about how someone is using the advice you shared. You don't need to mention a specific name or company; the idea is to communicate that others who are similar to the reader solved their problems by following your advice.

Message 5: Offer an additional tip or idea that was not included in the report.

Message 6: Answer a question that a client asked you recently. (If you don't have clients yet, you can just think of a question that prospective clients would likely ask.)

Message 7: Offer a free 30-minute consultation.

Okay, let's get started on developing your sequence of messages.

Message #1

Remember, in an autoresponder system, "days" refers to the length of time that has passed since a prospect signed up to get your free offer. The first email in the sequence is sent immediately, on what is referred to as "Day 0."

The subject line of your first email: "Here's the (**Title or Your Subject Matter**) Report You Requested."

Hi (**First name**),

I just wanted to write and introduce myself, and thank you for requesting (**Your Report's Title**).

You can get your copy by clicking here:

(**the link to where prospects can download your report**).

I'm (**your name**), and I've spent the last several years helping (**people in your niche**) get (**results to major problem**).

Now that you're a subscriber, I'm going to send you periodic information and share MANY of the secrets I've learned about how to (**achieve results your niche desires**).

By the way, if you ever want to stop receiving my newsletters, just click the link at the bottom and unsubscribe. Naturally, I'll NEVER share your email or other information with anyone.

Thanks for requesting the report and I look forward to helping you (**benefit you offer**).

Again, the link to download the free report is here: (**link to report**).

Thanks,

(**Your first name**)

Message #2

This message will go out on what the autoresponder calls Day 1, which is one day after your prospect signs up. Here's a simple template:

The subject line for this email could be "Quick Follow-up."

> Hi (**First name**),
>
> (**Your name**) here. I just wanted to check to make sure you successfully downloaded the free report you requested, (**Your Report's Title**). If for some reason it didn't make it to you, no worries, the link to download it again is here: (**link**).
>
> For over the past (**number of years**), I've assisted individuals like you in solving (**type of problem**). I offer some great insights into how others are solving these problems in the report and can virtually guarantee you'll put it down with some great ideas you can begin to implement immediately.
>
> Thanks, and I'll talk to you in a couple of days.
>
> All the best,
>
> (**Your first name**)

Message #3

In the third message we're going to focus on a particular section contained in the free report. Thus, the first step is to review what you're sending your subscribers and pick something that you will want to talk about.

It might be a particularly interesting story that you tell in the report—or the one nugget of information that you think is the most relevant to your particular niche audience. That's what you will refer to in this email.

An important point as you're writing this email is to make sure to describe specifically where the nugget can be found.

Here's the template with examples that illustrate the type of information to put in the blanks you will be filling in. This email goes out on Day 3.

The subject line for this email could be "A Quick Question, (First name)."

> Hi (**First name**),
>
> By now I hope you've had the chance to read (**Your Report's Title**).
>
> Many of my readers tell me that the story I shared about (**your story or information**) (*how I helped the woman I was sitting with at my sister's wedding get over a headache by pushing on a pressure point on her hand on p. 4*) was particularly helpful to them.
>
> I'm curious as to what you thought. Did it help you? Is it something you've tried before?
>
> If you wouldn't mind, I'd greatly appreciate some quick feedback on the report. The easiest way to do that is to simply hit "Reply."
>
> Next time, I'll share with you a real-life case example about how others in (**your niche**) (*people who are interested in alternative health*) are using this information to (**solve a particular problem**) (*get over all their aches and pains, particularly in their lower back*).
>
> All the best,
>
> (**Your first name**)

There are a few reasons I include this email in the series. The first is that you are more likely to convert a prospect into a client if they read your report, so this is another way to motivate them to look at it.

Also, anyone who emails you with feedback is beginning to engage with you on a personal level. When a prospect writes back, it's an indication that they are starting to know, like, and trust you. Not surprisingly, these are the people most likely to become your clients.

The last reason why I include this email in the series is that on some occasions the feedback is actually helpful.

If people send you feedback, regardless of whether you agree with it or not, the polite thing to do is acknowledge their comments. At the very least, write back something such as "Thanks for the feedback. I really appreciate your taking the time to share your ideas." You might even add "I really liked your comment about _____." You may also want to offer them a free consultation if they mention a problem or issue they're dealing with.

Message #4

In this message you'll be telling a story about someone who has used the information in your report. Since this is so individualized, it won't be as easy to copy from the template. I've done my best, though, to make it as simple as possible for you. This message goes out on Day 5.

If you don't want to use your customer's real name, you can write "a client of mine, who I'll call Rachel." Using names makes these emails more enjoyable to read and easier to write.

The subject line for this email could be "How (**Name**) (**What He or She Accomplished**)." For example, "How Sarah Made Her First Real Estate Sale" or "How Alice Got Her Kids to Stop Fighting."

Here's how this email might flow:

> Hi (**First name**),
> Here's an interesting story about how (**a person accomplished, fixed, or changed something in his or her life or business**) (*whatever you used in your subject line*).

Let me tell you about a client of mine named _____ (*or who I'll call* _____). (**Name**) is a (**job or some kind of description that applies based on the story you're telling**) (*chiropractor or mother of three toddlers or homeowner in Austin*) who had a problem. Every time she would (**something she wants to accomplish or have happen**), it wouldn't work out. Not only would she not (**accomplish it**), she would (**have something even worse happen**).

As you can imagine, (**Name**) was really frustrated. She didn't know what to do.

Luckily, she discovered (*or I taught her*) (**the information or technique that you're highlighting**) that I talk about in (**name of report**) on page ___.

It didn't take her long to understand the concept, and she was able to start implementing it right away. Soon, (**state what happened**) (*if you can break it down into three progressive successes that's ideal, but if you can't, that's okay, too*). Then (*or because of that*) (**some other positive result that happened**). And then (*or because of that*) (**yet another positive result that happened**). Until finally, (**Name did whatever it was she wanted to do in the first place**) (*make sure you're specific here*). And from then on, she never had a problem with (**whatever her problem was with**) again.

Her success isn't unique, but the key was that she took action. I'd love to hear about the results (or even the problems) you're experiencing as you move forward.

In my next email, I'm going to share something that I think you'll find extremely helpful that I haven't mentioned before.

All my best,

(**Your first name**)

Message #5

This is a message where you will share something that you "forgot" to include in the report. It goes out on Day 7 of your autoresponder series.

If you already have something in mind, skip this next section and start right in with the template.

But if you don't, here are some questions you can ask yourself to come up with a topic:

- What benefit or result do your clients or customers want that you might not have mentioned yet?
- Can you make a list of dos and don'ts?
- What's a big mistake people often make with your topic or product that they need to avoid?
- What success stories do you have that you haven't used yet? Is there one with a lesson you can add that would be helpful to your prospects?

Once you've selected something to write about, take a few minutes to jot down some notes. When you're ready, you can start working with the template below.

Use the subject line "(First name), I forgot to mention this."

Hi (**First name**),

I mentioned in my last email that I was going to tell you something I forgot to include in the report.

I want to share it with you now because I believe it's something you'll find really helpful.

(**Add your item here**).

I was recently asked a very interesting question (**insert question that you develop in the next email here**) and I'll share my thoughts on it with you next time.

Talk soon,

(**Your name**)

Message #6

This message goes out on Day 9 of your autoresponder series.

You'll need to come up with a good question to answer here. Ideally, you want to either show off another benefit that comes from working with you, answer a question that overcomes a typical objection that stops people from working with you, or pick something that adds to your credibility as an expert.

Your subject line on this could be "A question many (**in this niche**) are asking."

Hi (**First name**),

A client asked an interesting question the other day that I thought I'd share with you.

He was having a problem with (**some aspect of your topic**), and he asked me "(**Your question**)?"

That's a good question and one that many people in (**niche**) are concerned about.

Here's the answer I gave him:

(**Your answer**).

What do you think? I'd be interested in your perspective. Just hit "Reply" and share a couple of thoughts.

Next time, I have an interesting offer for you that won't cost you anything and could be the key that helps you (**achieve a specific goal**).

Look for it in two days.

All my best,

(**Your first name**)

Message #7

Congratulations. You are on the last message you need to write today. This one goes out on Day 11 of your autoresponder series and offers a free consultation.

It's important to think about marketing as a sequence. For most service businesses, the next step after your prospects get to know you through your emails and your report is to speak one-on-one with them. The reason we hold off until now is that a certain amount of trust and credibility needs to be established *before* you offer the consultation. After 20 years of testing various sequences, I've found that asking for the consultation in this sequence results in the highest percentage of acceptances.

The subject line on this could be "Of potential interest to some."

Here's your template:

> Hi (**First name**),
>
> Obviously, I don't know how serious you are about (**achieving a particular goal**). I've found that after (**number of years**) working with (**this niche market**) that only a very small percentage are truly committed to (**benefit this niche group wants**).
>
> However, if that's you, I have an offer that won't cost you any money and could be extremely beneficial.
>
> On a very limited basis, I offer complimentary consultations to readers such as you. In this 30-minute session, some of the issues I typically address include:
>
> (**List three questions on topics people might want to talk with you about in the consultation.**)
>
> If this interests you, simply hit "Reply" and put the words "Free Consultation" in the subject line, along with some convenient times, and the best number to reach you.

Thanks, and I look forward to speaking with you soon.
(**Your first name**)

With that, you are done with the writing portion of today's assignment.

Entering Your Messages into the Autoresponder

The next step is to load your messages in your autoresponder. It's quick and easy to do. You can do it yourself or you can ask your Web person to do it and it won't cost you very much.

As I mentioned before, there are many autoresponder services. The one I personally recommend was developed by industry leader 1AutomationWiz. You can sign up for a free 30-day trial at GentleRainAutomation.com. If you use a different autoresponder, follow their instructions, but the process won't be all that different from the steps I'm about to show you.

After you sign up for the free 30-day trial, here's what you will need to do:

1. Start by logging in to GentleRainAutomation.com.
2. Click on the tab for "Email & Marketing" at the top.
3. When the pulldown menu appears, select "Autoresponders."
4. On the top left-hand side, there will be two buttons. Click on the one that says "Create New."

Next, you'll be creating your campaign settings. Only fill in the parts I mention. Skip the ones I don't talk about.

1. Fill in the blank with the name of your campaign, e.g., "Free Gift Newsletter."

2. Click the "On" box next to the heading "Direct Subscribe."

3. In the next two boxes, fill in your name and the email from which you will be sending these newsletters. I highly suggest using a separate email account for this task. As your list grows, you could get a lot of automated replies from the people you're sending to that you don't want cluttering up your business or personal inbox.

4. Next to "Campaign Type," click on the arrow where it says "Select a Type." When the pulldown menu appears, select "Newsletter."

5. Next to "Shareable," click "Yes."

6. Click on the button that says "Save." Then click on the button that says "New Message." Wait for the new screen to appear.

7. Where it says "Days Delay," keep the default selection at zero for your first message. For the next six messages, you will change that number to 1, 3, 5, 7, 9, or 11 as indicated in the previous text.

8. Keep the default selection for "Message Type" as "text" unless you intend to send emails that are formatted in html, in which case, select that.

9. Paste your subject line in the box where the subject line goes and your message body in the box for that.

10. On the bottom of the page, click on "Save as New," then click on the button to the right of it that says "New Message."

11. Your message is now loaded, and you're ready to fill in the next one starting with step 7.

12. Continue until all seven messages are loaded.

Congratulations. You just finished today's task.

Additional Advice

Here's some advice for writing additional emails, or if you're not using the templates, some advice on creating your initial messages.

1. **Write to one person even though your email may be going to dozens, hundreds, or even thousands of people.** Picture someone in your life that resembles your ideal prospect. That's the person you're writing to. Remember that the tone of the message is just as important as the content. Be friendly. Be personable. Be encouraging.

2. **Have a point of view.** You don't have to have everyone agree with you. You're an expert—act like one. Stating your opinion without waffling is key. The biggest danger in marketing services is that you get ignored, which is unfortunately what happens to people who don't have a strong opinion.

3. **Share your stories.** The more you share your personal stories, the more you'll be remembered. There's an old (but true) saying, "People don't remember facts and figures; they remember stories." If you want more referrals, you need people to remember who you are and what you do. That's the power of stories. Also, the goal is to have subscribers who will be readers of your emails, newsletters, and blog posts for years. The ability to tell interesting stories is key to keeping people engaged with you.

4. **Give a preview of your upcoming email at the end of each email you write.** This is a secret borrowed from novelists, who work hard at the end of each chapter to get the reader to keep turning the page. You can do the same

thing with each of your emails. You'll notice that we use
this technique in the template emails.

Ideas for Additional Content

Here are some thoughts you can use to brainstorm ideas for
more emails to your list. Remember, the timed messages have
to be timeless—subjects that are true today and true tomorrow.
Timed message ideas:

- Additional client success stories and case studies
- Your opinion on long-standing controversies in your
  industry
- Tips on saving money and time at what you do (or any
  other tips you can think of)
- More questions that clients or potential clients ask

When it comes to broadcast messages, try to tie your message
to recent events. For example:

- Current industry controversies
- Stories that relate to the news (e.g., using the presidential
  elections as a metaphor for something that happens in
  your industry)
- Tying in to celebrity news related to your industry, or as a
  metaphor
- Messages that relate to national events like the Super Bowl
  or the Oscars
- Emails that relate to holidays
- Taking surveys (use SurveyMonkey.com) and sharing the
  information with your readers
- Links to news stories or blogs about your industry that
  your prospects will find helpful—personalized with your

comments about what you find important about what's being said

Congratulations on coming this far on your One Week Marketing Plan. Tomorrow you're going to write some very short advertisements, buy some inexpensive ads, and start the process of getting actual clients.

Chapter Five

DAY FIVE:
Get Traffic to Your Website

NOW THAT YOU HAVE the free offer, website, and auto-responder sequence completed, your next goal is to drive targeted traffic to your site to download your report. Today is about advertising.

One of the fastest ways to attract new qualified prospects is by using "pay-per-click" (PPC) advertising. Pay-per-click means exactly what it sounds like. The advertiser pays only when someone clicks on their ad. It is probably the best way to get immediate traffic.

When PPC first came out, it was revolutionary. With traditional advertising, you pay for the total number of people who are exposed to your ad, whether they are interested in it or not. If someone sees your ad for a deluxe refrigerator on TV or in a magazine, you have no idea if they want a refrigerator of any kind, let alone a deluxe one. You could pay thousands of dollars for an ad that absolutely no one has an interest in.

PPC, however, doesn't cost you anything when someone passively views your ad. You are only charged when someone takes action by clicking on it, which indicates that they have at least some interest in the topic.

Today I'm going to share with you how to do PPC on Google, Bing, Facebook, and LinkedIn. Your goal is to select one of these, set up an account, and get an ad running.

Where you choose to advertise is up to you. I'll give you some guidelines on the type of prospect you're most likely to attract with each venue. Ideally, as you become successful, I'd encourage you to experiment and advertise on several of these.

We will start with discussing how to advertise on the two main search engines—Google and Bing. With both of these, you advertise by bidding on keywords, which are the words or phrases people type into the search engines when they want to look something up. (I'll explain more about how that works in a moment.) About two-thirds of all searches take place on Google, according to Danny Goodwin of SearchEngineWatch .com. They are the 800-pound gorilla in the Internet advertising world, and for many businesses, they provide a substantial number of new clients.

Bing (which partners with Yahoo, so your ads will show up there, too) has its advantages as well. Some keywords tend to be less expensive on Bing. The reality is that since fewer people search on Bing and Yahoo (28% combined, according to Goodwin), there are fewer advertisers, and you'll tend to get clicks for less money. This may be very appealing if you're on a limited budget.

You can also advertise on many of the social media sites. Facebook is a good place if you market your products or services to consumers or are trying to reach women. LinkedIn is strong when your target market is professionals or if you're in the Business2Business space.

Advertising on the Search Engines

One of the big advantages of advertising on the search engines is immediacy. When someone searches for something using the keywords you've selected, your ad immediately appears. Unlike traditional advertising in general circulation magazines or on radio or television, you know with certainty that this person has at least some interest in your topic. If we do a good job with the design of the ad, we can reel lots of prospects into our marketing system. Finally, advertising on the search engines works for companies offering both products and services, so it's one of the best places to start your lead-generation activities.

Before we dive into developing our advertising campaign, let's take a moment and review precisely what appears when we do a search. We'll use Google in this example; the other search engines are pretty much the same.

There are two kinds of results that show up when someone searches: organic or natural search results and paid advertisements. Three of the ads usually appear at the top of the page (typically with a beige background) and another six to eight run down the right-hand side. The organic or natural search listings appear in the center of the page. In the screenshot on the next page, the top three listings are ads, as are those down the right-hand side. The natural search results begin with Debbie Montgomery's listing as an Atlanta Certified Financial Planner. This probably looks very familiar to you, but you may not have realized the differences among the results that appear.

There are some trade-offs whether you want your website to appear as an ad or as a natural search result. While there is some tendency for people to click more frequently on the natural search results, it is very difficult to get on the first page for many keywords. The process for achieving this is called SEO (search engine optimization), and while it can be effective, it

will typically require a minimum of three months before you see results. I'll discuss SEO and how to implement it a bit later. For the purposes of getting your marketing campaign up and running quickly, I suggest that you focus on PPC7 to get the proverbial ball rolling.

A secret that you might not be aware of is that where your ad appears on the page involves more than just how much you bid for each click. The search engines also take into consideration the percentage of people who click on an ad. Thus, the more your ad is directly relevant to the words people enter into the search engine, the better your position on the page. You may also wind up paying less money than someone whose ad doesn't relate as closely to the search terms. Later in this chapter, I'll show you how to write ads that are likely to get more clicks than those of your competitors.

Choosing Keywords with Google's Help

Your first step to a successful paid search campaign is to select the keywords or keyword phrases you want to advertise for.

When determining your list of keywords, the trick is to think like one of your customers. What would they type into the search box if they were either looking for your type of service or try-ing to solve a particular problem? For example, a lawyer who specializes in estate planning might use "estate planning," "estate planning lawyer," "estate planning attorney," "wills," and "trusts."

Google has a tool called the Google Keyword Planner that can be a huge help when it comes to selecting keywords. It provides additional suggestions for keywords and lets you know how often a keyword is searched for. It also gives you an idea of how competitive it is and how much that keyword costs for each click on Google.

All of these factors will help you decide which four to eight keywords to start advertising with. I would recommend you limit your initial list of keywords to just a handful and then add additional words as time goes on.

To use the keyword tool, you have to go through just the first few steps of creating an account with Google AdWords. Let's do that now. It's easy, takes just a couple of minutes, and won't cost you anything.

Creating a Google AdWords Account

Here's all you need to do to create your account: Go to google .com/adwords and click "Get started" at the top of the page.

On the next page, click on "Get started now." (I know it looks like the same instruction, but it's a different page.)

You'll be asked to either use a Google account if you already have one or create a new Google account by inputting an email address and password. Google will then send an email to verify your account. Click the link in the email that comes; a new browser window will open congratulating you and letting you click to continue.

The page that comes up is about helping you "Create your first campaign." Congratulations. You're on the site where the Google Keyword Planner can be found.

Using the Google Keyword Planner

At the top of the page, select the green tab that says "Tools and Analysis," then on the pulldown menu that appears, click on "Keyword Planner."

On the next page, select "Search for keyword and ad group ideas." As an example, I'm entering the phrases that I mentioned would be useful for an estate planning attorney: "estate planning," "estate planning lawyer," "estate planning attorney," "wills," and "trusts."

The next step is to submit this information by clicking on "Get Ideas."

Your results show up in the middle of the next page.

There are two tabs at the top of this section: "Ad group ideas," which is open by default, and "Keyword ideas," which you need to click on.

For our purposes, all you need to look at is the tab for keyword ideas, so click on that.

Keyword Planner Add ideas to your plan	Your product or service • estate planning				Get ideas	Modify search

Negative keywords ✎	Ad group ideas	Keyword ideas			↗	⬇ Download	Add all (801)

	Search terms		Avg. monthly searches ?	Competition ?	Suggested bid ?	Ad impr. share ?	Add to plan
Date range ? Show avg. monthly searches for: Last 12 months	estate planning	↗	9,900	High	$10.19	0%	»

1 - 1 of 1 keywords ▾ ‹ ›

	Keyword (by relevance)		Avg. monthly searches ?	Competition ?	Suggested bid ?	Ad impr. share ?	Add to plan
Customize your search ? Keyword filters ✎	estate planning checklist	↗	1,300	High	$3.18	0%	»
Keyword options ✎ Show broadly related ideas Hide keywords in my account	estate planning attorney	↗	2,400	High	$12.19	0%	»
Hide keywords in my plan	what is estate planning	↗	720	High	$6.97	0%	»

The first piece of information you'll see is the statistical information for the keywords you typed into the Keyword Planner. You are shown the average monthly searches, how competitive the keyword is, and the average CPC (cost-per-click). There's also a box with two little arrows or greater-than signs that you can click on to choose a keyword as one that you want to select for your campaign.

Edit locations

In what locations do you want your ads to appear?

Targeted locations	Reach ?	Remove all
Canada - country	45,000,000	Remove | Nearby
United States - country	378,000,000	Remove | Nearby
Enter a location to target or exclude.	Advanced search	

For example, a country, city, region, or postal code.

Save   Cancel

☐	Location	Bid adj. ?	+ Clicks ?	Impr. ?	CTR ?	Avg. CPC ?	Cost ?	Avg. Pos. ?	Conv. (1-per-click) ?	Cost / conv. (1-per-click) ?	Conv. rate (1-per-click) ?	View-through conv. ?
☐	Canada	--	0	0	0.00%	$0.00	$0.00	0.0	0	$0.00	0.00%	0
☐	United States	--	0	0	0.00%	$0.00	$0.00	0.0	0	$0.00	0.00%	0
	Total - other locations ?		0	0	0.00%	$0.00	$0.00	0.0	0	$0.00	0.00%	0
	Total		0	0	0.00%	$0.00	$0.00	0.0	0	$0.00	0.00%	0

After Google shows you the data for the keywords that you came up with, they give you suggestions for additional keywords based on what you typed into the Keyword Planner.

For the five estate planning keywords we came up with, Google has 800 additional suggestions. Some of these, like "estate planning software," aren't useful, but some are good ideas. "Irrevocable trust," for example, gets 14,400 clicks per month and only costs $.55 per click. Other terms that show up include "probate attorney," "elder law lawyer," and "testamentary trust" (which is a type of trust you use when you want to leave your assets to someone but don't want them to have access until a certain amount of time elapses, for example, until they are 25).

There are two other things worth noting: Your results will include variations of the term you're searching on. Some of these are tiny but important, such as adding the letter "s" to a word. By adding the plural version of a word like "estate planning attorneys" to the singular "estate planning attorney," you get additional searches and possibly additional clicks. ("Estate planning attorneys" adds another 320 searches per month to the 2,400 for "estate planning attorney.") Adding a location to a search term will give you additional clicks, sometimes at a lower cost. If you have a local business or are targeting a specific geographic area, including the name of the location is something worth doing.

Write down your keywords now. This list will be helpful as you write your actual ad. Let's continue to set up your AdWords campaign.

Building Your Campaign on Google

To continue this process, just go back to the green bar at the top of the page and select the tab that says "Campaigns" on the left-hand side.

When the new page loads, click on "Create your first campaign" and you'll arrive at a page where you can select your campaign settings.

Start by naming your campaign—the default is "Campaign #1." Since you may be adding additional campaigns in the future, it helps to come up with something that will remind you what this campaign is. You might use one of the keyword phrases you came up with previously.

Where it says "Type" underneath that slot, click on the arrow next to "Search and Display Networks." You want to change that setting to "Search Network Only."

Here's why: The search network is made up of Google-based sites. The display network operates on a wide variety of places outside of the traditional search websites. The conversion percentages from these sites usually aren't very good, so I'd advise you to avoid them until you become a more experienced advertiser

Next you need to choose between Google's "Standard Setting" and "All Features." The standard setting keeps things simpler, but allows you fewer choices. One nice component of going with all features is that, under "Advanced settings" it allows you to select what times of day your ad runs, which is called "Ad scheduling." Since my prospective clients are unlikely to be searching the Web at 2:00 A.M., I don't show ads at that time. But your best bet, for now, is to start off with the standard settings until you get more comfortable with AdWords.

Next, where it says "Networks," uncheck the box under "Google Search Networks" that says "Include Search Partners." Once again, these are places like Google Maps and Google

Shopping where your ads may not convert as well, so eliminate them for now.

After that, you get to select the locations where your ad shows. If you click on "Let me choose," you can pick a country, a city, a region, or a zip code.

Edit locations

In what locations do you want your ads to appear?

Targeted locations	Reach ?	Remove all
Canada - country	45,000,000	Remove	Nearby
United States - country	378,000,000	Remove	Nearby

Enter a location to target or exclude.   Advanced search

For example, a country, city, region, or postal code.

[Save]   [Cancel]

	Location	Bid adj. ?	+ Clicks ?	Impr. ?	CTR ?	Avg. CPC ?	Cost ?	Avg. Pos. ?	Conv. (1-per-click) ?	Cost / conv. (1-per-click) ?	Conv. rate (1-per-click) ?	View-through conv. ?
☐	Canada	--	0	0	0.00%	$0.00	$0.00	0.0	0	$0.00	0.00%	0
☐	United States	--	0	0	0.00%	$0.00	$0.00	0.0	0	$0.00	0.00%	0
	Total - other locations ?		0	0	0.00%	$0.00	$0.00	0.0	0	$0.00	0.00%	0
	Total		0	0	0.00%	$0.00	$0.00	0.0	0	$0.00	0.00%	0

If you enter a local area, Google offers you a pulldown menu with a number of options to choose from. For Albany, New York, for example, you can choose from the city itself, the 19th and 20th Congressional Districts, and the Albany-Schenectady-Troy region.

Your next decision is about how much you bid. Google's default is "AdWords will set my bids to help maximize clicks within my target budget." Keep that in place rather than choosing to set your bids by hand. They do a good job, and until you get more experience, let Google do it for you.

The box that follows is where you input your daily budget. Ideally you want to spend as much as you can, but $10 per day will be enough to get you started depending on which keywords you're using. One of the beautiful things about PPC advertising (regardless of whether it's on Google, Bing, or elsewhere) is that you completely control how much you spend. You can adjust it up or down in seconds.

After that, Google offers you the chance to extend your ads with your phone number and location. Let's start simply and skip this. Just click on "Save and Continue."

The page that comes up after that lets you name your ad group and write your ad.

Your Ad Group and Your Quality Score

Google's default setting for the name of your ad group is "Ad Group #1." Replace that and name your ad group something that reflects the keywords in it. For instance, in the example with the estate planning lawyer, the ad group name could be "Estate Planning." The keywords could be anything with estate planning in it: "estate planning," "estate planning lawyer," "estate planning attorney," "Albany estate planning," etc.

Keep in mind that Google issues a quality score for each keyword. One of the things Google measures to create this quality score is how relevant your keyword is to your ads. For your estate planning ad group, the ads should contain the words "estate planning" for a good quality score.

For that reason, the keywords about trusts ("irrevocable trust" and "testamentary trust") would be more effective in a second ad group. This way you could slightly modify your ad for this group and make sure it includes the word "trusts."

The reason Google issues a quality score is that they want their users to easily find what they are specifically searching for. Here's how they describe what they want on their website: "Suppose Sam is looking for a pair of striped socks. And let's say you own a website that specializes in socks. Wouldn't it be great if Sam types 'striped socks' into Google search, sees your ad about striped socks, clicks your ad, and then lands on your web page where he buys some spiffy new striped socks?"

The other element Google looks at for your quality score, besides the quality of your landing page, is how successful you are in getting people to click on your ads. There's a statistic that is commonly used by all the PPC programs called click-through rate (CTR). The CTR is the number of people who click on your ad divided by the number of times your ad was shown. If your ad is shown 100 times and 5 people click on it, your CTR would be 5/100, or 5%. If your ad is shown 1,000 times and 5 people click on it, your CTR would be .5%.

I will show you how to write ads that achieve a strong CTR in just a moment.

A high quality score means Google feels secure your ad and website are giving people what they are looking for when they search using the keyword you've selected. They reward that with lower CPCs for your keywords and better positions for your ads. Those benefits are worth having and can ultimately bring you more clients for less money.

Writing Your Ad

Now it's time to write your ad. You will be surprised at how easy this is.

Whether you're planning on advertising on Google or Bing, the ad formats are almost identical. Both give you a 25-character headline. You get 70 characters from Google for the body of your ad and 71 from Bing. Google splits your 70 characters into two even 35-character lines. (Bing gives you one line and will perform the split automatically.) You also receive 35 characters from each company for the URL (website address) that gets displayed in the ad.

It's important to note that characters include spaces as well as all typed marks.

When you write your ad, there are three things you should keep in mind:

1. **Include one of your keywords in the title line.** People find you because they searched for a particular keyword. They feel more comfortable clicking when your headline has the word they were searching for. It also helps with your quality score, as I just mentioned. This isn't absolutely necessary, but it can reduce your costs.

2. **Focus on benefits and forget about features.** You have 95 total characters to convince people to click. That's two-thirds of a tweet. You don't have the real estate to even mention a feature. People will choose your ad if they believe your free offer will give them something that's important to them. For example, "personal injury attorney" is one of the most expensive keyword phrases at an average cost of $47 per click. These firms can't afford not to have their ads convert so they make compelling offers such as "Find out how much your case may be worth." The more you appeal to the basic question that is running through the prospect's mind, the more effective the ad will be. Thus a Realtor who offers a free report on recent sales in a particular neighborhood might use "Find out how much your house is worth" in her ad.

3. **Use Title Case.** Title case is simply Capital Letters At The Beginning Of Each Word. Your CTR will go up just by using this technique. It makes your whole ad look like a headline, so it grabs the viewer's eye more than ads that are mostly in lower case.

Let's continue with the example of the estate planning attorney so you can see how Google AdWords works for a whole campaign. Let's say our free report is "7 Secrets for Lowering Your Estate Planning Costs As Well As the Inheritance Taxes for Your Loved Ones." Our pretend company is Cortiner Legal and we're based in Albany, New York.

Our first step is to write the headline for our ad. The purpose of a headline, even this very short 25-character one, is to grab people's attention—at least enough to get them to read the next line. We want our keyword phrase of "estate planning" to be included in the headline, since that is what people will be typing in the search box. That will help both our quality score and our CTR. Since "estate planning" and the space that will follow it take up 16 characters, we only have nine characters left to work with. Let's use the word "secrets," which is only seven characters.

"Secrets" is a word that will likely motivate people to read the next line of our ad. It's a human instinct to wonder what kind of secrets someone is talking about. That means our headline is "Estate Planning Secrets."

Next comes the body of the text. In Google, you get another seventy characters— two lines of thirty-five characters each. (In Bing, you get seventy-one characters that you fill in on one line, which Bing lays out as two lines.)

As you're filling in the form, Google (and Bing) will show you how your ad will appear (see screenshot on page 121).

For our Albany Estate Planner's ad, here's what we can do: First of all, the body of our ad needs to include a benefit. In this case, it would make sense to use either *cutting costs* or *cutting taxes*—or preferably both. After all, some people will be more attracted to click in order to cut their costs, while others will be more interested in cutting the inheritance taxes for their heirs.

How about "Lower Your Costs and Their Taxes." (Remember, we're capitalizing each word.) That's exactly 33 characters and spaces, including the period. That gets both benefits in easily. Your headline for an ad at the top of the page will now be: "Estate Planning Secrets—Lower Your Costs and Their Taxes."

At this point, we have 35 characters left on Google (and 36 characters remaining on Bing) to tell readers what they're going to get and what they're going to have to do to get it. We need the words "Free Report" and "Click Now." Ideally, we would say "Free Report Shows You How. Click Here Now!" But that's 42 characters. We just don't have the room. Let's get rid of some extra words. "Here" and "You" are easy choices since they don't change the meaning, although "You" is a big loss, as studies have shown that it increases CTR. But you can't have everything.

That leaves us with "Free Report Shows How. Click Now."

All that's left to complete the ad is to input your "Display URL" and your "Actual Destination." The display URL is the one that appears in the ad, and the actual destination is where people are actually going to be sent to. Unfortunately, they both have to have the same domain; otherwise we could make our display URL www.WorldsGreatestEstatePlanners.com or some other element to improve sales.

Here's what our ad will look like when it runs on the right-hand side of Google (or Bing):

ESTATE PLANNING SECRETS

WWW.CORTINERLEGAL.COM

LOWER YOUR COSTS AND THEIR TAXES.

FREE REPORT SHOWS HOW. CLICK NOW.

And if our ad shows up at the top, it will look like this:

ESTATE PLANNING SECRETS - LOWER YOUR COSTS AND THEIR TAXES.

WWW.CORTINERLEGAL.COM

FREE REPORT SHOWS HOW. CLICK NOW.

New text ad

Write your text ad below. Remember to be clear and specific. Learn how to write a great text ad

Headline	Estate Planning Secrets
Description line 1	Lower Your Costs and Their Taxes
Description line 2	Free Report Shows How. Click Now
Display URL ⁇	www.Cortinerlegal.com
Destination URL ⁇	http:// ▾ www.Cortinerlegal.com

Device preference ⁇ ☐ Mobile

Ad preview: The following ad previews may be formatted slightly differently from what is shown to users. Learn more

Side ad

Estate Planning Secrets
www.cortinerlegal.com
Lower Your Costs and Their Taxes
Free Report Shows How. Click Now

Top ad

Estate Planning Secrets
www.cortinerlegal.com
Lower Your Costs and Their Taxes Free Report Shows How. Click Now

That's what it takes to write an ad.

Some Other Observations

There are lots of ways to attract prospects with these ads. Here's an ad I've run that has worked consistently in the niche market of Certified Financial Planners:

SALES LETTERS FOR **CFPs**

WWW.GENTLERAINAFFLUENTMARKETING.COM

THIS SALES LETTER GENERATED 15 NEW
CLIENTS. CLICK FOR A FREE SAMPLE!

Obviously, the keyword phrases "sales letters for CFPs" or "Sales letters for financial advisors" will only show up sporadically as searches. There are only so many CFPs interested in sales letters. That can be frustrating. But the people who do click have a very specific need and are much more likely to sign up once they get to my website.

It comes down to quantity versus quality. You'd like one hundred people coming to your website, but if only ten of them are qualified as potential clients, you're wasting money. When a high percentage of people actually take action, that's a home run. Plus it reinforces the fact that the website you're taking people to has a great offer.

Another strategy that I've used is to create an ad using a very broad keyword phrase, which I target to a precise audience with the copy (words) in the ad, like this:

NEED MORE NEW CLIENTS?

WWW.GENTLERAINMARKETING.COM

EXCLUSIVELY FOR PROVIDERS OF

HIGH VALUE SERVICES. LEARN MORE

The phrase "exclusively for providers of high value services" keeps anyone who isn't an appropriate match from clicking. If I didn't define who I am targeting, it's likely I would waste a lot of money attracting visitors who would never convert into clients.

Adding Your Keywords

Your next step is to add your keywords.

Page down to just below where Google shows you your sample ads and you'll see "Select keywords" with a box with a plus sign. Click on the plus sign and Google will display some keyword tips. Move down the page and you'll see a box on the left-hand side that says, "Add your keywords here."

Just enter your keyword phrases, *one per line*. For most people, that's all you need to do.

If you want to get a little fancier, Google (and Bing) have different ways for you to list your keywords, which affects who sees your ads.

Let me explain. To make this easy to understand, let's say you want to advertise for the term "back pain."

Just typing those two words together, by themselves, will give you a "broad match," where Google will show your ads for searches for back pain, backaches, and maybe even back surgery.

If you type *+back +pain*, your ads will only show to people whose searches have the words "back" *and* "pain" in them. You won't get the people who search under "back surgery." Your ads will, however, show when people search under "pain in my back." Google calls this type of match a "broad match modifier."

If you only want your search to show up for people who include your exact phrase, you need to type "back pain" with the quotation marks in your keyword list. Your ad will reach people who search for "back pain doctors," but not people who search for "pain in my back side." This is referred to as a "phrase match."

Finally, if for some reason you want your ad to show to people who search for an "exact match," specifically for "back pain" without any modification, such as "lower back pain," put the two words in brackets like this: [back pain].

Some people say you can get a higher CTR by adding all of these matches to your keyword list. For now I'd just keep it simple.

Once you input your keywords, select either "Save and continue to billing" or "Set up bill later." If you choose the latter, eventually you will want to click on "Billing" at the top of the page and then "Billing preferences" to set up your credit card payments.

Your campaign will be set up and ready to go either way. It won't actually run until Google has your credit card information.

Adjusting Your Campaign on Google

Next you'll get to see all the keywords in your ad group in the form of a chart with information about each of your keywords, including:

- How many clicks you're getting
- The number of impressions your ad has received, which means how many times your ad was shown
- The CTR, which as you know is the percentage of clicks on the ad
- The average position it's been in when it has shown on searches
- The average cost-per-click (CPC)

At this point the numbers that are shown will be zeroes, as your ads won't have run yet. After your campaign runs for two days, you'll want to check to see your results in order to make adjustments or to congratulate yourself on a job well done. (To get back to the page, sign in to your AdWords account, and click on "Campaigns." On the new page, click on the name of your campaign and then on your ad group.)

There are three buttons that will let you make adjustments to your campaign:

1. **Edit:** This box lets you pause your keyword, or edit different aspects of it. You have to click on the box next to the keyword to allow this function to work. If you've chosen the automatic bidding, you won't be able to edit your bid here. You'll have to change to manual settings first by clicking on the tab for "Settings" about an inch down the page and then clicking on "Edit Settings." This will, however, turn manual bidding on for all your keywords in this ad group.

2. **Details:** This button lets you run an "Auction Analysis" as to how you are doing with your keywords compared to everyone else who advertises for that keyword phrase. It also lets you perform a "Keyword Diagnosis" to test if your ad is actually showing up when someone searches for your keyword. If it's not, this diagnosis will tell you why.

3. **Automate:** This menu lets you create automatic rules to change how your automated bidding works. It gives a list of suggested ideas such as "Change ad group default max when…" or "Pause ad group when." The page that shows up has several options on a pulldown menu for creating a variety of "if/then" scenarios. There are so many possibilities that you'll need to play around with it yourself. Just click all the down arrow buttons to see what options you can change.

If you decide you want to add some new keywords, click on the green button above the chart with your keyword information. You'll see a blank box like the one you initially filled in. To the right of that will be keyword suggestions that Google generates from the keywords you are already using. Enter your additional keywords, one per line, click "Save," and you'll be set.

That's your introduction to Google AdWords. Remember that you can have one of their employees walk you through your first campaign for free by calling the number they give you.

As an Alternative to Google, Try Bing

Bing is an interesting alternative to Google. There are a couple of good reasons to give them a try:

1. You may be able to get your keywords at a lower CPC.

2. If you want to maximize your traffic on a particular keyword, the Yahoo Bing Network can bring in additional prospects.

Getting Started on Bing

Go to Bing.com and at the bottom of the page, click on the word "Advertise." *Make sure you do this using Internet Explorer or Firefox* because, as of this writing, their PPC program doesn't work as well on the other browsers.

On the next page, on the right-hand side, click on the box that says "Sign Up Now." Then fill out the form and submit it. You now have an advertising account for the Yahoo Bing Network.

At the very bottom of the page that comes up next, in small text, you'll see "To get started, import your campaigns from Google AdWords or create a campaign." Click on "Create a campaign."

You will land on the form that sets up your ads on Bing.

Most of this is very much like Google. You start off by naming your campaign and selecting your time zone.

After that, Bing asks for your budget. One slight difference here is that you are given a choice between a daily and a monthly budget.

Underneath the budget box is a line that says "Daily budget options" with a little arrow. If you leave that alone, your ads will appear evenly throughout the day. If you'd like them to appear as frequently as possible until your money is spent, click on the little arrow and choose that option.

Your ads will run in English unless you say otherwise, and you can select the locations for where your ads run, as you did in Google.

Now you're ready to type in your keywords.

Adding Your Keywords

This is a little different on Bing than it is on Google.

Just type in the list you made earlier in the big box on the lower left-hand side—one keyword phrase per line—then click on the button that says "Add" underneath that box.

As soon as you press the button, you'll see that the field on the right is populated under the following topics: Keyword, Type, and Bid (USD).

Your keywords are listed under "Keyword." "Type" refers to the match types we talked about above with Google—"broad match," "phrase match," etc.

"Bid (USD)" has two pieces of information under it. The first is either a little box with a dollar amount, typically $0.05, or there's no box and just "----." The second item is a box with an arrow next to it where the default setting will be either "Ad group bid" or "First page bid."

Let's talk about match types first.

Match Types

If you click on the arrow in the box under "Type" on any key-word, a pulldown menu will appear with the words "Broad," "Phrase," "Exact," and "Content."

You can select one or more of these. A "Content" match, which isn't a match choice on Google, means your ad will show up on Bing's content network. Just as I said with Google, I suggest you ignore this option.

A broad match is your best option for now. You can experiment by changing this setting later if you discover your CTR is less than you want it to be. By the way, a CTR of .05% means you're doing reasonably well. The more you go over half a percent, the better you're doing. If your CTR is below that mark, it means you might want to change something.

Bidding

There are five terms that you will need to understand in order to bid on keywords the Yahoo Bing Network. Some of these are obvious:

- **Best position:** This is the very first ad you see at the top of the page.
- **Mainline position:** These are the ads that appear above the organic search results, but below that first ad at the top.
- **First page:** Any position on the first page, but the suggested bid is more likely to place your ad on the sidebar, rather than in the mainline.
- **Ad group:** Ad groups are created a little differently on Bing than on Google. Here you can select "Ad group" from the pulldown menu. All the words with "Ad group"

selected will use the same bid. If you want to change your bid, you can do it for the whole group at once.

- **Custom value:** "Custom value" lets you override your ad group bid for any keyword you choose to manage separately.

Now just decide how much you want to spend per click and put it in the box that says "Bid." The numbers on the pulldown menu on the right give you the bid that won for each category during the previous month.

Deciding How Much to Bid

Now that you have an idea as to what the highest bids were last month for each position, you need to decide how much you want to bid.

Bing and Google both work like eBay; you never pay more than what you bid, and in many cases, the actual amount of money you get charged is less. In other words, if you bid $2.00 per click to get the best position, you may only wind up spending $1.50 per click. It all depends on what the other bidders are doing, and this changes from month to month.

With that in mind, just bid the amount indicated for the position you want. As mentioned previously, the best position and the mainline positions get the lion's share of the clicks. If possible, bid whatever will get you closest to the top of the page.

Once you decide on your amounts, fill them in, hit "Submit," and your campaign will be ready to go.

Just like with Google, your campaign won't start until you click on "Accounts and Billing" and give Bing your credit card information.

Submit that and your campaign will be up and running.

Adjusting Your Campaign on Bing

Just like with Google, after your campaign runs for two days, you'll want to check your results.

When you sign in, click on the name of your campaign. When the next page appears, click on the name of your ad group. You'll get the same chart I described with Google.

People usually make adjustments when their ads are not achieving the top position or whichever position you were aiming for. If you want to change your bid, just highlight the bid amount and click. You'll have a blank box to fill in with a new dollar amount.

You can also pause keywords that aren't working by clicking on their status and selecting "Pause" from the pulldown menu.

If you decide you want to try some new keywords, go to the top of the page and click on "Campaigns." Then click on your campaign name and your ad group name. In a gray bar above the chart will be the phrase, "Add Keywords." This will take you to the spot where you originally entered your keywords. Follow the instructions above once again so you can make appropriate bids.

That's how you advertise on Bing.

Now that we've covered the main search engines, let's talk about advertising on two of the largest social media sites, starting with Facebook.

Advertising on Facebook

In June of 2013, Facebook became home to more than one million advertisers for the first time. That's a pretty clear indication that Facebook advertising has become increasingly popular. As I mentioned previously, Facebook is a particularly good place to be when you're advertising to consumers and women.

One unique feature Facebook includes is recommendations for your ad, in the form of "likes," by personal friends of the people who view the ad. For example, "John Martin likes this" will appear above an ad for which John clicked the "Like" button. This endorsement will only show up when John's friends are seeing the ad, but it's a nice feature and it can increase response.

Facebook also has some very interesting options in terms of letting you target who sees your ad, which I'll talk about in a moment.

To get started, click on "Create Advert." If you have a Facebook page, this appears on the top right-hand side of your main page, next to the word "Sponsored," just above where the ads appear. If you don't have a Facebook page, go to Facebook.com and you'll find that same link at the bottom of their signup page.

Once you click, you will be asked, "What do you want to advertise?" Though Facebook offers options that include your Facebook fan page or apps in the iTunes or Google Play store, for our purposes, just fill in the web address for your free report.

Once you type your URL in the blank space, Facebook will try to create your ad using text and an image from your website. While it's fun to see what they do, you're better off creating your own ad, which will be similar to the ad we developed for Google.

Facebook gives you 95 characters in the body of your text, which is 25 extra compared to Google. (The headline is the same at 25 characters.) It will be simple to make your advertisement a little bigger. For example, to change our estate planning ad on Google to a Facebook ad, we just have to include a few words that we left out previously. The adaptation below brings the ad up to 92 characters:

ESTATE PLANNING SECRETS
Lower your costs and their inheritance taxes.
Our free report shows you how. CLICK HERE NOW.

With Facebook ads, the text is smaller than on Google or Bing because there is also a picture next to the ad. Using title case for the whole ad makes it harder to read. Instead, write normal sentences for most of the text. Save the title case for just a few words that you want to emphasize.

After you type in the text of your ad, you need to upload the color image that will run next to it. Use a picture that includes a human being rather than your company logo. People click more when there is a person in the picture. Friends who have tested a variety of images tell me that pictures of women outperform pictures of men. If it's appropriate for your business, you might want to take that into consideration. As I mentioned in Chapter 3, you can find images to use inexpensively at 123rf.com.

Next to the words "Related Page" and below the image upload area, there's a little white square that says, "Show social activity next to my advert." Check this box, which then allows Facebook to show the people who "like" your website to their Facebook friends.

If you page down a bit, Facebook will show you what your finished ad will look like.

Targeting Your Audience

Continue to page down and you get to choose your audience demographics, including their location, age group, and gender.

Next, you'll see a blank space beside the words "Precise Interests." This is where Facebook has some extra features for you to use. You can target people with specific interests, such as finance—or people who are fans of companies such as Starbucks or individuals like Tony Robbins. Just type the name or term you want to use in the white box, and Facebook will create a pulldown menu with pages or topics you can select from. Once you pick a page whose fans you'd like to advertise to, Facebook makes additional suggestions based on what you typed. For example, if you select Tony Robbins, you get a list of other people including Dale Carnegie, Napoleon Hill, Robert Kiyosaki, John Gray, and other prominent individuals in the self-improvement world.

This gives you a whole new way to think about your prospective clients. Ask yourself, what are they reading, what topics are they interested in, and what other experts in this niche might they be following?

Below that box is a one for Facebook's broad categories to select who sees your ad. Choose one of the items on the left-hand side, and Facebook will give you a checklist of sub-categories on the right-hand side. Click on "Activities" and you'll see items like "Cooking" or "Dancing." Click on "Business/Technology" and you get a range of items that includes "Small Business Owners" and "Technology Early Adopters." Each menu item on the left triggers different categories on the right, so spend some time identifying the groups you'd like to advertise to.

If you click on "See Advanced Targeting Options," you can target people by their marital status, education, and even companies they have worked for.

Your next step is to create your campaign budget. You can either choose a daily budget, say $10 per day, or a lifetime budget where you select how much money you want to spend. Facebook will run your ad until that amount has been spent. Click on the arrows next to which method you prefer.

Once that's done, you choose whether you want to start your campaign immediately, which is the default setting, or to schedule a particular start and end date. This is simple to do.

Next there's a link about conversion tracking. This is a helpful feature that, if you decide not to do today, is worth doing in the immediate future. When you click on the link, make a copy of the URL that appears and send it to the person who made your website come alive. Ask them to add this code to your site. It will enable you to track what people do once they click on your ad and go to your website. That's good information to have, especially as you expand your marketing efforts.

Bidding on Facebook

Bidding on Facebook is a little different from bidding on Google or Bing. Facebook lets you pay each time someone clicks, or you can pay per each 1,000 impressions (showings), without regard for how many people click on it.

Interests	Additional Interests		1,100,000 people
	Tony Robbins	4,615,675 people	✓ You've defined your audience.
	Search for interests	Suggestions | Browse	Continue to the next section once you're happy with your audience.
Connections	Jim Rohn	2,591,330 people +	Your ad targets people:
	Napoleon Hill	1,970,901 people +	• Who live in United States
Interested In	Dale Carnegie	2,298,176 people +	• age exactly 30 and older
	Think and Grow Rich	1,896,636 people +	• Who like Tony Robbins
Relationship Status	Jack Canfield	2,210,804 people +	Suggested Bid
	Brian Tracy	1,541,295 people +	$0.59–$1.12 USD

I'd stay with the PPC option. Make sure you fill in the circle marked "Optimize for clicks." For Facebook, instead of letting them optimize your bids for you, I would suggest that you manually bid for clicks. Fill in the circle that allows you to do that as well.

Your last task on this page is to choose how much to bid. I'd recommend you start out by bidding 10 or 20 cents less than the minimum bid Facebook recommends, which is listed in small print underneath the box where you type in your bid, and also on the top right-hand side just above where the Campaign, Pricing, and Scheduling section begins.

Then just push the button that says "Review Advert." Since you're advertising a website, Facebook wants you to confirm that you "don't want to run your ad in the news feed." Click on that phrase in the box that shows up. Then click on the "Review Advert" button again. Once you give Facebook your billing information, your campaign will run.

The Facebook crowd is a bit more cautious about clicking on ads, so don't be surprised if your campaign starts off slowly.

However, over time, they will join your community and become subscribers.

LinkedIn

LinkedIn is a social media site aimed primarily at professionals. It lets you target your ad to people based on the type of job they hold, their industry, the specific company they work for, what they read, and a lot of other business-oriented criteria. You can also target prospects by which LinkedIn groups they belong to. Since it's more of a B2B site, the keywords tend to be more expensive, with a $2 minimum per click. If your products or services are directed at a high-end market or the business community, there's a good chance advertising will work well for you on LinkedIn.

To advertise, go to LinkedIn.com, click on the word "Advertising" at the bottom of the page, then click on the "Start Now" button on the page that comes up next. If you're not a member of LinkedIn, you'll have to join and set up a profile first. (See Chapter 6 for instructions on the best way to do that.)

The page you'll come to after you click the "Start Now" button will be similar to the ad setup pages for Google and Bing. Begin by naming your campaign, then type in your ad.

There are a few differences worth noting versus the sites we've covered so far:

1. You get 75 characters in the body of your text, so you have five more characters than Google to play with. (The headline is the standard 25 characters.)
2. Similar to Facebook, you can add a color image to your ad. Just click on the box that says "Image" to upload your picture.

3. LinkedIn makes it easy to test up to 15 variations of your ad to see which ones get the best results. For example, for our estate planning free report, you could change the headline to "Albany Estate Planning" as a variation on the original headline of "Estate Planning Secrets." If you'd like to test variations of your ad, just click on the green plus sign next to the words "Add a variation."

4. LinkedIn runs your ads in different configurations, depending on where on the page it appears. You can preview what your ad will look like in its "Square," "Tall," and "Long" versions by clicking on the preview panel.

When you write your ads, use title case, since the text is bigger than it is on Facebook. Then upload your images and click on "Next Step." You'll arrive at LinkedIn's targeting page.

LinkedIn gives you a wide range of options to target the professionals who are members. You can target by location, company, job title, schools, skills, and membership in various LinkedIn groups. You can also select based on gender and age.

LinkedIn's targeting menu is intuitive to work with, so you'll have an easy time exploring your options. Just click on the plus signs next to any category, and menus of sub-categories will appear. For example, if you click on the plus sign just to the left of the word "location," you start off with a list of continent-sized regions. Keep clicking on plus signs starting with North America, and you get to choose the United States, then individual states, then regions within each state such as the "Albany, New York area" or the "Greater Chicago area."

Here are some highlights with regard to your targeting options:

- You can select *companies* by name or by category. This means your ad will be shown to the people who are employees of these organizations. If you are picking by

name, just type the first few letters and LinkedIn will give
you a list of choices. If you want to advertise to companies
by categories, you can choose a big category like consumer
goods, or you can get more specific by selecting cosmetics
or sporting goods. You can also choose by size, letting you
select anything from one-person companies to organizations with 10,000 or more employees.

- You can show your ad by *job title*. If you're marketing a
  financial software product aimed at CFOs, you can enter
  "CFO" in the blank box, and LinkedIn will provide you
  with both "CFO" and a number of similar titles to select
  from such as finance director, controller, etc.

- You can select who sees your ad by *job function*. With that
  option, you pick a category like accounting or marketing
  and then choose who sees your ad by their levels of senior-
  ity, such as only showing your ad to directors or VPs.

Who's the audience for this campaign?

📍 Location	Please specify at least one location ⬍	**Audience**
🏢 Companies	⦿ All ○ By name ○ By category (industry, company size)	**6,117,908** LinkedIn Members 📇 **Job Function:** Finance
📇 Job Title	○ All ○ By title ⦿ By category (job function, seniority) Finance × ⬍	

- *Skills* works the same way as job titles. Your ad will show up to the people who list the skills you select. Type in the first few letters and you get a pulldown menu to choose from. Select something such as "brand management" and you'll get related suggestions like "brand advertising" and "consumer marketing."
- You can select the members of *groups*. Type the first few letters and you'll get a list to choose from. Pick a group, and you'll be prompted to select from a list of skills that group members might have as an additional way to target people.
- Alternatively, you can make a list of *groups* that you would like to advertise to by going to the search bar on any page of LinkedIn and typing a word that's part of the group name, such as "consultants." After you click on the search symbol, click on the word "Groups" on the left-hand side of the page, and you can compile a list of consultant groups to advertise to. This list will be more comprehensive than the one you can get using the targeting page.

Make sure you end up with at least 200,000 people in your target audience, or you won't reach a wide enough audience for your ads to be effective.

After you've made your choices, uncheck the box about the LinkedIn Audience Network. Similar to what I recommended about advertising on Google, these extended networks usually don't convert particularly well.

Click on the "Next Step" button and you'll be on LinkedIn's bidding page.

Bidding on LinkedIn

Bidding on LinkedIn is similar to bidding on Facebook. You're given the choice between PPC-style payments or paying per 1,000 impressions. You want to choose PPC.

LinkedIn suggests a bidding range for the list of people you've targeted. Start by bidding 10 or 20 cents below LinkedIn's lower suggestion. (You can always raise your bid later.) LinkedIn has a minimum bid requirement of $2.00 per click, so you can't bid any lower than that.

Next comes your daily budget. Fill that in with the amount you are willing to spend each day.

Finally, you can choose whether to show your ads continuously or to have an end date for your campaign. It's best if you let your campaign run continuously. Make sure your daily budget is something you can afford as an ongoing expense.

When you click on "Next Step," it's time to provide your payment information. Once you've done that, your LinkedIn campaign will begin.

You're Up and Running

Once you pull the trigger on an ad campaign, whether it's on Google, Bing, Facebook, or LinkedIn, you will begin to reap the immediate benefits of your One Week Marketing Plan. Prospects will come into your marketing funnel automatically, week after week.

The benefit of advertising your free report online is speed, but it is just one of many marketing options that are available to attract new clients. In the second half of this book, I'll show you how to add to the efforts you've already made by strategically using blogs, social media, video, public relations, and joint ventures to grow your business. I'll even take you behind the scenes to show you how I market my company using the same tools I'm showing you.

The goal is to add enough marketing activity, a little bit at a time, to allow you to earn the level of income you want, while you work with clients you like on projects you enjoy.

I'm looking forward to continuing our journey together in Part II.

Part Two

STRATEGIC MARKETING BOOSTS

Introduction to Part Two

JAMBA JUICE OFFERS "BOOSTS" for your mango smoothie that make it more powerful, either to fight a cold, improve your immune system, or even make your brain work better. Once you get a taste of how effective a marketing system can be for your business, you're going to want to continue to boost your marketing efforts as well.

There are many additional activities you can do that make your marketing more effective. You should be able to implement any of these within four to eight hours.

In this section I cover blogging, joint ventures, video marketing, and other methods you can use to drive highly targeted traffic to your website.

I suggest that you experiment with one boost each month after you implement the One Week Marketing Plan. They don't have to be done in order, and you can pick and choose which ones you want to focus on. My hope is that over time you'll try all of them and then expand your efforts on those that are producing the greatest results. The most important point is to make sure you do something every month.

To get started, I suggest that you read through all of the boosts one time. Then pick one and focus on implementing it. As I've done in the preceding chapters, you will find that each boost has complete "here's precisely how to implement this" information. I get frustrated when someone shares great information but fails to tell me how to turn a good idea into reality. I'm sure you're the same way, so rest assured, I won't leave you hanging.

Chapter Six

SOCIAL MEDIA:
Strategic Marketing Boosts 1 and 2

THE GOAL OF SOCIAL MEDIA, like most marketing, is to get more people to know, like, and trust you.

My personal philosophy is that just posting on the various social media sites for the sake of posting is a complete waste of time. Yes, you may have heard of someone who said, "I tweeted and as a result got Anheuser-Busch as a client." Though that may be true, out of the one billion tweets that are sent each week—what, realistically, are the odds of that happening?

I have a rule I always follow: *Never* focus your marketing efforts on low-probability events.

That's why my strategy has always been to use social media as a lead-generation tool to drive people to my blog posts. As a result of the blog, people engage with you.

We'll start with social media, then I'll show you how to set up your blog in the next chapter. This way, when you put up your first blog post, you can immediately drive traffic to it through your social media messages.

With your first two strategic marketing boosts, you're going to set up your business profiles on four of the major social media platforms: LinkedIn, Google+, Facebook, and Twitter. Even if you already have these social media sites set up for your business, I'm going to show you how to optimize key sections so that people will find you more easily.

You'll also set up an account with HootSuite, TweetDeck, or Sprout Social so that you can automate your posting to all of your social media. You'll literally be able to set up a week's worth of messages in less than an hour. I personally use HootSuite, but you won't go wrong with any of these services.

Your Overall Goal

These days, social media sites are becoming more and more like search engines. People go to Twitter, LinkedIn, and the others to search for information, not to just connect with others. Facebook even added Graph Search so that you can search on their site for individuals who have similar interests or specific areas of expertise.

The most important thing you can do as you're setting up your social media home pages is to make sure your bio or profile includes the keywords or phrases that potential customers would use if they were searching for the type of products or services you offer.

You already have your keywords prepared, since you'll most likely use the same ones as you used for your free report.

Now let's talk about each of the sites individually.

Google+

I'm big on prioritizing Google+ these days because these posts show up in Google search results more often than posts that are made on the other social media platforms. The primary reason for this is that since Google is far and away the largest search engine, your posts appear prominently whenever someone types in a relevant search term. This is a huge advantage since we know that when people type a search request, they usually have a serious interest in a particular topic. While posting on other social media platforms is certainly worth doing, you are likely to get greater visibility to your niche audience that has a specific need by using Google+.

If you don't have a Google+ page, you can create one by going to google.com/+/business. Click on "Create a Google+ page" at the top right-hand corner of the page.

If you're not already signed into a Google account, they'll ask you to either sign in or create an account.

Since Google and the other social media sites change on a regular basis, rather than give you step-by-step instructions for creating your Google+ page, I'll just talk about some of the ways you can make your Google+ page easy for people to find.

Your Story: This is one of the sections you fill in when you're creating your account. You've got ten words to come up with your tagline. It's your chance to make a small sales pitch, so convey benefits. Try to include as many keywords as you can, but don't try to jam them in just for the sake of jamming them in.

For example, a local dentist might say, "Affordable, pain-free dentistry by Milwaukee dentist." "Pain-free dentistry" is a keyword phrase, as is "Milwaukee dentist." If someone searches for either of these terms, there's a high probability that dentist will show up.

You'll also need to complete the introduction section for your page. This is where you include a thorough description of your business. Once again, use keywords as much as you can without making your copy difficult to read. Then link your keywords to your website by highlighting them and clicking on the word

"Link" at the top of the box you are writing in. A pop-up box will appear that says, "To what URL should this link go?" Fill in your web address, click "OK," and your link will be live. This is a pretty effective way to get people from the Google+ page to your website, where they can then download your free report and start getting your drip-marketing autoresponder sequence.

There's also a place to list your main website, plus your favorite links. Use this spot to link to the other social media sites you'll be setting up.

You get to add a cover photo for your page, which is one way to add color and differentiate yourself from everyone else's pages. Additionally, these cover images can be a great way to brand your company and differentiate yourself from the competition. Just click on "change cover."

You can also add a profile photo by clicking to the left of the name of your page. This can be very important, as you'll see in a few minutes.

To post to Google+ and actually have someone see it, you have to add people to your "circles," which is their name for your personal groups. This way, you can post business items to your business connections, and jokes and personal items to your friends. You can define these circles yourself, in the same way that you can create folders for your different documents.

To find people to add, place your cursor in the top left corner of the page. This will bring out the Google+ main menu, where you can select "People." Google+ gives you a lot of options that will allow you to find the people you want to connect with. If you have someone particular in mind, type their name into the search box, then go to their Google+ profile. Mouse over the button that says "Add to circles." Pick a circle for them, then click your "Return" or "Enter" button, and you will be connected. It's pretty simple to add precisely the people you want to connect with to your circles.

Google also lets you join groups of like-minded strangers through Google Communities. This is an important feature because you can share your latest blog posts. It's also a great way to develop relationships with people who could become interested in your products or services.

To join any group, use the menu as above, but click on "Communities." Put the appropriate keywords in the search box and you'll find a list of communities to join.

You post in Google+ by clicking on "Share" at the top of the page. Any post you create can also be sent to your communities by adding "+" and the name of the community you want to send to. For example, if you add "+Internet Marketing," your post will appear in your circles and the Internet Marketing community.

Google Authorship

Google+ has a program that will show a thumbnail of your profile picture next to your posts when they appear on Google's search engine results. This could be a considerable advantage in getting people to click, as results with pictures stand out. A photo also adds credibility.

The program is called Google Authorship and you have to apply to join. Pamela Vaughan of HubSpot says that she noticed a spike in the rankings of her posts that coincided with her approval for membership. Here are the steps Vaughan says you need to take in order to apply for the program:

1. The program only works with headshots, so make sure your profile picture is obviously a picture of your whole face.
2. You have to have an email address with the same domain name as the site you are linking the material you are posting from. In other words, if your material is posted

from your blog at www.yourcompany.com, you need a corresponding email address such as you@yourcompany .com.

3. Make sure the email address above is in the "About" section of your Google+ profile. This will make it clearer to Google that your domain is connected to their social media site.

4. While you're in the "About" section, confirm that the box between "Profile Discovery" and "Help others discover my profile in search" is checked.

5. Give all your blog posts on the domain for which you want to claim Google Authorship a byline, such as by "First name Last name." Vaughan says you can also use "Author: First name Last name." That name needs to match the name on your Google+ profile, so if you use a company name rather than a personal name for Google+, that's what you should use for the byline. In other words, if you write a blog post titled "How to Hire a Web Designer" and your Google+ profile is under Tamara Jones, you will add "by Tamara Jones" or "Author: Tamara Jones" below the title. But if your Google + profile is named "Jones Web Design," you would create a byline that says either "by Jones Web Design" or "Author: Jones Web Design."

6. Go to plus.google.com/authorship, Google's Authorship page. Fill in the blank box on that page with the email address mentioned above and click the button to sign up for authorship. You only have to do this once. You will hear back from Google when they approve you.

The screenshot on the next page shows you what the results look like. The listings with the authors' pictures really do stand out.

affluent marketing « Gentle Rain Marketing
gentlerainmarketing.com/tag/affluent-marketing/ ▾
by Mark Satterfield
I'm probably not telling you anything you don't know when I say that the
affluent market doesn't respond well to the direct head-on sales approach. If
for no other ...

marketing to the affluent « Gentle Rain Marketing
gentlerainmarketing.com/tag/marketing-to-the-affluent/ ▾
Social media has found a new resource for those targeting the ultra-affluent, and ten
nationally ranked firms, catering to the wealthy, have jumped on board.

How To Sell Services To The Very Affluent « Gentle Rain Marketing
gentlerainmarketing.com/affluent-marketing/how-to-sell-services-to-the-... ▾
Nov 27, 2013 - Although this appears on the surface to be a bit "counter-intuitive"
marketing to those who have worked with your competitors or bought ...

What Lady Gaga knows about marketing to the affluent http://bit.ly ...
https://plus.google.com/.../posts/FtmvRpEqCAp ▾
Gentle Rain Marketing
Oct 30, 2013 - What Lady Gaga knows about marketing to the affluent
http://bit.ly/1adw4BR What Lady Gaga Knows About Marketing To The
Affluent | Affluent ...

LinkedIn

LinkedIn provides lots of opportunities for you to be found by potential customers. If you're marketing products or services to businesses, this is definitely a social media channel you'll want to take advantage of. With LinkedIn you will be creating two profiles: one that's personal and one for your business. Your business profile connects or links from your personal profile.

There are numerous sections in your LinkedIn profile where you can add keywords to make sure you appear when people search under topics, experience, education, skills, and expertise. LinkedIn is heavily searched on by an increasing number of companies looking for consultants and experts, so it makes sense to take some time and ensure that your profile is as keyword-heavy as possible.

The first thing you'll be asked for is your current occupation. Whatever you write will appear under your name, in big print. This is your de facto headline in LinkedIn. It makes sense to insert a keyword phrase in here. Always keep in mind how people may be searching for you. For example, instead of just saying "financial planner," you might want to say "Boston Financial Planner."

Add the phrase "specializing in," and you are able to include whatever other keyword phrases you want. "Boston Financial Planner Specializing in Retirement Planning."

You could even do a little marketing here. What if you added the word "best"? Then your profile might say, "Steve Johnson, Best Boston Financial Planner Specializing in Retirement Planning." If someone's searching for "Boston financial planners," you will stand out from the pack. Also, a surprising number of searches are done with the word "best" in the query.

After your title, you'll be asked to put in your company name. Your listing headline will now read "Steve Johnson, Best Boston Financial Planner Specializing in Retirement Planning at Magic Money Matters."

You could also include a link to your free report after your company name. "Steve Johnson, Best Boston Financial Planner at Magic Money Matters/Free Report on Retiring More Quickly at www.YourWebsite.com." Or you could create a special URL that points to your website and say "Go here for www.FreeReportOnRetiringMoreQuickly.com." (You can register any URL you want at Godaddy.com or similar registration services and then forward it to any other URL you have.)

Once you're done writing about your current business or job, LinkedIn will let you write about previous jobs. In theory you are creating an online résumé, but you have complete discretion over what you include. One trick to consider if you're a consultant is to include the clients you've worked with. The advantage of this is that your profile will come up when people search for that company name. For each "job," make sure you include your keywords in the descriptions.

Next comes your education. Obviously you want to be truthful, but there's nothing wrong with including places you studied, even if you didn't receive a degree. Just keep in mind that it's very easy for people to check out the validity of what you claim, so there's a huge downside risk to being blatantly dishonest.

When you get to the Skills & Expertise category, LinkedIn will provide a menu once you begin typing. You can use the items from their list or create your own. You can include up to 50 of these, so you might want to use both their suggestions and your keyword phrase version of a particular skill. LinkedIn suggestions will be the skills most often entered into their system or the ones most commonly searched for. For example, if you enter the letters "pub" in the form, a dropdown menu will list "Public Speaking," "Public Relations," "Publishing," "Public Policy," and "Public Health," along with a host of other options.

Adding a Company Page

Adding a company page offers you another way to be found on LinkedIn. This page lets you tell more of your company's story, since it becomes a clickable link from your personal profile. It's also another place to add keyword phrases. You can add your company page on LinkedIn by going here: linkedin.com/company/add/show.

Recommendations

LinkedIn has a section where you can get personalized testimonials from people you've worked with. Click on "Profile" at the top of the page and you'll get a menu from which you can select

"Recommendations." The page that shows up lets you give a rec-ommendation, which often is the best way to get one.

At the top left of the page, there's a link that lets you "Ask for Recommendations." The new page will give you everything you need to send a message to any of your LinkedIn connections you want a testimonial from.

Here's a quick tip: You already have testimonials from clients that you've used on your website. Ask those people if they can repeat the recommendation on LinkedIn. You can say, "If you want to make it easy, use what you said before, which is…." If you have just LinkedIn recommendations, I would get permission for those to appear on your website as well.

Groups

It's also a smart idea to join LinkedIn Groups. All you have to do is put your keywords in the search box at the top of any LinkedIn page, and groups will show up in the results. Also, LinkedIn will suggest groups they think you will like based on the information you have filled out on your profile. Just click on the Groups menu at the top of the page.

In addition, there's a complete directory of LinkedIn Groups here: linkedin.com/directory/groups/.

Pick groups you think your prospective clients will be in, and you can send them links to your blog posts. I drive a huge amount of highly targeted traffic to my website by posting a one-sentence hooky headline for one of my blog posts. I find that many times, asking a mildly provocative question generates a lot of curiosity. For example, I posted *Is this segment of the affluent market worth focusing on?* (http://bit.ly/12gkaaQ.) This is a shortened link that I made on bitly (http://bitly.com) that connects to my blog page. In less than an hour, I had 53 new subscribers to my email mar-keting list. Since you can join up to 50 groups, this is one of the most effective methods I know for getting prospects from the social media sites over to your own website. I strongly encourage you to implement it.

Facebook

For business, you want a fan page on Facebook, not a personal page. Presently, the keyword searching on Facebook only goes through their Graph Search feature.

If you don't already have a Facebook account, the way to create this is to go to Facebook.com. Ignore the form that lets you sign up, and look just below the sign-up button where it says, "Create a page for a celebrity, band, or business." Click on the word "Create" and you'll be able to start your page.

If you're already signed in to Facebook, just search for any fan page, e.g., Brad Pitt or Angelina Jolie, and go to the bottom of the page. There will be links at the bottom, including one that says "Create a Page," which will enable you to set up your own fan page when you click it.

Facebook's fan pages are pretty simple. The places for your keywords are in the descriptions of your company. You also get to add a profile picture and a cover shot for the page.

People subscribe to your page by "liking" it. If you already have a personal page, you can start by getting your Facebook friends to like your fan page. You can also send an email out to your list to get them to like it.

If you want to add motivation, offer a free gift to people who like your page from your email list. Broadway producer Ken Davenport recently gave away two free tickets to see the opening night performance of Alan Cumming in *Macbeth* to one lucky subscriber who liked his fan page. Naturally you want to check Facebook's guidelines before launching a campaign.

Twitter

The right blog post sent or, in Twitter vernacular, "tweeted" to the right audience on Twitter has the potential to be seen by thousands of people.

The reason for this is that there is a culture of "retweeting" on this social media site. Retweeting simply means resending a tweet that you received from someone else to your own list of followers. Why retweeting (and replying directly to those who retweet your messages) is important is that it builds engagement with your connections. Twitter is one of the most social of the social media platforms, so this little bit of effort will go a long way. Plus, there's a very practical reason for retweeting as often as possible. The more you create engagement with a follower, the greater the likelihood that they will then become a subscriber on your website and eventually a client.

Because a tweet is only 140 characters, Twitter moves very fast. This is both good and bad. You can get immediate attention, but in order to have a sustained presence on Twitter you've got to commit to tweeting multiple times a day. Retweeting what others send you is one way to have something new to say to your followers. Sharing someone else's blog posts happens more frequently on this site than any other.

Twitter is about brevity, and as such there's only so much you can do in terms of using keywords. You get to pick your Twitter name, add a 160-character description about yourself, and select a profile picture. Make sure you speak in benefits and try to mention your niche.

For example, you could say, "Best Asheville chiropractor for people who play sports. Get rid of your back pain now so you can play and be your very best. Learn more at www.ChiroSolutions .com." That falls within the allotted character limit.

One thing you can do to make your page stand out is to use your own custom background and cover image. First, you have to confirm your Twitter account by clicking on the link in the email they send you. Then click on the little gear emblem on the top right-hand side, select "Settings" from the pulldown menu, and pick "Design" from the left-hand side of the page that comes up. Twitter offers a lot of their own artwork to choose from, but ideally some customized branding would make you stand out. Click on the arrow next to "Change background" and select "Choose existing background" to pick an image from your own computer.

Before you tweet, you need to get followers. A natural place to start is by emailing your list and asking your subscribers to follow you.

One thing that's unique to Twitter is that many people use a setting where they will automatically follow someone who follows them. If you follow those people, they will follow you back. The trick is to find people who serve the same audience as you do, then follow their followers.

Be careful, though. If you have a lot less followers than the number of people you follow, you will look less credible to the people who check you out on Twitter. Plus Twitter will stop letting you follow people at a certain point, usually 2,000, until the number of people who follow you catches up with that number.

One trick to get around this is to "unfollow" people who don't follow you back. There are a couple of pieces of software you can use for this task: Friend or Follow (friendorfollow.com) and Twidium (twidium.com).

Posting on Twitter is simple, but there are several tricks you need to know:

1. **Shorten the URLs for anything you're linking to by going to Bitly.** As I mentioned previously, Bitly is a website that will take your URL and make it shorter, and

it tracks how many people go to the link and where they come from. Shortening your links is necessary because you only have 140 characters to work with.

2. **In order to make it easy for people to retweet your material, make tweets that are 20 characters fewer than the 140 you are given.** Twitter's unwritten ethos is that credit is always given to the original tweeter. That means a retweet of your original tweet will look like this: "RT @ yourname. Here are 7 great ways to save money on your taxes http://bit.ly/yourlink."

   Then, if someone retweets the retweet of your material (and this happens a lot), he or she will give credit to both you and the person she received your retweet from. This adds RT @theirname to the tweet above. If your tweet is too long, people will have to edit it in order to give the proper credit before they re-retweet it, which may discourage them from doing so. Make it easy on them by using 120 characters or less on anything you'd like retweeted.

3. **Occasionally, you can get more retweets by adding the phrase "Please RT" at the end of your tweet.** Use this strategy sparingly, as it tends to wear thin if overused.

4. **Think strategically about each word you tweet.** Every word in your tweet is searchable, so include variations of your keywords in each one. That way people who are interested in your topic can find your tweets.

5. **Use hashtags to post to groups of tweets that are established topics in your field.** Hashtags are words preceded by "#," such as "#jobtips" and "#migrainehelp." Search on Twitter under your keywords and you may find regular topics to post under by adding a hashtag. Also, it's a good idea to follow the people who post under these hashtags in order to get them to follow you back. (Plus

you can check out who they are following and follow those people as well.)

Personally, I find that Twitter is the social media platform I have the hardest time justifying spending huge amounts of time on. My personal philosophy is that social media should be used to get more people to your website so they will opt in for your free offer and then become readers of your drip-marketing autoresponder sequence. People who are active on Twitter tend not to be of the mindset to visit websites and download information. Yes, there are exceptions, and as long as it's simple to post on Twitter (as I'll explain next), it makes sense to continue to have a presence. But I wouldn't put it at the top of my list.

Posting to the Social Media Sites

As I mentioned at the beginning of this chapter, the main point of social media in terms of your business is to drive traffic to your blog. That means you will need to come up with several different hooks for each blog you post.

Let me show you what I mean. Let's pretend you've written a blog post titled "5 Surprising Ways to Save on Your Taxes." Here are some items you could post that include a link to the blog:

1. Use a question: "Which of these tax saving ideas would save YOU the most money?"
2. Describe the blog in the most enticing way possible. Ideally, try to use the phrase "my clients" as part of your post: "Here are the tax savings ideas that always surprise my clients."
3. You can post one or two times with an actual quote from the blog: "The following five tax deductions save my average client about $1,000 a year."

4. Post two or three of the five ways: "Most people forget
    they can write off their _____ and four other ways
    to save on your taxes."
5. Use the phrase "Here's a way to" and include the benefit
    you're writing about: "Here's a way to write off your
    vacation as a business trip."
6. Show how your blog answers a question: "If you've ever
    had a question about _____, the answer is here."
7. Let your followers know that your blog provides a
    definition or a description of something they want to
    know about. "If you're curious about what _____
    really means (and a lot of people are), read this."

Scheduling Your Posts in Advance with HootSuite

If you're going to post to all the social media sites, you don't want
to have to do it manually. Fortunately, there are several tools that
automate the whole process and let you schedule your social
media messages in advance. One note of caution: It's important
to be aware that when setting up any automated posts, timing
can be essential. Try not to schedule a post during anticipated
breaking news (elections, for example), and suspend automated
posts for other breaking news. For example, a few companies
were criticized for tweeting about giveaways and special offers
directly after the Boston bombings. Suspending tweets is appropriate in a situation like that.

With that caveat in mind, one of the best tools to automate
your social media posts is HootSuite (HootSuite.com).

In the HootSuite platform, you start by importing all your
social media profiles. Once that's done, you can schedule your
posts.

The instructions on their website are easy to follow. Just enter
your messages and schedule the dates and times for those posts

to go out. They will automatically show up exactly at the time for which you schedule them.

Time to Implement

Now it's time to take what you've learned and apply it. Here are your first two assignments:

Strategic Marketing Boost 1

1. Set up your profiles on Google+, LinkedIn, and Facebook.
2. Search for and join the appropriate groups that you will eventually want to share your posts with.

Strategic Marketing Boost 2

1. Set up your Twitter account.
2. Search for hashtags that you might want to add to your posts.
3. Set up your HootSuite account with each of your social media accounts.

When you complete these tasks, you'll be ready to set up your blog and start using your social media sites to promote it. You'll find out how to do that in the next chapter.

Chapter Seven

START A BLOG:
Strategic Marketing Boost 3

WHEN THE INTERNET first became popular, there was only one entryway to your site—your home page. But with the advent of blogs, there's a great new way to attract lots of prospective clients to your site. While blogging is powerful and can be a great way to attract lots of great prospects, it does take a commitment. The last thing you want to do is to have visitors come to your blog and see that the most recent post is six months (or more) old. That will hurt your credibility and image. However, if you are willing to make a reasonable commitment, blogs can yield big results.

"Blog" is a shortened version of what these sites were originally called—"weblogs," which means quite literally a "log," as in journal, on the Web. A blog is the equivalent to your own personal op-ed page. It lets you editorialize on any aspect of your topic that you want. As a result, it's a great place to showcase what you know, what you think, and what kind of success you've had with clients.

While you may be familiar with blogs, the idea of starting one yourself might seem a bit overwhelming. Fortunately, the reality is that blogs are simple to set up. Today I'm going to show you how to quickly and easily get your blog started. I believe you'll find that your blog quickly becomes an essential component in your marketing arsenal. Here's why:

- A blog can help establish and sustain your position as a thought leader in your field.
- Each time you publish a blog post, it draws people to your site. If we correctly design the frame that appears around your blog post, your blog becomes a powerful tool for getting people to sign up for your email list and purchase other products and services you offer.
- As we discussed in the previous chapter, you can promote your blog posts on Twitter, LinkedIn, Facebook, and Google+. This enables you to attract prospects that you otherwise would miss.
- One of the biggest benefits of blogs is that they get passed along. If you write something that's interesting or even controversial, there's a strong chance that readers will send it to their friends, fans, circles, followers, and links on social media.
- Blogging can help increase your ranking in search engines. Google loves sites that have new, updated content, which you're providing every time you post a new blog.
- Google also rates your site based on how much time people spend when they visit. An interesting blog keeps people on your site much longer.
- Google also favors bigger sites. Since each blog post increases the size of your website by one page, your site grows with each post.

- The title of your blog post shows up in search results. If you include the terms that people search for in the title of your article, you'll almost immediately start to see your Internet traffic increase.

Ultimately, one of the largest benefits of a blog is that it deepens your relationship with your readers. If they enjoy an article, it's likely they'll say to themselves, "I like how this person thinks. Let me learn more about this person and the services they offer."

I recently acquired a new client through my blog in just this way. A large homebuilder in Australia read one of my blog posts, downloaded the free book offer that appears on the page, loved the book, called, and became a client. I landed a potential six-figure client, all as a result of a single blog post.

Many businesses find that their blogs produce a similarly positive result. My dentist says she gets a new patient for every few blog entries she posts. It's also a great way for her to stay connected with her current patients.

Think about it for a moment. When was the last time you received anything from your dentist aside from a reminder that you are overdue for a checkup?

The power of writing regular blog posts goes beyond building a brand for your business and attracting new clients. If you do it consistently, your blog becomes a powerful tool for cementing relationships with your existing clients and thwarting the attempts from your competitors to poach them.

Quick Tips for Your Web Designer

Let's start off with a little technical information for setting up your blog. Most of this is material you can tell your web designer, and he or she can run with it.

First of all, it's best if your designer uses WordPress to develop your blog. It's the leading website design platform, so most web developers are very familiar with it, and it's easy to use. It also enables you to design a page frame that appears each time someone goes to your blog. In this frame you can promote other services you offer. This is how we truly leverage the power of the blog. I'll show you how this works in just a moment.

One additional point; make sure you have your web designer use WordPress.*org* and not WordPress.*com*. You can do a lot more using the former.

If your website is on a platform other than WordPress, you don't have to start over and create a new website. You can set up a WordPress blog and just connect it to your existing site. WordPress specialist Chris Burbridge says, "The search engines will still consider it part of your main site, and you can still send links from your blog to the rest of your site."

Next, you will want to make sure your blog has the appropriate links to the places you want your visitor to go. These need to appear on the frame around your blog. When new visitors come and read your blog article, we don't want them to simply leave when they're done. By putting interesting information into the frame, we're motivating them to want to learn more about you and potentially become a client. One of the benefits of the WordPress platform is that it makes creating these elegant frames simple and easy.

What you put in the frame on your blog page will depend a great deal on your type of business, but there are numerous possibilities. I'm a subscriber to the theory that the greater the number of interesting offers we make, the greater the likelihood that people will be intrigued and decide to join our mailing list. That's crucially important since virtually all of my clients become subscribers first. I think the same will prove true for you as well. Here's what's on my blog frame.

- In the upper right-hand corner there's a link to my free report "How to Create a Steady Stream of New Clients Quickly and Easily" that includes a graphic with report covers.
- Moving down, there are graphics that link to my Facebook fan page, my Twitter Feed, my LinkedIn page, and my YouTube channel.
- Next comes a button that allows you to subscribe to the RSS feed for my blog.
- Finally, there are summaries of five previous blog posts, with a headline and the first 60 words for each one. Two of these are always the most recent ones and three are specifically chosen posts that I want visitors to see.

I've placed these links on the right-hand side because they are the most important. People tend to read the top line and the right-hand side of your site first. These links are all various free offers that are designed to motivate visitors to engage with me.

The various services I offer (which is how I make my money) have links on the left-hand side. I realize that when someone first comes to my site, the odds of them actually hiring me are slim. Thus my primary goal is to motivate them to opt in to my list. Once they're on my list, I have plenty of opportunities to send them lots of messages. If I don't get them to opt in, then it's up to them when (or if) they come back. We want to maintain control (as much as we can) over our marketing. That's why the very first step is always to get people to raise their hands and tell us that they have at least a teeny tiny bit of interest in what we do. Our drip-marketing sequence stokes that fire, so the two go hand in hand.

Let me walk you through what appears on the left-hand side of the frame. Much of what I'll be reviewing is applicable to your business, so feel free to model it.

The first button says "Will Gentle Rain Marketing Work for Me?" and connects to a web-based brochure that ends with an offer to call us for more information. This is an important link since it focuses on making a strong case for why this particular marketing system is one people should consider. You can do the same with your system for financial planning, manufacturing consulting, real estate marketing, legal services, or whatever you offer.

Other buttons link to my bio as a speaker, personal coaching, our home study course, and our Done For You marketing system, among others. The ninth button links to our blog, but it always goes to the post on "How to Drive Lots of Free Targeted Traffic to Your Website." That's the blog post that I most want potential clients to see. By the way, there's a special plugin that always puts today's date on that post, no matter when visitors click on that button.

That's followed by two testimonials, each of which gives specific results. In one our client says, "We tripled our inquiries from qualified prospects and doubled our contact-to-close ratio." The other mentions an additional $20,000 in revenue during the first 30 days of the program. Remember, you want your testimonials to focus on the results clients get when they hire you. Testimonials are often referred to as "social proof," and they are absolutely critical for your website. If you don't yet have a large number of them, put this high on your list of things to do.

There's one other automated item that shows up, not on the frame, but just under each blog post. It's a simple graphic, generated by a WordPress plugin, with a button you can click on to receive a free electronic copy of my book *Unique Sales Stories*. To get the book, you have to subscribe to my blog.

This button is particularly effective because it immediately follows the blog post. If my reader has enjoyed the blog, it's a very attractive offer made at precisely the right time. In fact, this offer is the most popular one on the page. If all you have is your free report, I would reiterate that offer at the bottom of each blog post.

Here's what this button looks like:

RECEIVE A COPY OF MARK'S #1 AMAZON BEST SELLER, UNIQUE SALES STORIES: HOW TO PERSUADE OTHERS THROUGH THE POWER OF STORIES   GET YOUR FREE BOOK
when you become a subscriber to the Gentle Rain Marketing Blog

I'll admit that I didn't think this technique up on my own, but rather "borrowed" the idea from other sites I was impressed with. One of my goals with this book is to make you more astute and aware of other people's websites. When you find that you are attracted to something on a website, pause for a moment and ask yourself, "Why has this gotten my attention?" It's likely you will pick up a lot of great ideas for your site as a result.

For example, Derek Halpern has a blog called Social Triggers (SocialTriggers.com), where he uses the entire first screen of his site to capture email addresses, as you can see below.

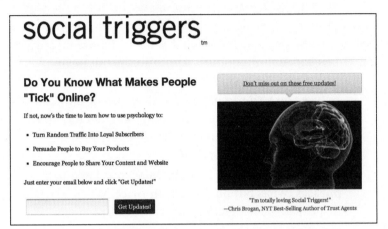

The beginning of the article appears below the opt-in box, but he never posts the full article; instead, he shows the first five to seven lines, then asks you to "click to continue."

At the top of the new page, where the actual article appears, he asks for your email address again. There's a banner that says, "Enter your email to get free updates" with a box for your email address and a button that says, "Get Instant Access!" It's a very clever approach that other businesses should consider modeling.

Halpern also uses a button to grab subscriptions at the bottom of each post. It says, "If you enjoyed this article, get email updates (it's free)." Again, a very effective technique that's worth considering for your own marketing.

SEO Tips Before You Write Your First Post

As I mentioned previously, in addition to attracting new subscribers, blogs help your entire site appear higher in the natural
search listings of Google and other search engines. However,
there are certain guidelines you'll want to follow in order to
make this happen:

1. **Before you write a post, pick one or two of the keyword
   phrases that you want to get highly ranked for.** You
   don't have to do this for every post you write, but try to
   do it for at least 50% of them.
2. **When you write your post, include your keyword
   phrases twice, but no more than twice.** When blogging
   first began, people put keywords in multiple times,
   sometimes to the point of ridiculousness. It wasn't
   long before Google caught on to this trick of "keyword
   stuffing," and they now penalize you for doing it.
3. **Your keyword phrase should appear within the first
   seven words of your headline.** If you're focusing on two
   different keyword phrases for a post, you'll have to choose
   which one is most important to you, since it's unlikely
   you'll fit both in the same headline. You can always
   highlight the other one in another post.
4. **One of the iterations of your keyword phrase should be
   in the first sentence, in bold typeface.** I'll show you how
   to do this when you're actually doing your first post.
5. **Add the keywords and phrases as "tags" to your post.**
   WordPress has a box that lets you create tags to let the
   search engines know about your post so they can add it to
   their index. Put in whatever keywords or subjects you find
   appropriate, even if you didn't emphasize them in your
   post.

6. **Make sure your post is at least 300 words.** A client of mine who was posting four times a week discovered that only the blogs with 300 words or more were having an effect on his ranking. Many social media experts agree that 300 words is the minimum number necessary to get SEO benefits for your blog.

7. **Periodically, take an original photo, post it on Flickr .com or Instagram.com and add it to your post.** Randall West of TapSuccess.com says, "Search engines are tired of seeing the same old photos and ideas floating around the Internet. Google's spiders will give you points for an original photo, as most posts use photos taken from somewhere else on the Internet, or stock photography that everyone uses." Also, the reason to post your photo on one of the big photography sites is that it provides a link from a highly ranked site, which will also help with your SEO.

8. **Give your picture a name that includes your keyword phrase.** This is pretty self-explanatory, and it makes a difference.

9. **Add your keyword phrase as an alt description.** A person can look at a photo and tell that it's the Empire State Building. A search engine spider doesn't know what it is. The alt description is where you tell the robots what the picture is. You can sneak your keyword phrase in at the same time. For example, let's say your keywords are "retirement plan" and you have a photo of a piggy bank. Your alt description could be "retirement plan piggy bank."

If you follow these instructions, you'll have used your main keyword phrase five times between the headline, the body of the post, and the photo you've added. Your secondary keyword phrase will be mentioned twice in the body of the post. This will give your SEO a significant boost.

One other tip: If you want to write a post that's 600 words or longer, break it up into Part I and Part II (using the same headline) and you'll get double the search engine benefits.

Finding Your Blogging Personality

There's an interesting paradox that takes place when you're writing a blog post for your business. On the one hand, your goal is to talk about your business. On the other, you want it to be entertaining enough for people to want to read it. Trust me, there's nothing as boring and unreadable as a blog that's written in 100% "corporate speak."

Your blog should read like you're having a one-to-one conversation with a prospect or customer you already like. Sharing personal details from your life accelerates the "know, like, and trust" factors that are crucial for building relationships. The trick is to insert things that have happened in your personal life and relate them to your business—like the vacation you just took to the Bahamas, where you collected shells on the beach with your four-year-old daughter, which reminded you of an important premise you wanted to share with your clients. Or it could be the movie you just saw, the restaurant you just ate in, or the conversation you just had with a client. In other words, sprinkle these moments in from time to time, and your blog will have plenty of personality.

Here's one more suggestion: Don't be afraid to be humorous—or even ever-so-slightly risqué. When a friend of mine tells the story of how he got his first ghostwriting deal on a book about hair color, he talks about how he inherently understood how to write for women: "When I was a kid, I read everything that fell under my nose, including my mom's *Cosmos*," he says. "Of course, that was before I really understood what the 'Foreplay Men Crave' was really about."

But after he makes the joke, he brings it back to business by adding, "That's how I knew how to write in a voice that resonated with women." You can do the same thing. Keep it light, but never forget to make sure you get back to business.

Your Tasks for Today

Understanding the benefits of having a blog is important, but it doesn't do us any good if you don't actually *have* one. So let's get started and set yours up.

Strategic Marketing Boost 3

1. If you haven't already done so, contact your web designer and have them create the blog for your website. Ask them to do all the items listed above in "Quick Tips for Your Web Designer." Don't forget to make sure they create a button on your blog frame that links to your free report.
2. Write your first post. It will need to be 300–500 words. Then, as soon as your web designer has installed your blog, upload the post to your site.
3. Follow the instructions in Chapter 6 and create a great hook that will make people want to read your blog post. Using HootSuite, post a message with that hook and a shortened link (that you make by going to Bitly). One of the great things about HootSuite is that you can post to all your social media sites and the groups you join on LinkedIn with a single message.

One of the easiest posts you can write is "How I Became a (**Whatever You Do**)." You'll get SEO benefit when people search for the job title that the post references, and there is usually a high degree of curiosity about these types of articles. That makes for a great combination.

I obviously can't give you an exact template for this story, but here are some items to think about using. Naturally, you'll want to write this in your own voice.

- One way to start off is to say either "I never expected to be a _____" (and if applicable, you might add, "I'd never even heard of one") or "I've wanted to be a _____ ever since I was ___ years old. It was because . . ." For example, "I never expected to be a chiropractor. I'd never even heard of one" or "I've wanted to be a chiropractor ever since I was 15 years old. It was because I saw a chiropractor change my brother's life."
- Talk about your journey. This can take two distinct paths: "The road wasn't easy" or "Everything about this profession came easily to me."
- Talk about your education. Was there anything a professor or a mentor told you that helped you feel like you could do this, or was there a lesson you learned that still influences you today?
- Mention your first big success and how it came to be. You could also mention some trials along the way to that success if you had difficulties. This humanizes you and will make you appear more accessible in the eyes of prospective clients.
- Sum up by saying, "Even though there have been ups and downs since then, I've never regretted my decision to enter this profession. Every time I help a client (achieve a result), it always makes me feel _____."

These are just suggestions. You don't need to use all of them, as that may create a longer post than you need. Here's an example of what a finished "How I Became" post might look like:

How I Became an Executive Recruiter

I never expected to be an executive recruiter, although I sort of knew what one was. My father always used to mention the recruiters or "headhunters" who called him. One recruiter got him a new job that moved us from Baltimore to New York when I was ten.

My father made a few big career and financial moves because of recruiters.

When I was 28, I answered a classified ad in the paper for a position as a Santa Cruz executive recruiter. When I heard what the pay was before commissions, I decided not to go to the interview I had set up; I only went because I forgot to cancel it. I planned to leave after ten minutes, but I stayed for an hour, leaving my poor fiancée, who had just moved from New York to California and didn't have a car yet, waiting.

The job, as my soon-to-be new boss described it, sounded just like me: Networking your way around an industry to find people who were as difficult to find as needles in haystacks. I had a lot of experience with that from my life already; I had networked my way into a job with a record label right out of college.

Though I was frightened about the money, I took the job.

The first step for a newbie Santa Cruz executive recruiter back then was to scan the ads for jobs in the Sunday papers, pick some you were interested in, and then weasel your way into talking directly to the managers of the companies that were advertising (instead of their Human Resources department) so you could work on the job.

One particular ad seemed to almost glow in the dark for me. It was for optical networking engineers for a company with military contracts. I didn't want to work with defense companies, so I put it aside. Oddly enough, though there were more than one hundred display ads in the Sunday paper, my boss specifically picked out that one and said, "Why don't you call them?"

It seemed like too much of a coincidence to ignore, so I called. Two months later, I had placed four optical engineers with that defense contractor. In just 60 days, I earned more than 60% of what my total income had been the previous year. It was a record haul for a newcomer in that company, a record that was never broken.

Even though there have been ups and downs since then, I've never regretted my decision to enter this profession. Every time I help a client improve their life with a new job, it always makes me feel like I'm doing something to make at least a few people in this world a little happier.

In addition to using this as a blog post, you might also add it to your website as the page that talks more about who you are.

Your Next Four Posts

Here are some suggestions for future blog posts:

1. Write a post about three to five items everyone should be doing on a regular basis when it comes to your topic, whether they're a client of yours or not. Ideally, you want this to be something that isn't commonly known. For example, if you're a dentist, you can say "You already know to brush and floss twice a day, but here are some things that you might not know." Then tell them something like "Instead of using toothpaste, you're much

better off brushing with a mixture that's half hydrogen peroxide and half mouthwash." Let them know what benefits this will give them, and briefly mention the fuller benefits they would get if they came to see you.

2. The post that follows should be a compilation of questions and answers that people ask you. This will be a fairly easy post to write.

3. Follow that up with a story about your work with a client and the benefits they achieved as a result of working with you.

4. Next, try the three biggest mistakes people make or bad habits they have regarding your area of expertise.

More Ideas to Pick and Choose From

Once you get a blog started, you'll find there's plenty more for you to write about. Here are several more ideas you can use as a starting point:

- **Tell the tale of a problem a real (or hypothetical) company in your industry is facing** and what they can do to make it better.
- **Talk about current trends in your industry,** or be really brave and talk about what those trends could lead to in the near future—or even ten years from now.
- **Report on articles you've read in trade publications** or items you've learned at conventions you've attended.
- **Debunk a myth.** Isn't it time to set the record straight? The truth starts with you.
- **Keep a diary of your day.** This may surprise you, but many readers will follow your posts simply because they become interested in you as a person. I did one of these types of posts on a dare, never thinking it would be of

interest, and received a surprisingly large amount of positive response.

- **Show off your world.** What's it look like where you work? Take photos and write about these photos, or better still, make a video. This builds on the previous point. Remember, people will hire you not simply because you can do what needs to be done. (Frankly, there are always a lot of people who can jump that bar.) They'll hire you because of your technical capabilities *and* because they feel connected to you. This is a great way to facilitate that process.

- **Write about someone you admire in your industry or a mentor.** I was initially reticent to mention others in my blog since I thought it would take away from my own credibility. I was wrong. Talking about the role that others have played in your life makes you more real in the eyes of your subscribers. It demonstrates that you're always learning and growing. People want to hire those who display these characteristics.

- **Discuss a mistake you've made and what you learned from it.** Let your readers know how you got through it and how it's influenced you today. Demonstrating that you have personally experienced the pain your prospective clients are facing shows that your knowledge is more than theoretical. My wife has said to me, "It would be great if you got it right the first time, just once," but the fact that I'm willing to share mistakes makes my recommended solution all the more credible.

- **Do a "Coming Attractions" piece.** When I go to the movies, I often like the previews as much as the actual picture I'm seeing. People love to know what's coming next. Give them an inside peek at what's on its way in your business. Internet marketer Ryan Deiss posts a blog entry every Friday about what he's reading that weekend. Even if my personal reading list is packed, I still find that I can't resist taking a peek at the blog.

- **Conduct a survey and then report the results.** This will give you two pieces, one in which you conduct the survey and one where you report on the results. SurveyMonkey .com is a great resource. A matchmaking company I know of got into *Time* magazine and *U.S. News & World Report* because of their surveys about dating. You can also make it super-simple and ask people to send their replies to your email address.

- **Write about a celebrity that everyone's talking about and relate it to your business.** If something happens that puts a celebrity in the news, whether it be a gaffe, an accomplishment, or even a death, lots of people are searching under their name. If you can find a way to make a comment about them that also relates to your business, you'll pick up new traffic for your blog. For example, when Steve Jobs passed away, I posted a blog that featured a video of the great commencement speech he made at Stanford. Since one of my subspecialties is how to use stories to influence others, the post related to my business.

- **Make a list that your readers will find useful.** Can you put together a convenient list that people in your niche will find relevant? It could be books and articles, but don't forget social media. Maybe you could make a list of groups on Facebook, LinkedIn, and Google+ that your audience should be members of. Or perhaps you can make a list of people they should follow. A client of mine put together a list of Twitter handles for literary agents that was retweeted heavily.

It's also a good idea to periodically include a video on your blog. Posting videos on WordPress is really easy. Upload the video on YouTube first and then simply copy the embed code and paste it into your blog. Make sure you go back to the YouTube page with the video and post the link to your blog. That way you'll have the double benefit of the video appearing both on your blog and YouTube. Remember, YouTube is the second largest search engine after Google, so make sure to add keywords in the descriptions of any videos you put up there.

A Cool Idea to Bring in Traffic

Google has a site called "Google Trends" (google.com/trends/), which lets you know on an hour-by-hour basis what the most popular searches are. Under the search bar that appears, it says "hot searches." Photos run next to an animation that shows the nine most popular topics one at a time.

If you write a post on one of these sought-after searches, you will get a quick traffic boost according to Jesse Peterson, quoted on iThemes.com by Cory Miller. Here's what happened to Peterson:

> I purposefully targeted the most popular Google trend of the hour one morning. I wrote a post, linked a video, and used appropriate keywords for my subject. That day, my traffic was *triple* that of the day before and the hit trail continues today. Keep in mind, this was *the* most popular topic of the day on July 8th, but it managed to get an immense amount of traffic despite the competition.

This might be a strategy you can use. But wait until you have at least five posts. You want people to see that you have a viable blog.

Coming Up with Your Own Ideas

You've now got ideas for your first 18 posts. If you only post once a month, that's a year and a half. But as you begin to see what a blog can do for you, I'm sure you'll want to post more often than that. Ideally I'd like to see you add a new blog post at least once a week.

For anyone who blogs regularly, the challenge is to come up with new topics. One helpful tip is that whenever a thought comes to mind, or you read something that might make a great post, keep a record of it. I use a program called Evernote that enables me to keep all these ideas readily available. Tadeusz Szewczyk, an SEO and blog consultant at Seoptimise.com, offers this advice that's worth keeping in mind:

> *Remember that business blogging is about value.* That's indeed the most crucial difference between private and business blogs. In private blogs people want to express themselves; business bloggers want to create value for others. So when writing a post for a business blog, always consider this question: *Of what use can this article be to potential clients, people in my industry, and the general public?*

While I agree with that statement, I think it's also important to let your personality come through, and there's nothing wrong with a bit of humor.

Back a few years ago, I was recording a video on implementing a marketing system. I'm usually pretty good in front of the camera and seldom require more than two takes. I don't know precisely what went wrong that day, but the words wouldn't come out of my mouth in a coherent manner. Finally when I completed take number eight, I managed to get through the presentation without messing it up.

However, unbeknownst to me, my cat Sam had walked across the back of the sofa I was sitting on, stopped above my head, yawned, and then walked off.

There was a part of me that said I should do this over again. After all, I'm a marketing consultant and I'm talking about serious marketing stuff. But I was tired and a bit lazy, so using my video-editing program, I simply inserted a card that said, "Well, that wasn't very professional, was it?" after Sam made her appearance.

Suffice it to say, the response was much greater than normal, and somewhat to my surprise, universally positive. Granted, I wouldn't do this every time, but it does underscore the benefits of not taking your work, or yourself, too seriously.

Getting to Your Blog's Dashboard So You Can Post

WordPress makes putting up your post very easy. Just sign in to your account. (If you're having trouble figuring out where to do that, input the name of the site your blog is hosted on, followed by a slash, followed by the name of your blog, and then add "/wp-admin" without the quotation marks. The whole thing will look like this: www.yourhostingsite.com/thenameofyourblog/wp-admin.

On the left-hand side of the page, there will be a list of items under "Dashboard."

Prepping to Add a Photo

If you're planning on adding a photo to your post, start by adding that photo to your media library. If not, you can skip this section and go to the next one about posting. (You can also skip ahead if you plan on posting a video but not a photo.)

Under "Dashboard," hover over the word "Media," then click on "Add New." A new page will appear that says "Upload New Media." Click on the button that says "Select File." A window will open with a directory of your files. Click on the one that holds your images, and double-click on the photo you want to use.

A miniature version of your picture will appear. On the far right of your picture, you'll see the word "Edit." Click on that.

A new page will appear where you can add a caption, alternative text, and a description of your photo for your own files.

Make sure you use your main keyword phrase in your caption. It needs to make sense, though, since everyone who reads your blog will see the caption under your photo. Depending on what your picture is, it might take a little creativity to make your keywords part of the caption.

As mentioned previously, the alternative text tells Google's spiders what's in the picture. So you can use both keyword phrases as well as whatever accurately describes the image.

Then click on "Update" on the right-hand side of the page, and your image and its corresponding information will be saved to your media library. Now your picture will be ready for you when you want it. I'll show you how to add it to a post in just a little bit.

Posting to Your Blog

Look under "Dashboard" again and you'll see the word "Posts." Click on that and a menu will appear. Select "New Post."

A new page will appear with a thin bar for your title and a box to put your post in.

Add your title to the thin bar. Remember, your main keyword phrase should be in the first seven words.

Then add the material for your post to the box.

If you want to add a video, just go to the website where the video is hosted, most likely YouTube, and copy the embed code.

You'll find that under the section that says "Share your video." Then paste the code wherever you want it to appear within the blog—above the text, below the text, or in the middle of the text.

If you want to add a photo, place your cursor where you want your photo to appear. Then click on "Add Media." Your photo library will appear. Click on the photo you wish to use, and it will have a check mark on it. Then place your cursor on the blue button that says "Insert Into Post," hit it, and your picture and its caption will appear in your blog post.

Now click on "Publish" (or you can click on "Preview" to see what your post will look like first), and you're done. Then follow the instructions in Chapter 6 to create hooks that will make people want to read your posts. Load up your Tweets and posts for Facebook and LinkedIn on HootSuite so you can publicize your blog on your social media sites.

Social Blogging

Blogging is something worth doing on a regular basis. Just make it fun. I have one friend who gathers a bunch of people together for Blog and Breakfast Thursdays. They get together, eat bagels, schmooze, and write. Nobody leaves until they've written a post. Usually everybody comments on, tweets, and posts about one another's blogs.

When they do leave, it's with a full belly and a full blog. And it really puts the social into social media.

But even if you blog alone, you'll still bring all kinds of new people into your business life as you attract new visitors.

In the next chapter, you'll learn how to create videos for your blog and YouTube, and you won't even have to appear on camera unless you want to.

Chapter Eight

VIDEO MARKETING:
Strategic Marketing Boosts 4, 5, and 6

THEY SAY A PICTURE'S worth a thousand words. So what do you think a video's worth?

Believe it or not, someone came up with an answer, at least in terms of Internet marketing. According to Dr. James McQuivey of Forrester Research, one minute of video is worth 1.8 million words.

That may be an exaggeration, but study after study shows video is more effective than text in terms of SEO, lead generation, attracting prospects to your website, keeping them engaged while they are there, and ultimately converting them into customers.

Since YouTube is now the second most searched site after Google, video takes on increased importance. When you do a search on Google or Bing, you'll notice an increasing number of the results are videos. A post that you make on Facebook, Twitter, LinkedIn, and other social media leading people to an interesting video has the potential to be viewed by tens or even hundreds of thousands of viewers. Having a video "go viral" is often considered the Holy Grail for Internet marketers.

Whether we like it or not, we have become a nation of viewers, not readers. This isn't to say that copy is dead. You can still have a highly effective marketing system by just using text. But if you're serious about maximizing the number of clients who do business with you, video is a tool that you'll definitely want to be using.

However, if the idea of appearing on camera makes your hands sweat, don't worry; there are options that enable you to take advantage of video marketing without having to become an online personality. You may have noticed that many YouTube clips feature just text and audio or just text and music.

To make your task less daunting, you've got three sessions to write your script, shoot it, and post the video so that it gets a lot of views.

In Strategic Marketing Boost 4, you'll pick your topic and write your script. You've now had experience in writing free reports and emails that capture attention. Writing a script is pretty similar, and I'll walk you through the process.

In Strategic Marketing Boost 5, you'll create your video. You can either film yourself on camera or create a video that's all text and record an audio to go with it. Most people film themselves, which is pretty easy to do. However, if you want to hire someone to do it for you, I'll share some inexpensive ways to do that.

In Strategic Marketing Boost 6, you'll post your video to You-Tube, create your own YouTube channel, and do a few technical things that will get you a lot of viewers. Trust me, none of this will be difficult, and I'm going to be with you through each step.

Let's get started.

Strategic Marketing Boost 4:
Writing Your Video Script

Today's task is to write a two-minute video script. The first step is to determine what your goal is for the video.

As I've mentioned before, the most effective lead generation is that which directs people to the place where they can opt in to get your free offer and join your list of subscribers. Although you can eventually use video as a method for disseminating information, for your first attempt, I'd focus on a very short and targeted video that motivates viewers to take this important next step in the relationship-building process.

In this video we want to welcome people, communicate that we understand a problem they're facing, and direct them to take action by going to your website and downloading the free report. The goal is to be both welcoming and very specific about what you want them to do. Although two minutes (or less) may not sound like a lot of time to convey this, if we follow a rather simple structure, you won't have any problems.

Legendary copywriter John Carlton (MarketingRebel.com) offered me some great advice that's relevant to writing this video script. He said that persuading someone to do something fundamentally boils down to three things:

1. Tell them what you've got.
2. Tell them why they need it.
3. Tell them what you want them to do next.

Interestingly, in many selling situations, we really don't need to be much more subtle than that. However, for this video, I suggest that we first make sure that viewers know that we understand their specific challenges and problems.

Thus a template for your script would read as follows:

Hi. I'm _____. Thanks for watching this short video. If you're a (**targeted niche you market to**), I'm sure one challenge you face is (**specific problem**). For the past (**number of years**), I've shown people just like you precisely how to (**solve that problem**), and I'd like to assist you as well.

That's the reason I wrote (**name of report**). You can get a copy by visiting (**name of your website**). In the report you'll learn:

1. **Benefit #1**
2. **Benefit #2, and**
3. **Benefit #3**

So go ahead and head over to (**name of website**), put your information in the form, and I'll send you the report immediately. I guarantee you'll find it to be helpful and useful. Again, this is (**Your name**), thanking you for watching this video, and I look forward to speaking with you soon.

That's a basic script that works quite well for creating your first video. As we'll discuss in more detail shortly, YouTube and other video distribution sites also enable you to include a link to your website that appears below the video. You can also tell people to click on that link, which will take them immediately to your site where they can access the free information.

You can also create a version of this video and put it on the landing page of your website. Just replace the text where you tell people the name of your website with "simply fill in the box on this page with your name and email and I'll send you the report immediately."

The real key is to create a script that sounds like you speaking in your authentic voice, so use this template as a jumping-off point, but don't feel constrained by it. Remember, the more conversational the tone, the better.

So go ahead and write out your script. Once you've done so, read it out loud a few times. If it sounds like you talking, then it's going to be fine. If it sounds awkward, adjust the language until it's something you're comfortable saying.

Strategic Marketing Boost 5: Creating Your Video

Now that your script is written, it's time to create your video. The first decision is if you want to appear in the video. I'd encourage you to do so. I'll show you how to create a video with just text and narration, but here's why I recommend that you appear on camera.

Clients are going to hire you based on two primary criteria. The first is if you can do the job they need to have done. That's the credibility factor, and the reason why testimonials and focusing on a specific niche are so important.

But clients make their decisions with both their heads and their hearts. By this I mean it's extremely important that they like and trust you. This is one of the reasons why speeches are such a powerful tool for business development. Seeing someone live on stage enables us to connect with them in a way that we just can't through the printed word.

That's why video is so powerful. I don't personally believe it's quite as strong as a live presentation, but it's a close second. A simple welcoming video on your website enables you to greatly accelerate the relationship-building process. Remember, this doesn't have to be anything elaborate. A simple, "talking head"-style video will do just fine. So unless the idea of being on camera absolutely terrifies you, I'd recommend you be the star of your video. (However, if being on camera just isn't for you, I'm also going to show you how to create a video with just text and narration in a minute.)

Preparing to Shoot Your Video

There are a few things to get ready before you start filming.

1. **Your camera:** You don't need a fancy camera, but I would personally not recommend using the one that's built into your computer or phone. That said, weight loss and fitness expert Andrea Albright (AmazingBodyNow.com) has carved out a very successful business in an extremely competitive niche by filming videos of herself on the beach using her iPad. This ultimately becomes a judgment call. My guideline would be that if you are marketing to professionals, or in the B2B space, I'd use a real video camera rather than a built-in one.

   The good news is that there's no need to invest a lot of money in your video equipment. A decent camera can be picked up for less than $200 at Best Buy and even less on craigslist or eBay. Make sure your camera films in HD (high definition), which will make your videos have the appropriate level of visual professionalism.

2. **A tripod:** From a practical standpoint, it's a lot easier to shoot your video if it's on a tripod rather than balancing precariously on a stack of books. I learned this the hard way when halfway through shooting, the camera ever so slowly slipped off the stack and crashed to the floor. Whenever I shoot a video of me behind a desk, I use a small 5' tripod that you can pick up online for around $10.

3. **Sound:** This is important. You don't want to sound like you're speaking from a cave. Unfortunately, the microphone on your camera usually won't be of the quality that enables you to have a professional level of audio. Sometimes you can get adequate sound by recording in a room with a good thick carpet. The carpet has the effect of muffling the sound bounces that create that annoying echoing effect. The best solution is to use a lavaliere mike that you can clip to your lapel. Search on Google and buy one from a company where you can actually call and speak to a sales rep. (I personally like the service at sweetwater.com). There are a lot of choices with a bewildering alphabet soup of acronyms that can immediately befuddle those of us who aren't audio experts. The good news is that every audio salesperson I've ever spoken to seems genuinely interested in helping me. Just be prepared to tell them what type of camera you're using and what your project is all about.

4. **Clothing:** The watchword is to wear something that's consistent with your industry. If you'd wear a suit and tie on a sales call, that's what you should wear on camera. As a general rule, opt for something that's not too busy. Solids are preferred, even for your tie. Don't wear jewelry that clanks or moves around too much. A good way to get a sense for how to dress is to watch CNN or the morning talk shows and pay attention to what the anchors are wearing.

I also learned this the hard way. When I sat down to film my welcoming video for GentleRainMarketing.com, I didn't pay much attention to what I had on. Personally, I thought the sweater, which is reminiscent of what Cliff Huxtable wore on *The Cosby Show*, was rather cool. I certainly wasn't prepared for the emails I got, both pro and con, about it. One lady even wrote saying that while she liked my advice, she could never take seriously someone who wore such an "awful sweater." On the other side of the equation were the guys who wrote, "Love the sweater, dude, where'd you get it?" I suppose a bit of controversy isn't necessarily a bad thing, but if I had to do it all over again, I'd probably opt for a plain blue shirt. (You can weigh in with your own opinion on my fashion choices by visiting GentleRainMarketing.com.)

5. **Location:** You want to pick a location with a background that isn't too busy. A blank wall is ideal, but as long as there isn't distracting art on the wall, you should be fine. According to Catie Foertsch of yesmediaworks.com, if you have dark skin, you shouldn't shoot against a light background. "The camera will adjust for the background," she says. "Place yourself against a darker background so the camera adjusts to your face and not the white wall behind you."

6. **Lighting:** According to Foertsch, this is one of the easiest ways to make your video look good. Here's her advice: "Don't shoot against a window because your camera will adjust to the outside light and you'll be way too dark. Don't place yourself directly under an overhead light because you'll get very nasty raccoon eyes, as the light casts shadows from your brow." Instead, she suggests that you point a light source directly at your face to counter the shadows that show up from overhead light. You don't need a fancy lighting setup. Foertsch has an easy solution. "You can take the lampshade off a table lamp so the light shines on your face, or point a desk lamp at yourself. Don't place it so close that you blind yourself; just use it to fill in the light on your face. It'll make a big difference."

7. **Your script:** Unfortunately, few of us are such good actors that a memorized script doesn't wind up sounding like, well, a memorized script. Your best bet is to know what you're going to say using the script you've developed, but not worry excessively about getting it word-for-word perfect when it comes time to film. Remember, the real power of using videos is that they accelerate the relationship-building process. Sounding canned will work to your disadvantage. If you make a complete mess of it, you can always start over. If you flub a word, that's no big deal. It happens all the time in daily conversation, so if anything, it will make you seem more real.

For some of the videos I do, I write out a short list of bullet points and post it slightly behind the camera. If truth be told, the list serves more as a safety net than an actual prompt, and just having it there makes me more comfortable. Like many things in life, the more you get in the habit of doing videos, the more comfortable and natural you'll appear.

Once you've taken care of the preparations, all that's left to do is to set up the room, put your mike on your lapel, point the camera at yourself, and shoot. Then plug your camera into your USB port and save your video to your computer.

If you want to edit your video, you can put it into iMovie on your Mac. If you have a PC, there are several free video-editing software packages you can download, including a program called Steeper and another called Jahshaka. You can download them here: http://tinyurl.com/FreeVideoEditingSoftwareForPC.

In a little bit I'll tell you how to upload your video to YouTube, create your own YouTube channel, and market it so you get lots of viewers.

Hiring a Low- or No-Cost Videographer

If you don't feel comfortable creating a video by yourself, you can hire someone to do it inexpensively. The easiest way to find someone is to advertise in the "Gigs" section of craigslist. By inexpensive, I mean $25 per hour or less, depending on where you live. A friend of mine advertised on craigslist in Los Angeles and found several people willing to film and edit his talk at a bookstore for about $50.

If you'd like to hire someone for free (or for a very nominal amount), you can also post the job with the video department of your local college or university. For a few dollars and perhaps some pizza, you'll get talent that really knows what they're doing.

Creating a Narrated Text Video

As mentioned previously, if you don't want to appear on camera, another option is to create a narrated text video, or even one that just shows text on the screen with some accompanying background music. Creating a text video is simple. All you have to do is create a series of slides using either PowerPoint or Keynote (for Mac users) and record a narration.

You can achieve an acceptable level of audio by recording through your computer's microphone, but I'd recommend using a microphone that you can plug into the USB port on your computer. The headset model I use from Plantronics (plantronics .com) provides high-quality audio, and costs less than $100.

The first thing you do for your narrated text video is to create the slides. You can add pictures if you want, but it works just as well with simple text. I've found that the percentage of people who take advantage of the offer I make at the end of the video doesn't increase if I include fancy graphics.

While we don't want the videos to look too amateurish, investing in slick production values, graphics, and pictures usually doesn't pay off with higher levels of response. Keep it simple, always make sure you have a call to action, and you'll find that viewers will become engaged. After all, prospects are more interested in finding a solution to their problems than watching a fancy movie.

Both PowerPoint and Keynote are formatted to make creating bullet-point presentations a snap. There are varying opinions about precisely how much information to put on a slide. Having only a few words appear on the page forces the viewer to pay attention to the narration. Conversely, having a lot of text on each page enables you to get your message across both visually and audibly. Proponents of neuro-linguistic programming, who research how people learn, suggest that the more senses we appeal to, the greater the likelihood that they will assimilate the information. Ultimately what's the best choice for you will largely depend on your style and what you're most comfortable with.

Creating Slides in PowerPoint

Creating text slides is very easy in PowerPoint. If you're not familiar with it, here's what you do:

1. Open the software.
2. You'll see a slide with two boxes. The top one says "Click to add title." Click it and add your title.
3. Underneath that is another box. Click on that and add a subtitle.
4. The subtitle will appear in gray. If you want it to be black, highlight the text, then click on the formatting palette.
   (If the formatting palette isn't open, click on the icon that says "Toolbox" and it will appear.)

5. On the formatting palette, on the font menu, there is a box with the letter "A" and a colored bar underneath. Click on the arrow next to that.

   There will be a big rectangle. If that says "Automatic" and has a black box next to it, click on that. If it doesn't, click on the black color box and then on the big rectangle. That will turn your gray text to black.

6. Create the next slides by right clicking on your mouse and selecting "New Slide." You'll get the chance to create another title or header and more subtext.

7. Keep going until you finish your presentation.

8. There will be a thumbnail of each of your slides in a thin bar on the left. If you want to go back to edit one of them, click on it. Then you can page down the slides on the left to get back to where you were.

9. Once you have finished all your slides, save your file. You now have your slide show for your video.

This is the simplest of explanations. From the second slide on, you have six boxes within the subtext box that allow you to create different presentation styles and add charts, graphics, or even video. Feel free to click on those and experiment. You only have to click Control + Z on the PC or Command + Z on the Mac to get back to your blank box.

There are also different tabs at the top of the web page that let you change the background on your slide and create different formats for what you add. Play around to discover new things you can do.

For more detailed instructions for PowerPoint for the PC, go to: http://bit.ly/1ccaVg4

For PowerPoint for the Mac, go to http://bit.ly/1bvfpQZ

Creating Slides in Keynote

The steps you take in Keynote (a product for Apple computers) are very similar to those you take with PowerPoint.

1. Open Keynote.
2. You will see a page that says "Theme Chooser" with a bunch of rectangles that represent slides. If you mouse slowly over each one, you will see what that theme looks like as text, as a graph, and with pictures. Double-click on the white one for now. Feel free to choose whichever you prefer when you are creating a video on your own.
3. Your first slide will appear. There will be two boxes. Double-click on the top box to enter a title. Double-click on the bottom box to enter a subtitle.
4. To add a slide, head to the top left-hand side of the page and click on "New." You can also go to the sidebar where the thumbnails of the slides you created appear and right-click on your mouse. You then select "New Slide" and another slide will appear.
5. Once again, there will be two boxes. Double-click on the top one for a header.
6. The default for the second box includes a bullet on the left. If you'd like to work with the bullet, enter your text. If you want to create a bulleted list, you will get a new bullet each time you hit "return" on your keyboard. If you don't hit "return," the line will continue without a bullet.
7. If you'd like to get rid of the bullet, just left-click on your mouse and drag the box (that whole section of the screen) so that the bullet doesn't show. Release your mouse and the bullet will be gone in all your future slides. If you want it back, just left-click and drag the box to your right until it appears.

8. If you get rid of the bullet, you'll notice that the bottom box appears to be narrower than the top box. If you'd like to make it as wide as the top box, move your mouse onto one of the small squares you see on the right side of the perimeter of the bottom rectangle. Left-click and an arrow will appear. Then drag the box to the right to make it as big as you'd like. Let go of the mouse button and you will have a box that's the size you want. This will be the default size for all the other slides you create.

9. Keep creating slides until you finish. Save the presentation and you've completed the slides for your video.

As with PowerPoint, Keynote has lots of menu items for you to experiment with, if you want to get more creative. For a more complete explanation of how Keynote works, go to http://bit.ly/11m6wmp.

Turning Your PowerPoint Slides into a Video

Here's how you take your PowerPoint slides and the narration you composed and turn them into a video:

1. Get your audio recording equipment and script set up exactly as you want them when you start recording.
2. Open PowerPoint.
3. Click on "Slide Show."
4. Under "Slide Show," on the right-hand side, click on "Record Slide Show."
5. Select the option to "Start recording from the beginning." You will get a menu that asks you to "Select what you want to record," which will have two options. Click on "Narrations and laser pointer" if you've done the simple text video described above. If you've created

something more complex using additional features, click on "Slide and animation timings" as well.

6. Click on "Start recording." You are now recording both your voice and your laser movements.

7. Click on the thumbnails of each slide as you speak your presentation to create your video.

8. To stop recording, press the "Escape" button. (If you stop before you're finished and you want to continue where you left off, start the process over but instead of choosing "Start recording from the beginning," select "Start recording from current slide."

9. If you are finished recording, click on "File," then "Save As."

10. Name your file, if you haven't already. Then go to the bottom of the screen, to where it says "Save As Type." The default selection is a PowerPoint file (*.pptx), but you need to save this as a Windows Media Video (*.wmv). Just click on the text in the box and you'll get a pulldown menu where you can select "Windows Media Video."

11. Select the folder where you want to save your video.

12. Click "Save."

13. At the bottom of the page, there will be a progress bar next to the words "Creating Video." That progress bar will fill up and then disappear. When it's gone, your video will be complete.

You're now ready to post your video to YouTube. If you'd like to see this in action, go to: http://bit.ly/14VwJem.

If you'd like some alternative ways to do this, go to http://bit.ly/12sF1dz.

Turning Your Keynote Slides into a Video

Recording a video in Keynote is a simple procedure. Here's what you do:

1. Get your audio recording equipment and script set up exactly as you want them when you start recording.
2. Open Keynote and the slide show you want to record. Make sure you have selected the first slide because your recording will start with whatever slide you have selected.
3. Click on "Play," then select "Record Slide Show."
4. Your computer will switch to a full-screen mode where all you see are slides. When the first slide appears, there will be a red light button on to show that you are recording. Start speaking.
5. Click with your mouse to change slides.
6. When you are finished, double-click on your mouse to stop recording.
7. To export this as video, click on "File" and then select "Export."
8. The following settings are the defaults, but in case they're not, here's what you should select:
   - Quicktime Video
   - Next to "Playback Uses," select "Recorded Timing."
   - Next to "Formats," pick "Full Quality. Large."
   - Next to "Audio," the boxes that will be selected should be "Include audio" and "Include the slideshow recording." You really only need the latter, unless you previously added outside audio, like a piece of music, directly to your slideshow.
9. Click "Next."

10. Choose where you want to save the file. Your desktop might be the easiest place to find it.

11. Wait while your file is exported to video. There will be a blue and white horizontal line that looks like a skinny barber's pole, then each of the slides will appear. When the last slide goes away, your video is complete.

If you'd like to see this in action, go to http://bit.ly/16ndbwc.

Strategic Marketing Boost 6: Posting Your Video to YouTube and Promoting It

If you haven't created an account with Google for Gmail or any of their other programs, you will have to create a new account on YouTube. Otherwise, you can sign in with your Google information and create your YouTube account with that.

To create your account, go to YouTube.com.

1. Click on "Sign In."
2. On the next page, at the top, select "Create an Account."
3. You'll be taken to a page where you fill out the following information:
   - Your name
   - A Google username
   - A password of at least eight characters
   - Your gender
   - Your birthday
   - Your mobile phone number
   - Your current email address (You'll receive an email from Google asking permission to add this email to your new Google account. Just click the link to approve.)
   - Two words to type to prove you're not a robot

- Your location (country)
- Terms of Service and Privacy box, which has a check-mark in it by default and you need to keep that checked
- Permission to let Google use their +1 program with you on non-Google sites (This is a program where social networking friends can click +1 to let their friends see that they recommend or like a product. You can uncheck this if you like.)

Once you've filled all this out, click on "Next Step" and Google will take you to a page where it tells you how to provide more information for your profile. You are also asked for a photo.

You can use a photo, or you could use a logo for your business that includes your services and contact information. That might be a more effective marketing tool. (If you don't have one, you can start with your picture and change it later. You can always hire someone on Fiverr.com to create one for you.)

Click on "Next Step" again and you'll be taken to a page with a button that lets you go back to YouTube.

Upload Your Video and Create Your Channel

Once you're back on YouTube's homepage, you'll see a button that says "Upload" on the top right-hand side. Click on that word, not on the arrow next to it.

A box will appear that says "Upload As" with your user name and photo prominently displayed. By uploading your video, you will also be creating a new YouTube channel for your public videos and playlists.

Here's something you need to pay attention to: In small print below that, it says, "To use a business or other name, click here." This is important. For a business channel, you may want to use your business name or give yourself a special nickname, possibly including your keywords. You could call your channel "NewHavenChiropractor." You only have 20 character spaces to work with, so NewHavenChiropractor just fits.

YouTube will check to see if the name you've picked is available. If it is, you'll see a button that says, "Okay, I'm ready to upload." Click on that.

All you'll have to do to get your video on YouTube is to select the file that you want to use. As soon as you do that, it will begin uploading.

While that's happening, you'll be asked to create some of the most important aspects of marketing your video: a title, a description, and tags. On the same page you'll get to select your privacy settings, pick a subject matter category from a list, and share your video on Google+, Facebook, and Twitter.

Here's what to do in each category:

- **Title:** Call your video something that includes your keywords. This will help it show up when people search for that term on YouTube. But you want the title to make sense and not just be a list of keywords. If you want to squeeze more keywords in without a long, run-on sentence, simply add additional keywords in parentheses. For example, you could call your video "The New Haven Chiropractor's Guide Solution for Back Pain (Spine, Spinal Stenosis, Lumbar, Lower Back, Back Spasm, and More). There is a trade-off. The parentheses approach adds SEO power, but to some eyes it may look less professional. You make the decision as to what's best for you.
- **Description:** Here's where you tell viewers what your video is about. They'll only see the first few lines, so start with the most important part—your website. In fact, you might want to start with "For a free report about (**your report's title**), go to **yourwebsite.com**." Next add your company

name. Then write a description of your video using key-word phrases. Make sure what you write makes sense and isn't just a list of keywords.

- **Tags:** This is where you get to go hog wild with your key-words and phrases. Just separate them with a comma. Remember, these are the terms that people will search for. You want to include all of the terms that you think are rel-evant to your video.
- **Privacy Settings:** The default setting is "Public." But if you ever want to create a private video, you can change this setting to "Private." You can also make sure only people with a link to this video see it by changing this setting to "Unlisted."
- **Category:** Select a subject matter category that's most rel-evant for your business.
- **Sharing:** Google+, which you joined when you set up your Google account, is automatically selected. Make sure you select Facebook and Twitter as well.
- **Category:** Click on the arrow to the right and you'll get a pulldown menu. If your video fits one of the main top-ics, pick that. Otherwise you can always use the "How to and style" category, since you are telling people how to do something.

Advanced Settings

On the top left-hand side, next to "Basic Info," there's a link for "Advanced Settings." Most of these are unimportant, but the first four allow you to choose how you handle comments and video replies.

The default setting for "Approve Comments" is "All," mean-ing all comments are automatically approved. I'd suggest chang-ing this to "Approved," which allows you to approve comments before they appear. This way you avoid a bunch of spam that is often generated on these posts, plus you can delete any inappropriate rant that you sometimes see in the comments on videos where all comments are approved.

The other setting I would also change from "All" to "Approved" is "Allow video replies." A video reply is when someone replies to your video with theirs. Generally, their video will appear in the side box next to your video, so you want to be able to control this. Once again, spam is an issue—and you also don't want to let your competitors list their videos next to yours. (However, this is a feature you can use liberally to market your video. I'll explain that in a little bit.)

Your Channel

As mentioned above, once you've uploaded your video, you have your own YouTube channel. To find it, click on your username on the top right-hand side of the page, then click on "My Channel" from the list of links that will appear. Highlight and copy the web address at the top of your browser so you can share it with other people.

Uploading Video to Vimeo

Vimeo is the second most popular video channel, so it would be worth posting your video there, too. Here's how you do it:

1. Join Vimeo by going to vimeo.com/join and filling in your name, email address, and password.
2. Click on the button that says "Join." When you click on this button, you are agreeing to Vimeo's terms of service.
3. You'll be taken to a site where they want you to pay to subscribe. Just page down to the bottom and click on "Continue with your Basic account."

4. Go to your email account and open the email from
    Vimeo. Click on the link inside to confirm your
    membership.
5. Click on the "Upload" button at the top of the page.
6. Click on the "Choose a Video to Upload" button.
7. Select your video.
8. Click on "Upload Selected Videos."
9. You'll come to a page that lets you input a title, a
    description, and tags. See instructions for YouTube
    discussed previously.
10. Vimeo will also let you set up automatic sharing. Click
    on the link on the top left-hand side of the page that
    says "Set up automatic sharing now." You'll be able to
    automatically link all your videos to your social media
    pages.

Promoting Your Video

Once you put your video up, you need to promote it. Putting it
up on the social media sites is a good start, but there's a lot more
you can do. There are a number of simple techniques you can
use to promote your video. The more you do, the more viewers
you will get.

Video Replies

One of my favorite techniques for getting viewers is creating
video replies on YouTube. As mentioned above, a video reply is
where you use your video as a comment on someone else's video.
Generally, your video will show up in the list of similar videos
that appears on the side of the video you reply to.

The trick to making this work is to find videos that relate to
yours. In other words, would people watching these other videos

also be interested in your video? If so, you will want to video reply to them.

Start by searching under your keyword phrase to find appropriate videos to reply to. Videos with tens of thousands of views work well. Those that have hundreds of thousands of views also have a lot of significant competition.

To create your video reply, just click on the comment box below the video you've selected. A link will appear with the words, "Create a video response." When you click on this, a box will appear that says, "Select the video you want to respond with." Simply add a link to your video and click on the button that says, "Use the video selected," and you're done.

By the way, on the top left-hand corner of the page, you'll see how many video responses have been made so far, so you'll have a sense of what you're up against.

The more videos you respond to, the more viewers you will get.

One way to really make this strategy work is to hire someone to do this for you on Fiverr.com. If you paid $5 for every 25 video replies, $200 would give you replies to 1,000 videos. That would get you a lot of traffic.

Traffic Geyser

Traffic Geyser will send your video to all the important places where videos are distributed on the Web. This will enable your video to appear on the first page of the search engines for a limited period of time. It's very effective and costs about $100 per month, but you can get a three-week trial for just $1. I've had great results with the service, and you can find out more at TrafficGeyser.com.

Fiverr.com

Fiverr.com is a great resource to get your video viewed and liked. You can also use it to get subscribers to your channel. Just go to Fiverr and then mouse over "Online Marketing." A menu will appear that includes "Video Marketing." There will be offers for everything from getting you 5,000 views to getting you dozens of comments and likes. If you can't afford Traffic Geyser, there are people who will hand-submit your video to 30 sites for $5.

That's it for video. Your next Strategic Marketing Boosts will help you get attention on TV, on the radio, and in newspapers and magazines.

Chapter Nine

PUBLICITY:
Strategic Marketing Boosts 7 and 8

SUZE ORMAN turned her appearances on *Oprah* into a huge television and book career.

A large part of Donald Trump's success is due to his masterful courting of the media.

Although most of us don't want to be that famous, appearing on the radio, on TV, and in the print media on an occasional or even a regular basis can be a very good thing for your business.

Publicity offers three major benefits:

1. Your business is exposed to new audiences who may go to your website or contact you directly.
2. It gives you additional credibility, especially if you appear on national or regional media.
3. Links from high-traffic media sites to your website will increase your search engine ranking.

Getting on the right media can get you exposed to either millions of people or a highly targeted niche audience of prospective clients for free. Additionally, visibility in the media gives you a level of credibility that you simply can't get from advertising.

The trick to getting publicity is to come up with story angles that attract the attention of producers and journalists. Unless you're in a new and unusual field, they won't just interview you about your business. We need to be creative to develop hooks that will be appealing to the audiences that the particular media outlet wants to reach.

I've separated this chapter into two different marketing boosts to give you plenty of time to create the kind of story angles that will get you media attention.

In Strategic Marketing Boost 7, after you learn about what story angles most appeal to the media, you'll come up with several "hooks" to pitch the media. I'll show you the websites where you can distribute your press release. We'll also take a look at sites where you can advertise in publications that TV and radio producers read. This is a way to get them to invite you to appear on their shows.

You'll also do research to find some of the best blogs on your topic. Finally, you'll subscribe to email lists where reporters and producers look for people to interview for stories or shows they are working on.

In Strategic Marketing Boost 8, you'll actually write your press release or hire someone to write it for you. To make the process easy, I'll provide you with a template to use. Once that's done, you'll distribute your press release through one of the services you looked at previously. To ensure maximum exposure, you will also want to personally contact the media you most want to reach. Finally, since social media plays an increasingly larger role in publicity, you'll want to email some bloggers who focus on your area of specialization.

Story Ideas That the Media Loves

It may seem ironic, but the biggest mistake most business owners make with a press release is that they focus it on what *they* want to communicate about their business and their products. However, when you're pitching the media, the reality is that they don't care about your book, business, or free report. The media wants story ideas that will get people to watch or listen to their show, buy their paper or magazine, or visit their website. Thus, the trick to getting lots of media attention is to position what your business does in a way that appeals to the specific audience that the media outlet is trying to reach. Creativity is key.

Here are eight types of story ideas that get the media's attention:

- Stories that tie in to current events or have a specific local angle
- Stories that are related to holidays, annual events, and seasons
- Stories that tie to celebrities
- Trend pieces and surveys
- Numbered lists
- How-to pieces
- Stories that create controversy or debunk a myth
- Anniversaries of major events and smaller anniversaries with an interesting angle

This may seem complicated, but it's not. You've already listened to and read hundreds of media hooks. Every time a news anchor says "Coming up" or a talk show announcer says "Next on *Dr. Phil*," or *Ellen*, or *The View*, the phrase that follows is a hook.

A great way to test your story idea in terms of its newsworthiness is to actually say "Coming up" or "Next on" and then insert a summary of your idea afterward. If it sounds right, you've got a good hook.

For example, "Next on *Dr. Phil*: Seven signs your spouse is cheating" is a winner. It sounds just like something you would hear on the show. However, "Coming up: Local dentist offers anniversary special of half off on first visit" sounds more like an advertisement than a news or feature story. Yet it's very common for press releases to be focused on these types of messages. The results are inevitably disappointing.

So how might our dentist reposition her offer? If she was to celebrate her anniversary by giving away free dental work to poor children, that could very well be a story that the media might run with. "Coming Up: Local Dentist Celebrates Anniversary by Giving Free Dental Work to Underprivileged Children" is a more interesting story. The media is always interested in charity work, particularly involving children.

Tying Your Story to the News

You know the old saying that if you're a hammer, everything you see is a nail? That's the approach you need to take when you try to tie your pitch to current events.

The question to ask is "How can I relate what I do to this current event?"

Sometimes it's obvious, sometimes not. Not meaning to sound ghoulish, but when there's a story about a tragedy, if you're a psychologist, there are lots of ways you can approach the story. One very simple approach would be to create a release around "How to Talk to Your Children About (the tragic event)." One psychologist I know actually has a template created that she immediately modifies and sends out when (yet again) some tragedy occurs. In these instances, the media has a ravenous hunger for stories, and it's quite possible for experts to gain national exposure simply by being prepared.

You don't have to go after national media to tie into a news story. Especially when you're starting out, focusing on local coverage should be your goal. When a big story hits, the local news channels want to find ways to cover the same story as the major networks, but with a different, often local, perspective. If you pitch the media and say that you have a local angle for the story, it's likely you'll find a positive ear.

I've seen restaurants get media coverage during elections by offering two versions of the same item, be it coffee or pizza, with a Republican vs. Democrat twist, as a kind of survey. The only difference in the product would be that the Republican food or beverage would be served with red paper goods and the Democrat version with blue. There are two press releases in this—one announcing the food-based survey, the other giving the results. It usually gets attention.

Tying Your Story to a Holiday, an Annual Event, or a Season

The nice thing about this approach is that you've got plenty of time to prepare. New Year's Eve, the Oscars, the Super Bowl, and Back-To-School occur every year at pretty much the same time.

An added bonus is that with the right story idea, you can use the same pitch annually and even get the same national show to bring you back again and again.

You want to come up with something that's both unique and also a comfortable fit for the event you're targeting. Beware, though; everybody tries to get coverage around Christmas, so it's much more difficult than any other holiday.

I used the annual event strategy to promote my book *Unique Sales Stories*, which focuses on how to use stories to differentiate yourself and get more referrals for your business.

I was struggling with how to get more mainstream media attention for what was a niche business book. The Super Bowl was coming up when Steve Harrison, from Bradley Communications, mentioned to me that a lot of people watch the big game just for the commercials.

His thought was that a good commercial tells a good story—so why not pitch me as the Super Bowl advertising expert? I could talk about which ads did well and which were complete wastes of money.

We developed a press release and ran an ad in *RTIR*, a publication that goes out to hundreds of radio and television producers who are looking for guests to book on their shows. The idea was to have me on their shows the week before the Super Bowl to talk about which ads worked in the past, then to have me back the week after to evaluate the most recent Super Bowl commercials.

I had no idea if this was going to fly.

It didn't just fly. It soared. I was on 40 shows the week before the Super Bowl, ranging from small local affiliates to ESPN and ABC. I did another 15 shows after the game. It sold a lot of books, and I also got several client calls.

I also wound up with a lot of new subscribers to my mailing list. I used a trick that Steve taught me. I said that after the break, I'd share with viewers or listeners precisely how they could get a free chapter from my book, so they needed to get a pencil and paper. Then, when the commercials ended, I sent them to a website where they had to opt in to get the chapter. It was a PDF, so it didn't cost me anything. It generated a lot of requests, which ultimately led to a lot of book sales.

That was my big home run. Plus I got to be on most of the media outlets the following year. That's the wonderful thing about a holiday or event-based strategy. You can repeat it year after year.

Create Your Own Holiday

There are lots of holidays for you to tie in to that you've never heard of. As I'm writing this on May 11, it's not just the day before Mother's Day, but it's also National Babysitters Day, Eat What You Want Day, and Stay Up All Night Night, which actually makes a pretty good combination, especially if you have kids.

You can find these little-known holidays at Chases.com.

If you can't find your own holiday to tie in to, make up your own (with a creative way everyone can celebrate it) at Chases .com. Every year they publish *Chase's Calendar of Events*, a book that's chock full of unusual days, weeks, and months that people have created. Make sure you are committed to publicizing and celebrating it (even if it's just at your office) because Chase is looking for real events, not imaginary ones.

Just go to their website and click on "Submit an Entry" on the left-hand side of the page, then fill out the form that shows up. *Abracadabra!* You've made your own holiday appear out of thin air.

One quick tip about timing: Their deadline for submissions to the next year's calendar is April 15, so submit your holiday ASAP if you're reading this book close to that date.

Celebrity Tie-Ins

The media knows that the mere mention of a celebrity attracts attention. Plus television producers are always looking for ways to add visual interest to an interview, and they know they can easily find photos and video clips of a celebrity to show while a guest is speaking. Finding a tie-in to a celebrity can increase your chances to get interviewed.

This strategy works best when a celebrity is already in the news. A retail store owner could pitch a story on "How to Create Sandra Bullock's $2,000 Oscar Ensemble for under $100." When a political candidate gives a particularly great speech, if you're a public speaking coach, your hook could be "5 Speaking Tips You Can Learn from Governor Smith." (You could also comment on the mistakes a candidate made.)

Watch the local news and the morning shows and you'll see how often this strategy is used.

Trend Pieces and Surveys

The hard part about trend pieces is that you have to be one of the first people to notice the trend. You have to be aware of it before the media reports heavily on it, but not so early that no one knows the trend exists. Timing is crucial.

Sometimes the best way to pick up on trends is to simply pay attention to your customers.

In 2010, a little product called Silly Bandz and the companies doing knock-offs were selling huge numbers of animal and character-shaped silicone rubber bands each week. Kids were wearing dozens of these rubber bands on their arms and spending lunch periods trading them.

The first people to notice what was going on were the stores that were selling them. Whenever they put a new order on the shelves, it would sell out within a few hours. Silly Bandz started off as a regional story and eventually became a national one. Many store owners got into newspapers and on television as the first to spot this trend.

You didn't have to be a retailer, however, to benefit from this trend. A number of doctors made it into the news on this story as well. How? They talked about the health risks to children of wearing too many tight rubber bands on their arms. (They didn't have to make this story up, as there were kids coming into their offices with injuries due to wearing excessive numbers of these bands.) Several doctors made it onto national TV and major news magazines talking about this.

Sometimes a trend is noticeable in your industry and covered by your industry periodicals, but the general media hasn't yet noticed it. That's another item to pitch to the media. Use statistics to prove your point where possible.

Surveys, which are a good strategy to get media attention in and of themselves, can also be used to detect trends. The dating service It's Just Lunch has done a number of surveys that indicate that men and women are beginning to reverse roles in terms of their attitudes about dating. This is a new trend, and they've gotten a lot of media coverage issuing press releases with headlines like "Men More Likely to Prioritize Dating Over Work Than Women."

A survey doesn't always have to show a trend in order to attract media attention. It only has to ask questions that show what people think about something that everyone might have some curiosity about. As mentioned previously, SurveyMonkey .com is a great resource if you want to conduct a survey online.

Numbered Lists

Numbered lists are a favorite of the media whether they're about smart moves, stupid mistakes, or the biggest myths on any topic you can imagine.

You see numbered lists everywhere from the Internet to the newsstand. Here are just a few from a range of magazines I spied on a recent tour of the magazine stand at Barnes & Noble:

- 7 Traits of True Leaders
- 25 Life-Changing Road Trips
- 6 Instant Weight Loss Tricks

- Fresh Corn 50 Ways
- The 4 Keys to Pulling Yourself Out of a Rut

You get the idea.

These are relatively easy to do. Just find a benefit that everyone wants or some kind of difficulty people want to avoid. It's also a good way to share tips about one topic.

You can do the numbered list press release in two different ways, depending on the result you want. If you'd just like major websites to post your article as is, write a press release that includes the five or seven tips you want to share. But if you want to be interviewed on TV or the radio or by print publications, you want to write the tips as teasers that arouse curiosity. Instead of a bullet point saying "The simple solution to wrinkle-free skin is a crème containing the same antioxidants you find in the vitamins in your medicine cabinet," you would write, "How to achieve wrinkle-free skin with a surprisingly simple vitamin formula."

Make sure your list isn't something everybody outside your profession already knows. (If it's aimed at media for the general public, it's perfectly fine if it's things everyone in your field is already aware of.)

How-To Pieces

We're all curious about how to do things we don't know how to do. That's the allure of how-to pieces.

The secret to these is to find a way to make them a little bit different. Sometimes you can add a modifier to the basic idea that will make it more appealing. For example, I recently saw a cover story with the subhead, "How to Stand Up for Yourself—In the Nicest Way Possible." The second half, "In the Nicest Way Possible," is what gives this piece a little extra flavor.

How-to pieces can give an extra boost to any of the other strategies. For example, suppose you are an acupuncturist who knows which herbs and pressure points can help you get over being drunk faster. You could pitch a piece for New Year's Eve with the headline "How to Drink on New Year's Eve Without Getting a Hangover." If you have three or more tips, the same release could also be a numbered list.

Creating Controversy or Debunking a Myth

The basic premise under both of these concepts is the same: You have to say something that goes against the prevailing wisdom or standards.

This is a particularly good strategy for alternative health professionals and health food store owners, since there are lots of disagreements between these groups and traditional medical views.

One website that often has great headlines with either controversial positions or articles that debunk myths is mercola.com.

They got more than 182,000 views on the first day they posted "Statin Nation: The Great Cholesterol Cover-Up," a piece about a documentary that says cholesterol is good for your health, not bad, and that the real culprit in heart disease is sugar. You can see it here: http://bit.ly/ZbVu1V.

The one thing you need to be careful about when using controversy in your press releases is making sure you don't offend your customer base. Sometimes there's a fine line that you need to walk between doing something to get media attention and staying professional.

Name-calling and character assassination tend to be over the line. The headline "All Western Medical Doctors Are Cholesterol Quacks" might get a lot of attention, but most people wouldn't feel comfortable working with a doctor who is so undiplomatic.

Anniversaries

The media loves anniversaries. According to Tom Searcy of CBS Moneywatch, "Major news events are re-examined one, five, 10, 20, and 25 years later." Major events, births, and cultural icons will also show up for fiftieth, seventy-fifth, and hundredth anniversaries. When *The Wizard of Oz* turns 75, as it will soon, there will be media coverage.

An anniversary can also be a personal one, if it has a human interest angle or even a canine interest angle to it.

Publicist Anthony Mora, author of *Spin to Win*, was having a difficult time pitching stories for a client who owned a long-term health care facility. They were getting a little bit of traction, but most of the media didn't want to cover depressing stories about dementia and Alzheimer's or the usual topics of long-term care and baby boomers getting older.

Mora discovered that there was a dog at the facility that was being used for pet therapy. He did a press release about the dog celebrating her first anniversary working for the center. "We had a picture of the dog and there was an anecdotal story of how the dog jumped on one of the patient's laps and the patient talked for the first time in about a year," he says. "We pitched the story nationally, not just locally, and we were able to get the *L.A. Times*, the *New York Times*, we got *Time* magazine, we got NPR, we got Discovery—a huge amount of media that really wasn't listening to us before, because we were pitching them a story they couldn't hear."

A Sample Press Release

Before I give you my take on writing a press release, I thought I'd share a release that got a lot of media play after it was sent out. This one comes from It's Just Lunch, the dating company. Their hook is that they finally discovered what singles mean when they talk about dating "chemistry," and it's not what you would expect. This is a terrific angle for a story because everybody talks about "chemistry" and no one had really defined it before this release.

Notice that although they're announcing a free e-magazine, that's not what the press release is about:

CONTACT: Irene LaCota   FOR IMMEDIATE RELEASE
Phone: (555) 555-5555
Email: Irene.LaCota@IJLCorp.com

SINGLES PROVIDE CHEMISTRY LESSON
IN NEW DATING SURVEY
72% Define Chemistry as Comfort
and Good Conversation Rather Than Physical Attraction

A new survey by It's Just Lunch reveals that most singles believe in a different version of romantic chemistry than the one portrayed in the movies and on their iPod. The specialty dating service asked 5,000 singles, "When you think of chemistry on a first date, which of the following do you think is the most important component?" Though 20% were sparked by physical attractiveness and 7% by flirty or sexy banter, the clear winner was neither of those. Instead, it was "feeling comfortable together," the answer selected by 44% of singles—and, surprisingly, 49% of men. "Great conversation" was the runner-up, selected by 28%.

The question was part of research conducted at ItsJust-Lunch.com for a new e-magazine, *Twenty Years of First Dates: What Other Singles Want You to Know*, that the dating company is giving away (at the same site) in honor of its twentieth anniversary.

"We all have certain people that we feel at ease with, from the moment we meet them," says Irene LaCota, president of It's Just Lunch. "Most singles find that rarer and more meaningful than just physical attraction."

Comfort was also the number one factor in another area It's Just Lunch surveyed. When singles were asked how they judge the success of a first date, 43% chose "I felt comfortable being myself." Other top answers: 29% of singles chose "I walked away with a smile," and 15% selected "There was never a lull in the conversation."

"There are strategies you can use to be more relaxed on a date and make the conversation flow," says LaCota. "But how comfortable two people are with each other still comes down to something indefinable that you can't really plan—chemistry."

It's Just Lunch is a personalized dating service for busy professionals. The company has coordinated over two million dates for clients since opening in 1991. IJL minimizes the stress and maximizes the efficiency of dating by sending people on casual, no-pressure dates over lunch, brunch, or drinks after work. IJL's team of dating specialists, not a computer, performs the matchmaking. The company has over 150 locations in the US, Canada, and internationally.

# # #

For more information about IJL on this and other story angles, please contact Irene LaCota at (555)555-5555 or Irene.LaCota@IJLCorp.com

Writing Your Press Release

Now that you've seen a successful release, let's analyze the content. We'll discuss the traditional press release format in a little bit. (I'll also give you a template.)

Here are some things to pay attention to:

1. **The headline is catchy and sums up the article in a
   way that creates curiosity.** The "chemistry lesson" pun
   is a nice touch. Puns can be tricky, but if you can pull
   them off, they're often quite effective. The headline tells
   enough of the story to make you want to keep reading.
   Remember, that's the purpose of a great headline—to get
   the reader started down the slippery slope.

   That's all you need to do with it. There's no
   need to tell the whole story. You can't possibly do that.

   The headline is the most important part of your press
   release. It's how the media decides whether they want to
   read it or not.

2. **The sub-headline gives more detail that makes the
   headline easier to understand.** In this case, the headline
   tells readers that there's a chemistry lesson, the subhead
   tells them what it is, including a statistic that 72%
   employ a particular definition of chemistry. Simple
   statistics are always welcome in a press release, and the
   subhead is a great place to use one. Again, the subhead
   needs to keep readers interested and justify their
   decision to keep reading.

3. **The first sentence reiterates what the story is and why
   it's news.** This sentence can be general, like the one in
   the It's Just Lunch release, or more specific. Start with
   the most important part of your story. There's an old
   newsroom axiom, "Don't bury the lead," which refers
   to burying the most important parts deep in the article.
   The first sentence should give you a pretty good idea
   of what the story is about and make you want to keep
   reading.

If you're doing a soft story like the one above, make it clear why it's news. "Most singles believe in a different version of romantic chemistry than the one in the movies" shows the media that they're seeing something different. If most singles thought chemistry was physical attraction, that would be old hat, not news.

4. **The first paragraph gives a detailed explanation of the "who" and the "what."** This release does a good job of getting right to the meat of the story. You should, too. Your first paragraph should tell the main story.

5. **The second paragraph explains the "how, when, and where."** The second paragraph fills in the details. It's useful information for the reader once they know what the story is about from the first paragraph.

6. **The third paragraph is a quote that adds an explanation.** Quotations make a story more interesting, and by the time a reader gets to the third paragraph, they're ready for one. The idea is to make a comment on the story—maybe even explain why this story is happening, which is what the quote does in this release.

7. **The fourth paragraph adds some additional related information.** In this case, it's another survey question that yielded similar results. In your case it could be a historical note or something else you want the reader to know. Think of this paragraph as what you would say in a conversation after the word "also."

8. **The fifth paragraph is a two-sentence quote by the same company representative that summarizes the whole piece.** This is your chance to say either "This is what it all comes down to" or "This is what it all means." This is the end of the actual story.

9. **The final paragraph is a brief description of your company.** It's Just Lunch describes who they are, what

they've done, the benefits of working with them, how long they've been in business, and in broad terms, where their offices are. Make sure you include all of these items in your company bio, too.

10. **Contact information is provided at the end as well, so it's easy for the producer, editor, or writer to quickly request more information.** Right after the three number signs, there's a sentence that says: "For more information about IJL or this and other story angles, please contact," etc. Though this is a format item rather than a content item, I don't want you to forget it, so I'm listing it here. Media people are busy, so it's important to make this information easy to find without scrolling back up.

One other tip: If you want to use your release for SEO purposes, use the keyword phrases you want to optimize two times each in the release. Then, one time for each one, highlight them and create a hyperlink back to the website you want to optimize. You can do this by right-clicking on the phrase (after you highlight it) and selecting "hyperlink" at the bottom of the pulldown menu that appears. A form will show up called "Request Hyperlink." It will ask for the website you want to link to. Just fill in the box at the top with the site address and click "OK." Your hyperlink will instantly be created.

Formatting Your Release

The IJL sample is exactly what your release should look like. One page up to about one and a half pages is ideal. Here's what to take note of:

- Your name, your phone number, and your email address make up the top three lines on the left-hand side

- The top line on the right-hand side of the page should say "FOR IMMEDIATE RELEASE" in all capital letters
- At the end of the text of your press release, which should be your company description, type three number signs at the center of the page, with a space between each one, so they look like this, without the quotation marks: " # # # "
- After the number signs, include your contact information again

Here's a template you can use:

CONTACT: First name Last name   FOR IMMEDIATE RELEASE
Phone: (555)555-5555
Email: You@youremailaddress.com

CATCHY HEADLINE IN BOLD CAPITAL LETTERS THAT SUMS UP STORY
Sub-Headline in Normal Type
With First Letters Capitalized That Provides More Detail

The first sentence reiterates what the story is and why it's news. The rest of the first paragraph gives a detailed explanation of the who and the what. Make sure you add hyperlinks to a few of your keyword phrases that lead to your website in this paragraph and the second and fourth paragraphs, if applicable.

The second paragraph explains the how, the when, and the where. This can be a shorter paragraph.

"The third paragraph is a quote from someone at your company," according to First name Last name, President of

---

Your Company. "Break up the two sentences exactly as they are broken up in this template."

The fourth paragraph adds some additional related information. Think of this paragraph as what you would say in a conversation after the word "also."

"The fifth paragraph is a two-sentence quote that summarizes the whole piece," says Last name. "This is your chance to tell your reader what it all comes down to or what it all means."

Your Company gets to tell its story in this final paragraph, after the main story is over. Describe who they are, what they've done, the benefits of working with them, how long they've been in business, and in broad terms, where their offices are.

# # #

For more information about Your Company on this and other story angles, please contact First name Last name at (555)555-5555 or You@youremailaddress.com

That's your press release template. The format at the top and the bottom (starting with the number signs) never changes.

According to a publicist friend of mine, using a template makes it much easier to write a one-page release. He says he always pulls out the last one he wrote and types over it using the exact same style, including the quote format, over and over again.

You can download a copy of this template to use on your computer at gentlerainmarketing.com/pr/press-release-template/.

Determining Where to Send Your Press Release

Once the release is completed, your focus naturally turns to which media you want to pitch it to. As one would guess, large mainstream media such as *Good Morning America*, CNN, the *Wall Street Journal*, or *USA Today* are the most competitive.

While being featured in a national publication can be helpful from a credibility perspective, they may not result in attracting as much new business as a local or industry-specific media campaign will. That said, if you do appear on national media, make sure you feature the media logos and the clips on your website.

For anyone starting a publicity campaign, it is far easier to appear on local TV and radio, as well as in your local newspaper. Producers and editors in your town are particularly interested in local success stories. The fact that it's local is a primary criterion. (However, if you have a customer base that's national and you find an angle that's interesting to a wide audience, you can go puddle-jumping from one local morning show to the next. For example, Fox has many shows like *Good Day Atlanta*, with the same title but a different city name.)

In terms of print, an article about you in a Michigan health weekly is likely to bring you more patients than an article on the American Medical Association website. If you're in the business-to-business space, you will be better off in a trade publication geared to your customers than appearing in an article aimed at the general public.

Even if you have a national customer base, it's always worthwhile to start locally. Your local newspaper is designed to write about the people who live there, so they are the most likely to write about you. Many local business publications, such as the *Atlanta Business Chronicle*, are owned by larger companies (such as bizjournals.com), so if one paper writes a story about you, others may pick up the story. It's quite possible for what was originally a local story to go national in this manner.

Finding Local Media Contact Info

There are lots of ways to find local media people:

- Many reporters and columnists include their email address in their byline, and don't think they don't read their email. I struck up a very pleasant email relationship with Craig Wilson of *USA Today* simply by sending him a note congratulating him on his marriage. Commenting or congratulating a writer before you pitch them something is always a smart move. Ultimately, getting a lot of press is about cultivating relationships. *The Patch*, which has news websites for most cities, also is a great resource to find lists of editors you can contact.
- Check with your local Chamber of Commerce. They may have a media list already developed for your city. (If you work in the arts, your local cultural council may have a list of media people who cover culture.)
- You can record local television shows, and there's usually a list of producers at the end of the show.
- If that doesn't work, do a search on LinkedIn under the name of the TV show. This will work for radio as well.
- You can get a list of radio stations in your area by selecting the appropriate state and then clicking your way to your city or county using this website: http://bit.ly/117VCA1. Check out each station's website and the shows they broadcast. If they don't list the producer for a show you'd like to appear on, call the station and ask who the producer is. You can also Google the show and the word "producer."

- The Internet Public Library offers a great list of local newspapers as well as trade magazines here: http://bit. ly/142y4ui.
- You can buy a state-by-state guide to media at gebbieinc .com.

Finding National and Regional Media Contacts

For regional media, if you are willing to do your homework on a location-by-location basis, just follow the instructions above. With a bit of effort you should be able to find any producer's name either through a LinkedIn search or by Googling the channel name or the show name and the word "producer."

An inexpensive way to build a contact list of editors at popular and trade magazines is to get a weeklong pass to the database at Wooden Horse (woodenhorsepub.com). It's geared to freelance writers, so it gives you a feel for what each magazine is looking for, which is extremely handy information to know.

If you can afford to spend some money to gain access to contacts across a full range of media, here are some resources you can use to find both regional and national media contacts:

- Gebbie's (gebbieinc.com) offers a complete national list of contacts. Another good resource is Cision (cision.com), formerly known as Bacon's. They are a big player in the field. Also check out Vocus (Vocus.com).
- *Bradley's Guide to the Top National TV Talk and Interview Shows* is very comprehensive, with detailed information and articles about who national talk show producers are interested in and, equally important, who they're not. If you're serious about getting on national TV, this is a great resource. It's at: rtir.com/reports/TopTVBk.pdf.

- Alex Carroll has put together a list of radio shows with more than 100,000 listeners. It's available at radiopublicity .com.

News Release Services

The easiest way to get your release distributed is to use a press release service. Most highly reputable companies in this field will charge you per press release, which enables you to test an idea with a modest budget.

The granddaddy of these companies is PR Newswire (PRNewswire.com). Everyone from the nation's largest corporations to solo entrepreneurs uses this company. Prices range from $400 to $1,000 or more depending on how long your release is and where you want it to be sent to. Although they are not the least expensive service, they are highly reputable and you can rest assured that your release will actually be sent to the people you are trying to reach. PR Newswire also has a great analytical tool that tracks who picked up your release and used your story.

One of my personal favorites is PRWeb (PRWeb.com), which gives you a lot of bang for your buck. Their analytical tools are not quite as robust as PR Newswire, but you'll still be able to track the results of your release. Many reporters and bloggers subscribe to this service, which is a testament to its effectiveness.

eReleases.com is similar to PRWeb. They offer discounted bundle packages if you intend to send several releases. (See screenshot on page 234.) As media is increasingly being consumed online, they're a good resource to consider.

There are also less expensive services and even some free ones, but the old adage of "you get what you pay for" really does apply. Most only reach a small number of media contacts and they don't permanently host your release. This means it disappears after a period of time. That said, if you're on a tight budget, check out PR.com, which costs about $50 per release. Two free services that get generally good reviews are Newsvine.com and PRLog .com.

Also make sure to post your release on your website. Have your web designer add a page to your site that says "Press Room" and include them in chronological order. You never know when a journalist or producer may be doing a search for a piece they're putting together about your topic. Although there's no guarantee that the press will find you this way, it's easy to do and you never know precisely what will get the media to call. Plus, it makes your website look even more professional and adds to your credibility as an expert in your field.

Earlier in my career I wrote a syndicated career and professional advice column for the *Atlanta Journal-Constitution.* Although I knew my deadline was Wednesday at 9:00 A.M., you would typically find me scrambling each Tuesday night seeking sources for the particular article I was writing. The press-room pages on sites were a great resource for me and for many other columnists I know.

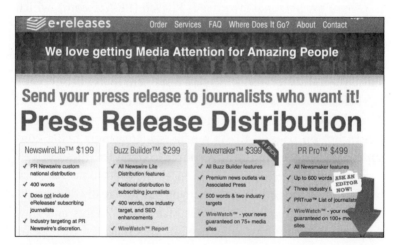

Getting the Media to Call You

There are three resources I recommend that have the potential to get the media to book or interview you almost immediately.

- Twice a year in Manhattan, the National Publicity Summit (http://bit.ly/13jBD5x) gathers 100 TV and radio producers as well as editors and freelance writers over a few days. You get to meet with them one-on-one to pitch your stories. It's like speed dating with the media. The cast of producers and editors changes from summit to summit, but among the shows and media that are often included are several big ones such as *The View*, *Time*, *O*, and *USA Weekend*. There is an investment to participate, but not only do you get in front of very hard-to-reach media, you also receive two days of comprehensive media training. If you're serious about playing on the national stage, this is something worth considering.
- *Radio-TV Interview Report* (RTIR.com) is a newsletter and website that reaches 4,000 producers looking for guests for their shows. It's published by the same company that puts on the Publicity Summit. You can either use your ad for the release you've written or let one of their copywriters write an ad for you. This publication has been a staple for bestselling authors like Robert Kiyosaki of the Rich Dad, Poor Dad series and the team behind Chicken Soup for the Soul, Jack Canfield and Mark Victor Hansen. This was a valuable resource for me when I did the Super Bowl promotion I mentioned earlier.

- *HARO* (HelpAReporter.com) is a newsletter that goes out three times a day with requests by reporters who need quotes or interviews from experts on the topics they are covering. You sign up, get the listings, and then respond to the ones you are qualified for. It's distributed to a large number of subscribers, so here are some tips on the best ways to get a reporter to choose you:

  - Be one of the first responses
  - Give the reporters answers that are exactly what they are asking for, not what you want to tell them
  - Tell a short but colorful story that illustrates your point
  - Since reporters need to tell two sides of every story, come up with an answer that's likely to be less popular
  - Reporters are always worried about finding an ending to their story, so come up with a quote that can be used as the last sentence for their article, using the ideas you utilized to create the last quote in your press release

Guest Blogging

You can also use your press release to get prominent bloggers in your field to let you submit a guest blog post or get them to write a post for yours. I recently did a guest post for Daftblogger.com, and when the article ran, we got 60 opt-ins, which is good for a niche business. More opt-ins continue to trickle in from that effort.

I found this blog by searching the keyword phrase "business development blog." You can also go to Technorati.com to find the most influential blogs and blog posts in your category. Choose the category your business best fits into from the list at the top of the page, and then select the sub-category that makes the most sense. You'll get a list of the top five blogs in your subject area, as well as five up-and-comers.

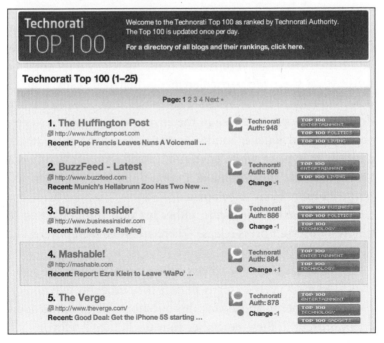

Pitching the Media

Once you have your press release written and you've decided which specific media you want to be in or on, it's time to make your pitch.

Here's how you do it:

If you're pitching by email, the first part of your subject line should say "Story Idea" or "Show Pitch," followed by a colon. There's so much spam that you need to make it clear to the media that you are a live person sending them an email with an interesting idea. Next to the colon, put a condensed version of your headline. For example, in the It's Just Lunch example, the subject line could be "Story Idea: Singles Provide Surprising Chemistry Lesson."

Then just paste your release into the body of the email, since most people won't open attachments from strangers. Hit "Send," and your release will be on its way.

"Snail mail" may seem like an old-fashioned way to do things, but since producers and editors have crowded inboxes, it may be a better way to get your release read, especially if it's not time sensitive. If there are particular media that you really want to land, send your release by email *and* snail mail. All you have to do is stick the press release in the envelope. If you want to give yourself an advantage, handwrite the address and your return address on a plain white envelope. Leave your name off your return address. This will make it seem more like a personal letter, so it's more likely to be opened.

You can also call the media, either for your initial pitch or to follow up on your press release. There are three secrets here:

1. Never ask if they've received the press release you've sent. The media gets so many pitches they probably will not remember it, and asking this question will mark you as an amateur. If they remember your pitch, they'll tell you.

2. Work on the assumption that they will not remember what you sent them. Be prepared to pitch the idea to what is likely to be a cold audience.
3. Be energetic. Every time you talk to the media, it's an audition for their show. These days, even newspapers host videos and podcasts. Regardless of whether it's print or broadcast, the media responds well to energy and enthusiasm.

Start off the phone call this way: "Hi, (**reporter's first name**), this is (**your name**) from (**your company**). Is this an okay time for a 30-second pitch?" If he or she says no, ask if there's a particular time of day that's generally better. Don't push.

If he or she says yes, go into your pitch. Do the highlights of your press release, without the quotes. (Make sure you rehearse it so that it can be delivered within the 30-second timeframe.) Finish off with a sentence as to why you're an expert in this topic. Then wait for the reporter's response.

You'll get a "no" on the spot, but sometimes a "yes" takes time. He or she may have to run your idea by the executive producer. Or the reporter may ask for more materials, such as a press kit. Remember that the media is interested in interesting ideas just as long as your pitch is well delivered and concise. Don't feel worried that you're wasting the reporters' time. They need great story ideas just as much as you want publicity.

Feel free to follow up every few days. Remember, you can keep going until someone tells you no. In that case, it's time to stop and come up with another release idea.

Always be polite and friendly. Your current pitch may not work, but you're building a relationship and you want to make a good impression.

If you do get booked, it's a nice touch to send a handwritten thank-you note.

Your Two Assignments

Now that you know the lay of the land in terms of publicity, here are your specific assignments for your next two marketing boosts:

Strategic Marketing Boost 7

1. **Come up with three to five ideas for hooks you can use to pitch the media.** Use at least three of the different types of story angles mentioned in the beginning of this chapter. Don't just think about them in your head; write them down.

2. **Make a list of at least seven publications or shows you would like to be included in.** Do the necessary research to get the names of people to contact. Make sure you include your local print media.

3. **Start an account with one of the press release distribution services and get familiar with their website.** PRWeb also has free material you can download that you may find useful in terms of writing your release. It's definitely worth reading.

4. **Check out the websites for the National Publicity Summit and Radio-TV Interview Report.** They are at nationalpublicitysummit.com and RTIR.com, respectively. There are two ways to enter the RTIR site—as someone who wants to be a guest on a show and as someone who wants to book a guest. You should check out both sides of the website. The guest-booking side has lots of ads that are great examples of content for the press release you'll be writing.

5. **Sign up for *HARO* and start looking to see if there are any news stories you can comment on.** The site is at HelpAReporter.com. Make it a priority to read these emails as soon as they come in, and send off your comments ASAP. You could land in the media tomorrow—these stories can be that hot.

6. **Do research to find some of the best blogs on your topic.** Perform a search on Google and learn your way around Technorati.com. Over the next month, read the blogs that interest you and leave comments. That's a great way to begin a relationship with bloggers before you ask them if you can do a guest post.

Strategic Marketing Boost 8

You might want to schedule two days for this one—the first to write your press release and the next to edit it and do all the marketing tasks. This way you've got a night to get a bit of objectivity about what you wrote and give it a little polish.

Here are your tasks:

1. **Pick one of the story angles you wrote down and create your press release, or hire someone to do it for you.** There is information in Appendix A about how and where to hire someone if you decide to outsource the task.
2. **Write or call your ideal media targets.**
3. **Distribute your press release through one of the press release services.**
4. **Email at least two bloggers about doing a guest blog for them.** If you're not comfortable with this at first, start by asking them if they would like for you to publish something they've written on your blog.

Chapter Ten

DIRECT MAIL:
Strategic Marketing Boosts 9 and 10

FOR YOUR NEXT TWO marketing strategy boosts, you are going to experiment with direct mail.

Maybe that sounds a little old-school to you, but direct mail is still a highly effective workhorse, even in today's electronic world of email, texting, and social media.

There are several reasons for that. The first is that *there is less competition in your mailbox than in your inbox.* As email increasingly becomes the communication vehicle of choice, there's less mail than ever. What does show up is mostly bills and junk mail.

Yet as human beings, we still have the eternal hope that something interesting is going to be in the mailbox. Thus, if you can create a sales letter that's different from the ordinary junk mail everybody gets from the big insurance and telephone companies, you can get attention and ultimately a lot of new customers.

There's also more engagement with physical mail than there is with email. As reported by *Forbes* magazine contributor Steve Olenski, a survey conducted by research agency Millward Brown showed that "physical media–AKA direct mail–left a 'deeper footprint' in the brain."

That means the tangible quality of a piece of physical mail can pack a more measurable emotional punch on the brain than an email. That's important, especially if you're offering high-value or high-price items. A one- or two-page letter delivered to a prospect's mailbox can convey the elegance and quality of the products you offer in a way that an email never can. The paper, the envelope, and the letterhead can all be used to communicate the value of what you're selling.

Another factor that makes direct mail such a winning proposition is that you can pinpoint your target audience with laser-like precision. Finally, since you only look at one envelope at a time, there's less information overload with physical mail than when your inbox is crowded with email subject lines.

To put direct mail in its proper context, it's important to understand that marketing is all about reducing waste. What this means is that you want to avoid marketing to people who will never buy from you, hire you, or refer business to you. The more money you spend communicating with those who will never become customers, the more money you are throwing directly into the trash. By contrast, with direct mail, if you buy the right list of prospective clients, you'll only be sending mail to people who are most likely to be interested in what you're offering.

Another great aspect of direct mail, particularly compared to advertising in the media, is that you have greater control over how much you spend. You can choose to send out a hundred, a thousand, or ten thousand letters. Since you have that control, it's easy to test if your message is working. If it is, you can do bigger mailings. If it's not, you can cut it off and test a new message.

Your next two marketing boosts will be to create and implement a direct mail campaign.

In Marketing Strategy Boost 9, you'll learn about the world of mailing lists. Then, using a format I've prepared, you'll write a sales letter to your ideal clients. I'll provide you with a template that will make it easy to motivate readers to go to your website and download your free report.

After you complete Marketing Strategy Boost 9, there are two things I want you to do: First, open and examine all the sales letters you receive during the month. I want you to get in the habit of reading the direct mail that's being sent to you. If there is a letter or even a part of one you think is compelling, put it into a folder. This is your "swipe file," and all great marketing copywriters have one. In the future, it will be a snap to create additional sales letters simply by cutting and pasting from what's in your file.

Secondly, I want you to purchase a mailing list from one of the vendors that you'll find as we're working through Boost 9. This is important so that you're ready to put your mailing campaign into action by the time you get to Boost 10.

Naturally, you're not going to want to sit in your living room licking stamps and stuffing envelopes, so in Marketing Strategy Boost 10, I'll show you how to contact direct mail vendors and get bids for someone to print and mail your sales letter for you. You'll find these companies are easy to work with. You can either send them a copy of the letter in the format you want or ask them to lay it out for you. Once the bids are in, you'll test out the company by having them mail a small test run of 100 to 250 pieces. The key to making direct mail work is to start small, monitor your results, and expand as you achieve success.

It All Starts with the Right List

Your first step is to find the best mailing list, so let's dig in and learn about the sometimes confusing world of mailing lists.

There's a truism in direct mail that the more you can precisely identify who your target client is, the more successful you'll likely be. Your odds of buying the right list that is hyper-responsive to your message increase the more you can narrowly define the people that make up your niche market. This might include their age, where they live, their gender, how much they earn, who they work for, and what their job title is. Naturally, depending on what you're selling, some of these factors will be more important than others. Mailing lists are becoming increasingly sophisticated, so the more we can define who is most likely to buy from us, the better the list we can buy. An additional benefit of having a very clear vision of your prospect is that it will actually make the writing process easy.

There are two types of mailing lists you need to be familiar with.

The first are what are referred to as "Compiled." As the name would indicate, these lists are compiled from directories and other information that is readily available.

The good news is that Compiled lists are inexpensive and widely available. Probably the best resource for these types of lists is InfoUSA.com.

You can create your list by selecting different parameters. These include job titles, type and size of companies, zip codes, headquarters or branch locations, home addresses, industries, and credit ratings, among many others.

What I like about InfoUSA.com is that they have an online tool that enables you to compile your list quickly and easily. They are the largest supplier of mailing lists and the overall quality is quite good.

The disadvantage is that their lists tend to get mailed to a lot. Thus, your letter is likely to be one of many that the prospect has received. That isn't too big an issue if you are using a great sales letter (which you will be), but it is something to keep in mind. (Tip: For some lists you'll see an option often referred to as "Hot

List." This refers to people who have recently been added to the list. Since they're new, they won't have been mailed to as often, and the response rate tends to be higher.)

The second type of mailing list is called a "Response" list. This is a list of people who have responded to particular offers in the past. The premise behind the power of these lists is that individuals who have responded to an offer similar to but not the same as yours are likely to be receptive to your offer as well. For example, if I sell baseball gloves, buying a Response list of people who bought baseball bats would be a smart move.

As a general rule, Response lists will pull larger numbers; however, they tend to be more expensive. This is a trade-off that needs to be considered, but if your budget allows for it, I'd try to use Response lists as much as possible. It probably won't come as any great surprise that there are Response lists for practically everything. However, what may be less well known is how some of them are developed.

For example, have you ever wondered how some of those companies advertising on TV manage to sell their products so cheaply? For instance, you might see an ad where you can purchase 15 fishing lures for a buck—plus if you buy in the next 30 minutes, you'll get a case and a reel. It's hard to believe they can even manufacture all those items for a dollar, let alone make a profit on them.

The truth is in many instances they're not making a profit on the products at all. They may even be taking a loss. What they're doing is collecting names of people who fish.

Fishermen and women are an extremely responsive group of people when it comes to direct mail. The companies advertising these products capture the contact information of purchasers and then call on companies that sell boats, fishing rods, clothing for fishermen, and duck calls. The pitch is, "We have a list of responsive buyers of fishing materials; would you like to rent our list?"

Obviously, a lot of companies say yes and pay big money for the opportunity to do so; otherwise the list creators wouldn't be able to afford the commercials.

Direct Mail Success Stories

My company did a very successful mailing to a Response list made up of people who had bought Michael Gerber's book *The E-Myth*. One of Gerber's key points is that far too many small business owners focus on day-to-day activities rather than how they are going to keep their pipeline full of new business.

That's exactly the same premise that we hold here at Gentle Rain Marketing. What makes us different is that we provide a step-by-step blueprint for precisely how to do that.

It seemed obvious to us that people who bought his book were primed and ready for the marketing system we offer. That assumption turned out to be correct, and mailing to those who bought Gerber's book was one of the most successful direct mail campaigns we've ever run.

Sometimes it takes a bit of work to figure out just who to mail to. We were working with a client who was selling career advice for recent college grads. He had an unusual problem: Recent college grads loved what he offered, but they couldn't afford to pay for it. Virtually all of his clients had the service paid for by their parents. When we started looking for a mailing list, the question we needed to answer was, "How can we find parents of recent college graduates?" On the surface, there didn't appear to be any magazine subscription list we could rent or an association that parents of recent college graduates belonged to. Ultimately we started to think about what else do Mom and Dad buy college graduates?

And then it hit us. Class rings.

From there it was a simple matter to purchase a customer list from several of the largest manufacturers of class rings. We mailed to that list with great results. Thus, one question you want to ask when thinking about what list to buy is, "What else is this group of prospects purchasing?"

There are many list brokers who offer highly specialized Response lists. The best way to find them is by going on Google and searching for "(**Your Topic**) Response Mailing Lists."

Mailing lists are sold with a minimum of 1,000 names. That doesn't mean you need to mail to 1,000 names; it just means that you'll pay the same for 250 names as you will for 1,000. Lists from InfoUSA.com tend to be quite inexpensive, while Response lists, which often give you better results on a per-name basis, usually cost more. Shop around, since the same list is often available from multiple sources. You may be able to find the list you want at a lower cost if you contact multiple vendors.

You can buy email lists as well, but the rules are slightly different. You are still charged on a per-name basis, but you never actually receive the email addresses. Instead, you send your email sales letter to the broker. The broker then sends your emails out for you. The good news is that anyone who responds to your email and opts in for your free product then becomes your subscriber, who you can mail to as often as you wish.

However, the number of people who respond to an email marketing campaign is quite small, so it really only makes sense if you have a market that's large and a fairly substantial budget. Personally, I would put a hold on email marketing until your business is well established. If you do decide to try it, make sure your email offer drives people to a website that encourages people to opt in for some sort of free information.

Writing Your Sales Letter

I'm about to show you step by step how to create your sales letter, which raises the question of whether letters are more effective than postcards or not. In an ideal world you would want to test both, but here are some pros and cons.

Postcards offer the advantage of being less expensive to mail than letters and can be eye-catching if you choose the right visual image for the front of the card. However, they have only a limited amount of space to communicate your message. If your target market is businesses, postcards usually don't make it past the screener due to their obvious promotional appearance. However, if you're marketing your services directly to consumers, they may be worth testing.

What has worked the best for me has been a sales letter that has the image of professional correspondence. In tests we've run they've outperformed postcards by a considerable margin. So let's turn our attention to developing your sales letter.

You can use this template as is or as a jumping-off point for your own creative endeavors. Again, one of the benefits of direct mail is that you are easily able to track the response. If you get a lot of new clients, keep mailing it. If the response is less than desired, you can cut things off without having invested a lot of money.

Nothing is worse than staring at a blank sheet of paper or an empty Word document, so allow me to guide you through the process of creating a powerful sales letter.

Following the same thought process we used when we created your giveaway, your sales letter needs to initially focus on your reader, not on you and the services you offer. That's why you want to tap into the emotional triggers of what they desire and what they are afraid of. Tapping into these triggers is what separates sales letters that get read and acted on from those that get dismissed.

It bears repeating that fear of pain and desire for gain have been documented as the two most powerful ways to motivate your prospect to take the action you want.

Focusing on the desire for gain refers to your reader's aspirations, goals, and ambitions. It is the positive outcome they desire. What makes this technique even more powerful is that it is closely linked with hope. Providing readers with hope is crucial if we expect them to take action.

If readers do not feel that they can achieve the goal, if they feel that attainment is outside of their capabilities, then inertia will take over. That's deadly, since our goal at the conclusion of the message is to motivate our readers to do something. Unless they feel hope and aspire to the "gain" that is communicated in the copy, they won't act. Thus you want to ensure that your copy is filled with emotion-laden statements that emphasize the gain that can be achieved by taking action.

However, as powerful as the emotion of gain is, it is pain that initially gets people's attention. In my opinion, when you start to write your sales letter, it's pain that you want to focus on.

So how do we communicate pain? It's most effectively done through a two-step process. First, you want to communicate what the problem is that your readers are facing. I'm assuming that you're writing to a niche market or offering a very specific service to a larger group of prospects. People pay attention to problems that either they suffer from or that those who are similar to them face. Thus the more you niche your audience, the better.

However, just stating the problem by itself is usually not enough. You need to build on it. Make your readers really care about it to the point where they are willing to take action. In order to do that, you need to communicate consequences. As I've discussed previously, these are simply the answer to "What happens if the problem isn't addressed?" As you can imagine, this is where we really make the reader care about the problem.

So if you focus on these items, you can create sales letters that not only are read but also motivate people to take *action*. And ultimately that's what it's all about.

Before You Write Your Sales Letter

Just as with the free report you created, you need to do a little homework before you sit down and begin writing. The more you invest a little bit of time at this stage, the higher the quality of the marketing message you'll create.

As I mentioned in Chapter 4, the style and tone of the message needs to seem like you're writing just for your prospects. It should feel personal, not like a letter that's written in what I call "corporate-speak." Those are the letters that make you feel like you're hearing from a company, not an individual, and are very impersonal in tone. Writing in that type of voice doesn't allow you to convey that you truly understand the needs, wants, hopes, and desires of your reader.

To create a sales letter with the appropriate level of intimacy, you need to be able to answer the following three questions. These will look familiar from the exercise you did in Chapter 2 when creating your free report:

1. Who are you writing to?
2. What is the specific problem they are facing for which you offer a solution? It's important to keep in mind that everyone thinks their problems are unique. The more you are able to micro-target specific issues that the reader faces, the greater the likelihood that your letter will be read.
3. What are the *consequences* if the problem isn't addressed? We have to elevate the problem in the reader's mind to make them care enough to prioritize it. We do this by

communicating the consequences that are likely to occur if it isn't addressed.

(Note of caution: While consequences are extremely important, you must take care not to sound like Chicken Little. Communicate that this is an issue that warrants action while at the same time not making it appear as if the proverbial sky is falling.)

Your First Sentence

You have two important objectives when you write the first sentence of a direct mail piece. First off, as legendary copywriter John Caples puts it, "the goal of the first sentence is simply to get the reader to read the second sentence."

I would add that not only should it hook the reader's attention, but it should also build credibility for the company or individual writing it.

Here's a simple opening sentence you can use as a template. It accomplishes both those tasks and has worked extremely well for my clients.

Dear (**Prospect**),
I know from speaking with (**others in the niche**) that many of them are concerned about (**problem**).

Here are a few examples of how this might appear:

- I know from speaking with other Boston retailers that many of them are concerned about inventory control.
- I know from speaking with other community banking executives that many of them are concerned about reducing technology costs.

- I know from speaking with other small business owners that many of them are concerned about attracting more new clients.

This is one of my favorite opening lines, and based on my tracking, it's very successful.

The other interesting point about this opening sentence is that it gets your letter past the secretary or screener and has a high probability of being passed along to the decision maker. The reason for this is that it very clearly articulates that you are someone who 1) focuses on their industry and 2) apparently has the ear of other executives in the field.

Make sure the first sentence appears as a single paragraph. This makes it easier for the eye to focus on it and increases the likelihood that it will be read—and that the reader will go on to the next paragraph.

Your Second Paragraph

According to the *Direct Marketing News*, if we can get people to read the second paragraph, then we have an excellent chance of getting them down the slippery slope of reading the entire message.

In this second paragraph you want to expand on the problem that you communicated in the first sentence. This is where the exercise I had you complete on developing consequences for your free report will really come in handy. Remember, simply stating that a problem exists is usually not enough to get people to take action. In order to do that, we need to reinforce what may occur if they just lie there like slugs and fail to take the necessary steps.

For example, if I were writing a sales letter about...sales letters, I'd emphasize that if they don't learn how to write a compelling letter, it's likely their business will remain little more than "a well-kept secret." It's fine to have a superior product or service, but if no one knows about it, it doesn't do you any good. (In fact, according to one study, over-reliance on referrals and word of mouth was the most common reason why solo consultants and small businesses went under.)

I'd then go on to discuss how most sales letters get screened out by secretaries, get dumped in spam files, never get read beyond the opening sentence, etc.

You get the idea.

One thing to consider is using bullet points when you discuss the consequences. I find that they break up the blocks of text and make the message more appealing to the eye. Don't overlook the visual layout of your letter since it influences if it gets read.

Your Offer

Remember, the whole point of the sales letter is to get readers to visit your website or request the free report. This differs from the traditional offer of a typical sales letter that encourages the reader to call for more information or to "speak with a representative."

Unfortunately, asking someone to call to speak with you usually doesn't generate much of a response. It is simply too big a request, too early in the relationship. Most of your readers think that if they call, they'll be subjecting themselves to a hard-core sales pitch. That's why you should always make a soft offer when you are contacting new prospects. We want to make it easy for them to say "yes."

Your Credibility Statement

Although we hook attention by focusing on fear, pain, and hope, your letter needs to have a credibility statement so that readers will feel comfortable that you have the skills necessary to solve their problems. Interestingly, you will establish a lot of credibility by simply demonstrating that you understand their specific problems, but you will need to add a bit more. What you emphasize in the letter is a judgment call based on what you think your niche audience would be most impressed with.

This might include your education, special training, or number of years in the field. If you've written any articles or books on the topic of your expertise, this is often worth mentioning.

Depending on your business and amount of experience, you may want to focus more on your company's expertise. In that case mention the number of years the company's been in business, results that clients get from working with you, the number and location of branch offices, as well as any other relevant information that you think is important to your prospect.

Another way to approach the topic of credibility is to ask yourself, "Why don't clients hire me?" The more you can address those issues in your credibility statement (and elsewhere in your sales copy), the more you will proactively defuse rejection. If you have a short testimonial that addresses the concern, it can be a helpful addition to the letter.

The Power of the P.S.

A lot of research shows that the P.S. is the second most often read part of the sales letter (after the opening sentence). I suggest that you reiterate what you want the reader to do. Thus the offer of your free report appears twice—once in the body of the letter, and once in the P.S. In tests we've run, repeating the call to action in the P.S. has increased response rates by as much as 33%.

Creating Your Sales Letter

Okay—that's everything that needs to go into a sales letter that will get you a lot more new prospects. However, knowing what goes into a sales letter and actually having a finished one ready to be mailed are two different things, so let's get yours written.

To do this I'm going to provide you with a template that will cover almost everything you need. Feel free to edit it to fit your own voice. Templates are best when they're used as guides, so feel free to be creative.

Let's get started.

Letter #1

Dear (**First name**),

I know from speaking with (**others in the niche**) that many of them are concerned about (**problem**).

It's an understandable concern since (**biggest consequence**) can often occur. In fact, we've noticed that within (**niche field**) it's very common to observe the following:

- **Consequence 1**
- **Consequence 2**
- **Consequence 3**

That's why I thought our latest publication, (**name of your free report**), would be of interest to you. This report will take you less than 15 minutes to read, and in that time you will learn:

- **Benefit 1**
- **Benefit 2**
- **Benefit 3**

At (**your company name**) we specialize in assisting (**niche market**) (**in solving biggest problem**). My personal background includes (**years of experience working with niche clients**) (*if appropriate, drop names and/or mention awards, publications, etc.*).

I guarantee that you will find useful and profitable information in (**name of report**) and that you'll put it down with new ideas and perspectives. It's free and you can receive your copy by visiting our website (**www.yourwebsite.com**) or calling (**your phone number**).

Thanks for investing your time in reading this letter, and I look forward to hearing from you soon.

Best Regards,

(**Your Full Name**)

(**Your Title**)

P.S. If (**solving particular problem**) is mission critical for you, I hope you'll take advantage of the information that's available for free at (**www.yourwebsite.com**). Thanks.

Beyond the First Letter

A single letter is a good start, but a three-letter sequence will get a significantly better response. Our clients have seen as much as an 85% increase compared to just mailing a single letter. If you are marketing to businesses, mail letter #2 thirty days after letter #1, and letter #3 thirty days after that. If marketing to consumers, you can send the letters out in two-week intervals. Make sure you track who has responded and delete those names from the subsequent mailing lists.

Here are two additional templates you can use.

Letter #2

Dear (**First name**),

Back in (**month you sent letter #1**) I sent you a letter offering you a copy of our latest free report, (**name of free report**).

Amid all the mail you get on a typical day, perhaps my letter got overlooked or maybe you were just too busy at the time to respond. However, since we specialize in working with (**niche market**), I wanted to write you again. I firmly believe that the information in the report will be particularly valuable to you.

I know from speaking with others (**in the niche market**) that ideas for (**solving problem**) are likely to be very important to you. (**Name of report**) will take you less than 15 minutes to read, and I guarantee it will stimulate your thinking about

- **Specific Benefit 1**
- **Specific Benefit 2**
- **Specific Benefit 3**

At (**your company name**) we specialize in assisting (**niche market**) (**in solving biggest problem**). My personal background includes (**years of experience working with niche clients**) (*if appropriate, drop names and/or mention awards, publications, etc.*).

Again, the report is free and you can receive your copy by visiting our website (**www.yourwebsite.com**) or calling us at (**your phone number**).

Thanks again.

Best Regards,

(**Your Full Name**)

(**Your Title**)

Letter #3

Dear (**First name**),

Take two (**companies of the type you're writing to**). Both (**similar in specific ways**). Both trying to (**accomplish a particular task**). One (**type of company**) chugs along at an okay pace, but the nagging feeling that "We could be doing better" never quite goes away.

By contrast, the second (**type of company**) continues to (**achieve a particular result**).

Why is one (**company**) so successful and the other so *average*?

We believe a large part of the answer revolves around the power and potential of (**the type of work your company does**). When you dig down and really examine what accounts for the success of (**these types of companies**), a key differentiator is (**how they effectively utilize or implement a particular solution**). The bottom line is that the right type of (**solutions**) can give you an enormous competitive advantage over your rivals, both big and small.

That's the reason I felt compelled to write you this last time to make you a final offer of our free special (**report**). The report will take you less than 15 minutes to read, and it will stimulate your thinking about

- What you should be doing to (**achieve a particular solution**).
- How to zero in on what's probably making your (**current solution**) needlessly (**expensive or ineffective**).
- The most important factor to focus on during any (**occurrence that's likely to happen**).
- What the most progressive (**companies in this industry**) are doing to drive new business results.

At (**your company**), we help (**companies in this industry**) (**accomplish a specific goal**). We know that at the end of
the day, what you care about most are solutions to the most
vexing business problems you face.

Even if you're completely satisfied with your current
(**approach to the particular business problem**), I guarantee
that you will find some useful and profitable information in
this report. It's free and you can receive your copy by visiting
our website (**www.yourwebsite.com**) or calling us at (**your
phone number**).

I look forward to hearing from you.

Best Regards,

(**Your Full Name**)

(**Your Title**)

Getting Your Direct Mail Printed and Sent

Once your sales letter is written and ready to go, you need to
have it printed and mailed. Since you want each letter to be written specifically to an individual prospect, as opposed to "Dear
Insurance Agent," you'll need to use a direct mail printing service. You can find these companies by searching on Google for
"Direct Mail Printing" or "Direct Mail Agency."

If you're using a list from InfoUsa.com, you can simplify your life
by letting them do everything for you. You might, however, want
to get a few other bids to make sure you're getting the best price
possible.

In most cases, it will make sense to print the letter on your statio-
nery. If you want to use some other format, most of these printing
companies have graphic artists who can design whatever you want.

You now know everything you need to know about direct mail
sales letters. As I mentioned before, they may seem old-school,
but they're still a reliable workhorse for growing your business.

Here's what I want you to do next.

Marketing Strategy Boost 9

1. Explore the mailing lists at InfoUsa.com.
2. Google "(**Your Topic**) Direct Response Lists." Remember, the results of your mailing will be heavily influenced by the quality of the list you buy. It's a good investment of time to fully explore your options.
3. Based on your research, select a mailing list and purchase the minimum number of names and addresses.
4. Use my template to write a sales letter, or create a sales letter on your own. Remember, the call to action is to motivate prospects to request your free report.

Marketing Strategy Boost 10

1. Review your sales letter and make any changes you think will make it better. One technique I use is to read my letter out loud. Since we are striving for a conversational tone, if it sounds like you speaking, it's probably fine.
2. Do a search under "Direct Mail Printer" or "Direct Mail Agency" and call for bids. If you're using InfoUSA.com for your list, also get a bid from them.
3. Hire one of the printing companies.
4. Have them lay out your sales letter, or send a copy to them in the format you want.
5. Set up a test run of 100 to 250 sales letters to be sent out immediately.
6. Within a couple of weeks of the mail being sent, you should have a good idea if you are satisfied with the results. If you are, continue to send mail to the rest of your names.

Chapter Eleven

JOINT VENTURES:
Strategic Marketing Boosts 11 and 12

I'VE SAVED THESE FINAL Strategic Marketing Boosts on joint ventures until last for a reason. It's been my experience that joint ventures work best once you have your initial marketing campaign up and running. There are a number of different types of joint venture relationships, some of which require that you have a substantial list of subscribers. Granted, the term "substantial" is relative and will vary depending on what niche you're in. As your list grows, you'll find that our next Strategic Marketing Boosts will produce solid results.

A joint venture is simply a collaboration with someone else with the goal of making money for both of you. In order to identify good joint venture (JV) partners, you want to ask yourself, "Who else has relationships with the types of people I want as customers or clients?"

These are the people you want to connect with to determine if there is some way that you can jointly market your services. I'll show you how to identify these people and build a relationship with them shortly.

Once you've developed these relationships, there are lots of joint-marketing activities you can engage in. You can

- Share a booth at a trade show
- Do a webinar or a teleseminar together
- Combine the products or services that each of you offers individually into a collaborative new program
- Refer business to one another and receive referral fees

The process can be as simple as having a JV partner introduce you to their contacts and vice versa. Alternatively, you might create a whole new business and market it together. I entered the training business largely due to a joint venture relationship. I had the content, my partner had the training expertise, and together we developed a highly profitable seminar business based on my book about using stories to more effectively sell services.

In Strategic Marketing Boost 11, you'll do the preparatory work of researching and identifying joint venture partners. It's important that you learn as much as you can about who might be good JV partners well in advance of going into business together. As part of this due diligence process, it's a smart move to get on their mailing list and, as much as your budget allows, invest in their products. You want to feel comfortable that what they're offering is something you can recommend with a clear conscience.

In Strategic Marketing Boost 12, we begin to build relationships with these potential JV partners. This may include directly reaching out to them by phone or email, attending conferences where they are likely to be, or even proactively recommending their products or services to your list of subscribers. (This strategy can be highly effective if someone with whom you want to build a relationship is difficult to reach.) The goal of this boost is to begin the process for getting these people to trust you enough to recommend your products and services.

The success of any joint venture relationship ultimately hinges on trust, and this takes time. Simply calling someone and suggesting that you cross-promote each other's products or services seldom has a positive result. However, if you can develop the right relationships, joint ventures can be extremely effective and add significant dollars to your bottom line.

Finding the Right Partners

The ideal JV partners are people selling complementary (as opposed to directly competitive) products or services to the same customer base as you. Finding these people starts with the questions, "Who already has relationships with the people that I'm trying to sell to? How does what I have fit with what these people are already selling to their market?"

Sometimes there's a natural fit: Realtors are a natural JV partner for mortgage brokers. Financial advisors and estate-planning lawyers make obvious sense. Chiropractors fit nicely with personal injury attorneys and sports coaches. Sometimes the connection is obvious; sometimes it's buried a bit deeper.

Keep in mind that the most obvious joint venture partnerships will also have been obvious to your competitors. Most Realtors know that developing referral relationships with mortgage brokers makes a lot of sense. Thus, if you're going to pursue the most obvious connections, you're going to have to think of creative or compelling ways to get them to pay attention to you. In many cases, putting in the time to develop a list of less obvious JV partners makes a lot of sense since there is less competition.

This is what we refer to as the fishing-hole analogy. Do you want to fish at a pond where you know there are lots of fish, but so does everyone else—so the banks are teeming with other fishermen; or do you want to seek out the ponds where there are perhaps fewer fish, but far less competition? There are advantages and disadvantages to both approaches, but it's worth developing a list of potential JV partners that's beyond just the obvious ones.

One great idea if you're having trouble is to talk with some of your customers. What types of products or services (aside from your own) would they be interested in? Is there anything that comes *before* the sale of your service that would be helpful for them? Is there anything they need *after* they have bought your product or service? Thinking and asking your current clients about these "before" and "after" scenarios may unlock some creative ideas for potential JV partners.

For example, one of the first things people do when they buy a new home is redecorate. Thus, developing relationships with Realtors may make sense for some interior decorators. How about chiropractors and health food store owners? Those that are open to alternative methods of medical treatment are also likely to be interested in natural and healthy foods.

In recent years an increasing amount of new business has come to me through joint ventures. Since we focus on developing and implementing marketing campaigns for our clients, great JV partners for us are marketing consultants who sell "how to" information to small businesses. After clients have bought their books and audio programs or attended their seminars, it is likely there will be a percentage who want someone to actually *do* the work for them. When these JV partners refer these clients to us, it's a win/win/win for everyone. The JV partner gets a commission, we get new business, and the client gets a marketing program that helps him or her grow their business. Thinking about this model may unlock some ideas for the types of businesses you should be contacting.

Another approach is to research the types of associations potential JV partners belong to. It's surprisingly easy to find out. Simply Google whatever their business is and the word "association." Alternatively, you can do this the old-fashioned way and check the *Encyclopedia of Associations*, which is available in many public libraries.

Most associations publish a list of members. Sometimes you can purchase the list directly; other times you have to be a member. Personally, if I discover a group that has a lot of JV partner potential, I'll go ahead and join. There are a number of benefits for doing so.

One of the main ones, which surprisingly few people take advantage of, is attending the meetings and conferences. I know that I told you earlier that attending conferences was largely a waste of effort, and that's true if you're there seeking customers. However, when you're looking for JV partners, attending meetings actually enables you to stand out from the other attendees and can be a great investment of time. For example, let's say that you decide the sales promotion industry offers some great potential for joint venture relationships. At the conferences, the vast majority of people will be in that particular field. The halls and meeting areas will be chock-a-block with people who make their living selling pens, T-shirts, and coffee cups. However, if you're a sales trainer, an Internet marketer, or a copywriter, it's conceivable that you'll be the only person there in your particular field. One of the frustrations people have at industry conferences is that all day long the only people they're meeting are the competition. If you're there with a pitch about how the two of you can partner together to help grow each other's businesses, you'll get a lot of welcome attention. In fact, we've had a number of clients who have further leveraged this idea by speaking at industry conferences about how to establish joint venture relationships. It's an idea definitely worth considering.

The Mindset of Your Potential Joint Venture Partners

On the surface, setting up joint ventures seems so obvious that one wonders why so few of them produce much in the way of tangible results. After all, there's a compelling financial proposition that's hard to argue against: "Let's refer each other clients and make money together." However, there's a huge barrier to successful joint ventures that can be summed up in one word: *trust*.

I remember the first time I attempted to establish some joint venture relationships. With the benefit of hindsight, I realize my strategy was flawed from the beginning. I never focused on the "relationship." To my way of thinking, if I could make a strong financial argument for what I proposed, it should be a "no-brainer." (As an aside, if you ever come up with an idea that seems like a no-brainer, that's usually an indication that you haven't thought it through enough.)

Much to my dismay, my no-brainer joint venture business proposal fell completely on deaf ears. For a long time I couldn't quite figure out what was wrong. Then I noticed that the few joint venture relationships I had that worked were exactly that—relationships.

This is an important point. While there are undoubtedly exceptions, the most valuable joint venture partnerships are those in which the relationship already exists before you decide to do business together.

When you think about it, that's the overall theme to the One Week Marketing Plan. We're not trying to get people to immediately buy from us, since all that's going to do is scare people away. Rather, we focus first on building a relationship and establishing trust.

That same lesson holds true for building mutually rewarding joint ventures.

Think about the clients you currently have. I would imagine that you worked hard to get them. Now suppose I (whom you've never met) called you up and said words to the effect of, "Hi, I realize you don't know me and have no idea about the quality of what I do, but I can give you a really big commission if you'll let me offer my very cool gizmo-service to your clients."

Okay, I'd say it a bit more elegantly, but I'm sure you get my point.

Although common sense would dictate otherwise, this some-what exaggerated example is what most people do when they attempt to develop joint ventures. They think of them as purely financial transactions and forget how important the bond of trust is between a company and their clients. Sure, we all want to make more money, but potentially damaging the relationships with our current clients by referring them to someone offering shoddy services trumps any short-term financial benefit that might occur.

There's an old saying in relationship building: "Go slow to go long." We'd all love to build a dozen great joint venture rela-tionships by tomorrow, but realistically, that just isn't going to happen. This is why cold calling people you don't know saying why they should joint venture with you is a rather pointless exercise.

Although you don't necessarily have to meet all your JV part-ners face-to-face, it certainly helps if you can. This underscores the benefits of attending the conferences and events where large numbers of potential JV partners may be. However, there's another angle that's often underutilized, which is to volunteer to be a resource in other people's marketing activities. Let me share an example.

An increasingly popular way to get the word out about your services (as well as stay in touch with your existing clients) is through teleseminars and webinars. People who use these methods are always on the lookout for people who can be guests on their programs. (As Internet radio continues to grow, this same strategy applies for business owners who host shows at places such as BlogTalkRadio and need guests.) Volunteering to be a guest, with no expectation of any personal benefit, can be an excellent way to start building a relationship.

This was a strategy that proved to be successful when I set out to develop a joint venture relationship with financial advisor/marketing guru Annette Bau. My research on potential JV partners identified Annette as someone who marketed her services to one of the niches I also focus on (financial advisors), but who did not offer a "Done For You" type of marketing service. Annette is very successful, with a huge list of followers, and would probably respond with disinterest if I were to instantly ask her to introduce my services to her clients.

However, what I noticed once I subscribed to her list (the importance of doing this for everyone who you might want to joint-venture with cannot be overstated) was that she conducted a number of teleseminars. Further research uncovered a couple of areas in which I might be able to provide value to her listeners that hadn't been previously covered. Thus, when I reached out to Annette, my pitch was completely focused on how I could be of assistance to her. As one might guess, approaching her in this way was positively received.

There are a couple of benefits to this type of approach. First, there's a greater likelihood of a positive outcome if your focus is on how you can help the other person, rather than on your personal agenda. But there's a somewhat sneaky benefit that also occurs that greatly accelerates the potential joint venture relationship. Having me on the teleseminar was a relatively low-risk proposition for Annette. If it was apparent that I didn't know much, she could easily jump in and take control of the conversation. However, since I did provide value during the program, I built up considerable credibility with Annette. Almost immediately, I became someone Annette could trust.

Thus, when I later approached Annette with the idea of promoting my services to her list of subscribers, it was greeted positively. Today, Annette and I have a very mutually beneficial joint venture relationship. I can trace its origins to appearing on that initial teleseminar. However, none of the later financial benefits would have occurred if I hadn't first offered to be of assistance to her.

We often hear the saying "you have to give before you get." To be perfectly honest, for years I was never exactly sure how one did that. However, if you take the time to learn about your potential JV partners, you can often also identify ways in which you can be helpful to them.

The flip side of volunteering to be a guest on other people's teleseminars or webinars is to invite potential JV partners to be on your programs or to be interviewed for your blog. While this may not be a compelling invitation for the celebrities in your field, most people will be flattered by your interest in having them share their knowledge and perspective. You can gain some additional goodwill by making sure their website, products, or services are heavily promoted during your program.

However, sometimes these strategies won't work. The person who could take your business to the next level of success already has countless numbers of people banging on the door asking him or her to appear on their teleseminars or webinars or speak at his or her conferences. But, you know that if only you could somehow develop a relationship with this person, it would dramatically elevate your business. How can you ascend Olympus and play with Zeus and the rest of the gang?

It's actually rather simple, but fair warning, it's not for the faint of heart.

You buy your way in.

If you want to build joint venture relationships with the Super A-Level players, it sometimes means bringing out the checkbook. There's a long history of people joining charitable groups and making contributions just so they can be put on committees where they will rub shoulders with those who have the potential to be extremely attractive JV partners.

Again, the focus initially needs to be on building the relationship. You can't write the check, join the committee, and not be expected to do any work. Your fellow committee members will view how seriously and diligently you fulfill your volunteer tasks as a free preview of the overall quality of the work you do in your day job.

You can also buy your way in by joining high-level Mastermind groups or specialized training programs. For example, I very much wanted to meet former Kodak chief marketing officer and author Jeffrey Hayzlett. Based on my research, I thought he would be an ideal potential JV partner. But I didn't know Jeff, nor did I know anyone who knew him. However, I went to Twitter and started to follow people he was following. That put me on the radar screen of a person named Larry Benet, who was developing a high-end Mastermind group. The fee to join wasn't inexpensive, but I noticed that Jeff, legendary marketer Jay Abraham, and book publicity gurus Steve & Bill Harrison were all members. These were all people who, if I approached them cold, would likely ignore my overture. However, after spending a year with them as part of the Mastermind group, I was able to build extremely profitable relationships with all of them.

Again, that word "relationships" is key. One factor that's often overlooked when you start to put this plan into action is that you need to make the commitment to stay in regular and frequent contact. Making a great connection at a conference is only the first step. You can't call the person up six months later and expect that his or her remember you if that's the only time you've been in touch since the original meeting. In much the same way as we develop relationships with prospective clients through the use of a drip-marketing sequence, you want to make sure that you're being proactive in communicating with potential JV partners. This is where writing frequent blog entries can pay dividends. I've found that by simply adding my JV partners and prospects to the distribution list for my blog, I remain top of mind.

Creating a Letter to Promote Their Product

As I've mentioned, one of the best strategies for developing long-term joint venture relationships is to promote their products or services *before* you ask them to promote yours. One of the easiest ways to do this is to send an email or letter to your subscribers introducing their services. Here's a template that works quite well:

> Hi (**First name**),
>
> Lately, a lot of my clients have been talking to me about a problem they're having. They want to (**achieve some type of result**), but they can't because of (**a particular reason**).
>
> I decided to do a little research to see if I could help—and I found a resource I want to share with you. As you know, I don't make recommendations lightly, but I'd encourage you to learn more about (**the joint venture's products or services**).
>
> If (**the problem**) is something you're struggling to address, I'd encourage you to learn more by going to (**website of your potential JV partner**).
>
> I found (**name of product or service**) to be extremely helpful, and I think you will, too.

This is also highly effective once you've established a joint venture partnership and are receiving (and paying) referral commissions. Many businesses that offer products or services over the Internet will set you up with what's called an affiliate code. It's simply a specialized URL (that's www.websiteaddress .com) that tracks the purchasing history of anyone who refers business to a JV partner. You would insert that affiliate link into the email when you send it out to your list. In other instances, referral fees are done on an honor system. It's been my experience that most JV partners are pretty honest in this regard. After all, there's little incentive for them to shortchange you a few dollars and risk killing a long-term profitable relationship.

Special Considerations for Internet Joint Venture Partners

As we've been discussing, joint ventures can take a number of different forms. If you're seeking JV partners to promote your products or services largely through the Internet, there are some considerations you need to be aware of.

The size of your subscriber list (the number of people who have opted in to receive your free offer) will play a large role in the types of JV partners you will be able to attract. As a general rule, people will be interested in partnering with you if the size of your list is roughly equal to theirs. It's difficult for me to get much enthusiasm from someone who has a list of 10,000 subscribers if I only have 100 people on my list. This emphasizes the importance of continuing to add people to your list. The more people you've got, the bigger the joint venture arena you'll be able to play in.

It's like the dating physical appearance scale, where sixes date sixes, eights are usually dating eights, and tens date tens. If you have a list of 10,000, the best people to approach are people with lists of up to 15,000 subscribers. If your list is 40,000, you can easily approach people with lists of 50,000 on down. If your list is around 1,000 people, you can probably easily approach people with lists of up to 2,000 people. (You have a little more flexibility percentage-wise with smaller lists. People with under 2,000 subscribers will probably say yes to almost anybody. At that point, every new subscriber counts for a lot more.)

That doesn't mean you can't "date up." With joint ventures, just as in the world of romance, the more of a relationship you build, the more you get them to like you, the less the relative size of your list matters. Also, if you develop a list in a very specific niche market, that may be very appealing to others who are also focused on that niche, regardless of your list's size.

When promoting your joint venture via the Internet, you also want to make sure there is an appropriate financial incentive for others to get involved. Offering someone a 10% commission on your $10 ebook isn't likely to generate much excitement.

You are much better off creating products or services where you can offer a significantly higher commission on more expensive products and services. There are three ways to do this:

1. Bundle together several products and services so that you create a higher-value product with a higher price. This allows you to offer a bigger commission. I would recommend that you sell this product package for a minimum of $500.
2. Create a $100 product or service that you're willing to use as a loss leader to get more customers. Offer 100% commission to your partners. If it's a physical product, charge separately for shipping so you don't get hit with the additional expense. This strategy works best if the "product" is one that can be delivered electronically. Ebooks, PDFs, podcasts, and recorded webinars can be nicely bundled into a $99 package. The advantage of

electronic products is that while you're foregoing making money from the sale, you don't incur fulfillment costs.

3. Develop a continuity product, where the customer gets billed every month for more of your product or service. For instance, you could have a main product and add a monthly teleseminar where you interview people from your industry who can give your customers inside information and charge $50 a month. Or you could offer a monthly chiropractic program where clients get one free treatment plus a discount on additional ones, for a monthly fee. Even if your JV partner is only getting $20 for the initial sale, they get an additional $20 per month as long as your customer stays in the program. That works out to $240 per year, which is significantly more lucrative than a one-time $20 commission.

There are no rules in terms of what percentage to give to your referring partner, but there are some guidelines. For a physical product, it's typical to give between 40% and 50%. To get a person to attend a conference, a seminar, or group coaching, 25–50% is common. If, however, you are giving a commission on something such as individual coaching or a service that requires a significant amount of work on your part, or one in which you have to pay an employee or subcontractor, 10% is a typical commission.

For some people, the total amount that is being paid is more important than the actual percentage. I know one list owner who does lots of joint venture partnerships but requires that her commission be at least $800. She doesn't particularly care whether that's 10% or 24% of the retail price—it's the number that she believes is fair for programs she promotes to her list. While that's the exception, it does underscore the fact that when it comes to commissions, everything is negotiable.

However, there is one potential issue that you need to keep in the back of your mind. If the joint venture is extremely successful, your partner might start to think that they could make more money if they just offered your service to their list themselves. You don't want to create your own competition, but unfortunately this sometimes happens.

There's an easy way to avoid this. Pay your JV partner a large enough incentive so that they feel it's not worth the bother to become your competitor. For example, let's pretend I'm successfully partnering with a dental supply company to promote a "How to Market a Dental Business" program. If I only offer this partner a $1,000 commission on a $50,000 product, they're likely to think, "Hmm, we're leaving $49,000 on the table every time we refer a client to Mark. It might be worth the effort on our part to create a program where we make all of the money." But if I offer them $15,000 per sale, they're more likely to conclude, "It's just not worth my while to go into this. The time and money required would be better spent on my core business."

The moral of the story is that the more you make your joint venture partnerships a true win-win, the greater the likelihood that these will become a long-term relationship that can last for years.

The Long-Term JV Partner

One of the nice things about business is finding people you can work with over the long term. When you find someone who you personally like, has high ethics, and has a business that's complementary to yours, that's an ideal joint venture relationship. It's even better when you find someone who is good at the things you're weak at and vice versa. If you're fortunate enough to find that person, you may want to consider going beyond just selling each other's products and services. You could create a new product and perhaps a business to sell it together.

After all, not only are two heads better than one, but if your personalities and capabilities are complementary, you will get more done faster—and better—together than you would by yourself.

Since you each have your own list, you'll have more people to launch your new service or product to. Plus you will each have your own networks of people to contact for joint ventures, so you can double your capacity that way as well.

Obviously, this is not the kind of thing you want to do right away with someone. However, it's something to consider as the joint venture relationship builds.

Joint Ventures Versus Subcontracting

In a sense, subcontracting is a very specific type of joint venture. When your business becomes established, you may have a number of subcontractors who implement specific components of the services you offer. Alternatively, you can serve as a subcontractor to others. There are a lot of people who make their living this way and never have clients on their own.

Subcontracts are great when you are starting out and you want to get your feet wet. They give you the opportunity to do the work you want to do, understand the marketplace you're in, and get paid while you're still learning.

When I wanted to start out as a speaker to the small business community, I began by working with SkillPath, a company that hires speakers to offer business training seminars and sell various products from the stage. I made some extra money, but more importantly, I learned what it was like to be a professional speaker. Ultimately I decided that while I enjoyed speaking to groups, the demands the profession makes on one's lifestyle were not a good long-term fit for me. That was extremely valuable knowledge, which I never would have known had I not started out as a subcontractor.

The problem with subcontracting is that you take a hit financially. You earn only a fraction of what you would if the client was yours, plus there are often limits on how much you are allowed to engage with the client.

Although you're doing a lot of work with the client, the harsh reality is that they are not yours. You didn't find them and get them to sign the contract. As a result, you'll earn less and may not even be able to tell others that you've worked with a prestigious client. These are some of the greatest frustrations that people experience who only work as a subcontractor. It's a bit like the old joke about what's the most important part of chicken soup? It's the chicken. It's important, once you've identified the niche you want to work with, that you put in place the One Week Marketing Plan so that you have clients of your own.

Your Marketing Tasks

Now that you know what goes into developing joint venture relationships, here are the tasks I want you to implement:

Strategic Marketing Boost 11

1. Make a list of businesses that complement but don't compete with yours.
2. Think about people you already know that you can approach.
3. Search Google or head to the public library to find associations that these people belong to.
4. Select people that you have found who might be good JV partners. Follow them on Facebook, Twitter, LinkedIn, etc., and subscribe to their newsletters and blogs.

That's all you need to do immediately. But this boost has homework. Take time to read and analyze the information these potential JV partners are sending you. If they offer programs or products you can afford, make that investment. One of the first questions I ask people who approach me is whether they have read any of my books or invested in my information products.

If they haven't, a huge red flag goes up.

Once you get comfortable that this is a person you want to joint-venture with, begin to interact with them. Along with the other ideas I've suggested, make sure you pay attention to their blog and what they're posting on social media. Make intelligent, supportive comments as often as you can. People read these comments, and it's a great way to start building the relationship.

Strategic Marketing Boost 12

1. The next step is to actually reach out to one or two of the people you would like to joint-venture with. Ask them if they would like to do a guest article on your blog, or if you could interview them, or perhaps if you could write something for their blog. Consider inviting them to participate in a webinar or teleseminar you have scheduled. Talk to them about promoting a product of theirs to your list. In other words, to paraphrase President Kennedy, "Ask not what your potential JV partner can do for you, ask what you can do for your potential JV partner."

   If they ask about your products and services, you can tell them, but don't ask them to promote you to their list yet. Wait until they've gotten to know you better. (However, if they offer to do so, don't turn them down.) The idea is to build a long-term relationship, and if you let it nurture a bit slower than you might ideally want, it's likely to yield a better long-term result. You'll know when you have enough of their trust to ask them to do a promotion for you.

2. Continue to build your connections with potential JV partners by scheduling to attend one of the association meetings or conferences you researched during Strategic Marketing Boost 11.

Chapter Twelve

THE NEXT STEP

CONGRATULATIONS. If you've followed the plan laid out in this book, you now have your marketing system up and running. I hope that you've been motivated as a result of what we've covered and that a lot of the uncertainty around marketing has disappeared.

However, there are a lot of people who like to read a book all the way through before they dig in and get started. If that's you, I hope you're excited about beginning. Without meaning to state the obvious, reading about marketing is a bit like reading about swimming. It doesn't really do you any good until you actually jump into the pool.

Which brings me to a couple of important points.

The first is what I alluded to a moment ago. One of the biggest obstacles you'll face is actually *implementing* the system I've been discussing. It's terribly easy to put down this book, saying to yourself, "Those were some good ideas." While I'm glad you found the ideas interesting, I doubt that's the reason you invested in this book in the first place. My guess is that you did so because you were tired of being one of the "best-kept secrets" in your particular field. You probably have also grown tired of continually chasing after clients.

Both of those frustrations are very real and quite common—especially for those who don't have a marketing system.

Perhaps you tried to implement a marketing program in the past and gave up. Again, this is common and usually occurs when one focuses on activities rather than a holistic system. Hopefully by now, you see how the components of attracting new prospects and converting them into actual paying clients fit together. I also hope you see that it doesn't have to be complicated, take a lot of time, or cost a lot of money.

But while realizing all these things is important, actually doing something is crucial. Getting started simply requires that you go back to Day One and begin to work on the tasks that I've given you. And if it takes you more than a day—so what? The important thing is that you've started. You're taking action.

One other thing I want to share with you.

If you make the decision to implement a marketing system, you need to also make the commitment to have marketing be a part of your life for as long as you run or own your business. This is especially true in the early stages for the first-time marketer. There will be an enormous temptation to quit. Even though new prospects are signing up for your free offer, none may have turned into paying clients.

You need to resist that temptation to quit.

If you are serious about implementing a marketing system, you need to make a commitment to keep at it for a minimum of six months. That will enable you to attract enough prospects so that the law of large numbers starts to work in your favor. If you only have three prospects, you're putting enormous pressure on your marketing system to convert that small number. What never works is when someone tries this program for 30 days and then shuts it down because they didn't get immediate results.

Unfortunately, I've seen far too many entrepreneurs, consultants, and small business owners get discouraged and quit at precisely the time when I just knew they were about to turn the corner and achieve real success.

If you're not attracting consistent streams of new prospects after six months, then it means you've either got the wrong offer or perhaps you're marketing to the wrong niche. If that's the case, I'd recommend changing one or both of those variables. The system that I've described in this book is a tried-and-true marketing method that's been working for businesses since the Direct Marketing Association was formed way back in 1917.

The beauty of this marketing system is that you can build your business to whatever size you want. Not only that, but also for me and for many of my clients, the greatest benefit is being able to pick and choose who we decide to work with. As anyone who has ever had a jerk as a client knows, this is huge. I think that one of the things I most cherish about having a marketing system is that I approach every potential client with the mindset of "I'm interested in their business, I might even want their business, but I don't *need* their business."

Remember, how people behave during the sales process is a free preview of how they will behave as a client. If they're jerks during the "getting to know you" sales stage, there's no reason to think they'll be different if they become clients. Once you have your marketing system in place, every day new people enter your system, so the pressure to work with anyone who just has money goes away.

There's a desperation that shows up when you have only one customer in your pipeline and you *need* the business. People pick up on that, and often either they use it to negotiate a lower price or, sensing desperation, they don't hire you at all.

I remember sitting next to a partner of a very large international consulting firm who said, "The one bad thing about the consulting business is that I don't particularly like my clients." That's sad.

I would have to say that I genuinely like all my clients. That's not to say they aren't frustrating at times, but I thoroughly enjoy working with them. As I alluded to earlier, I turn down way more business than I accept, and it's all because I have this marketing system working behind the scenes, 24 hours a day, 365 days a year.

From purely a financial perspective, it's possible to use the One Week Marketing Plan and take your income from $100,000 to $200,000, or from $200,000 to $500,000 or even more. For most of us, however, there's a plateau effect when it comes to money. Once you're able to afford a certain lifestyle, working with interesting and fun clients becomes increasingly important. But whether you're primarily interested in more money or better clients, or even more free time, the One Week Marketing Plan will get you there.

As long as you implement it.

Your Marketing Focus for the Coming Year

If you are returning to this book after implementing the marketing system for the past year, it's safe to say that your business is in better shape than it has ever been. I imagine that you've probably never had such a steady flow of prospects and clients.

However, every successful milestone offers new challenges. Two come to mind that are worth thinking about.

One is to think about how personally involved you want to be in your business. How much do you want your business to depend on *you* to deliver its services?

Some people want to take themselves entirely or mostly out of their business equation so they can make money with very little personal involvement. If that's the case, ask yourself, "How do I create this business without me having to show up?"

The truth is, sometimes you can and sometimes you can't.

I have a friend who is a speaker, who became frustrated that he only makes money when he speaks. Although he loves many of the aspects of the speaking lifestyle, the question increasingly became, "How can I add on a service or reconfigure what I'm doing now so it doesn't have to be just the 'me' show?"

His solution was to go from just speaking about customer service to developing a customer service training program that companies could license from him and implement on their own. Now he's able to speak less and make more money from these new ancillary services.

The second area that's worth thinking about is how do you take your One Week Marketing Plan to the next level? Marketing is continually evolving and changing, which for those of us who are "marketing nerds" provides an endless source of stimulation.

Technology evolves in wonderful and unexpected ways, offering methods for reaching our niche markets that were unimaginable a few years earlier. When I started my company in the 1990s, who could have imagined the power of today's social media platforms as tools for engaging with our customers and clients? Conversely, changes in the law can sometimes eliminate highly effective methods. I remember when broadcast fax was an amazingly powerful tool for lead generation. It cost only pennies to send a fax, people actually read them, and the response rates were incredible.

Then, one day, it became illegal.

Thus, in your goal to take your marketing plan to the next level, it's extremely helpful to become a student of marketing. Many of my clients who initially embarked on implementing a marketing system simply to grow their business discovered that the process by which they attract new clients was endlessly fascinating. Hopefully you will become a student of marketing as well.

On a more tangible level, growing your marketing program is often simply a matter of tracking what is proving to yield the greatest results. There's an old joke that marketing is simply "Try a lot of stuff, see what works, and do more of that."

There's actually a lot of truth to that, which is one of the reasons why you want to always be promoting your free offer so you can "see what works."

You might also take the One Week Marketing Plan and adapt it to another niche. For example, if you've focused on certified financial planners for the past year, you could now start with insurance sales people. The model is the same regardless of the niche you are focusing on. In fact, what my clients typically discover is that setting up the first One Week Marketing Plan is the most challenging. (That's usually the case with anything new.) However, as they expand into different niche markets, the process becomes almost second nature to them.

It's also important to remember that you don't need to do all the work yourself. We've talked about outsourcing, so that you only take on the tasks that you really enjoy doing and have others do the rest. Outsourcing also makes a lot of sense for the repetitive (albeit important) tasks such as posting on social media sites, tweeting, or sending out press releases. The important point is that with a little thought about how much you personally want to do, you'll be in a position to work as much or as little as you want.

Our Marketing Regimen at Gentle Rain

Many people ask, "To what extent do you actually use this system at Gentle Rain Marketing?" I've always found it a bit ironic that most marketing firms rarely do much marketing themselves. Ask them where they get new clients and you'll often hear, "Word of mouth and referrals." Now, there's nothing inherently wrong with referrals and word of mouth, but it seems to me that if you're a marketing firm, you ought to . . . market.

I'm a big believer in drinking our own Kool-Aid, and there isn't anything I've recommended in this book that we haven't done ourselves.

Our approach will sound familiar. The overall strategy is to drive people to our main site (GentleRainMarketing.com) or to our blog. They can opt in for various free information at either location.

In order to attract lots of prospects, I try to be as visible as possible where my niche audiences may be:

- We run ads on Google, Facebook, and LinkedIn to drive people to our main landing page at GentleRainMarketing .com.
- At least twice a week I write a new blog, which gets added to the site. About 20% of these are videos, which enables me to create a different type of bond with my visitors than I could with just a text post. I'll admit that there are days when I struggle with finding something to write about. However, there's usually an article or a post in the news that I can reference and it serves as a "jumping off" point for some commentary. This is where setting up Google alerts pays huge dividends. You can get automatic emails with the current news around any topic by setting up your own alerts at google.com/alerts.
- For the blog post I'll create some sort of hooky headline, which is posted to more than 150 LinkedIn groups. LinkedIn limits you to 50 groups per person, so I enlist the support of team members to post to groups they've joined. People who are in the groups read the headline and click on the link, which takes them to the post on my blog. If they like what they read, it's likely they'll sign up for a free report or one of the other offers. This is one of our most effective methods for attracting new prospects.

- We also post the hooky headline and a link to the blog post on Facebook and Google+ and tweet about them multiple times per day on Twitter.
- Twice a week people who've signed up for our mailing list get broadcasts about new blogs on the site. Staying connected with people is of huge importance for us.

Which leads to the next question: "Okay, all this staying in touch is great, but how do you make any money from this?"

Fundamentally, we make our money by developing and implementing One Week Marketing Plan–style campaigns for clients. While I'm a passionate believer that anyone can set up a highly effective marketing system, there will always be a percentage of people who would prefer to outsource the process. So most of the daily activities of our team are creating websites and free reports, developing drip-marketing campaigns, writing blog posts, creating ads, and implementing social media marketing campaigns. (You can learn more about the specifics at Gentle-RainDone4You.com.)

In terms of how we convert prospects into actual paying clients, I'll admit that we take a fairly passive approach. When I first started my business, I would follow up personally with everyone who requested the free report. Over time, as my list of prospects grew, I increasingly relied on the drip-marketing email system to motivate prospects who were interested in my services to initiate contact.

For many years, that was how my client attraction and conversion process worked. Then I discovered something interesting. The "free" consultation turned out to be a bit of mixed blessing. On the plus side, it enabled me to talk with prospects without forcing myself on them. I enjoyed the consultative nature of the calls.

However, there were a lot of people who signed up for the free session who would never become clients. In some cases it was purely a financial issue. They couldn't afford to pay for services. Others just wanted free advice. Unfortunately, I discovered that I was spending a growing percentage of my time talking with those who I'll politely refer to as "Time Vampires." I started to track the percentage of people I spoke with who became clients and was dismayed to learn that it was only 1 out of 15. Pretty miserable statistics, and clearly something needed to change.

After much thought, I decided to eliminate the free consultation.

In its place I offered a paid consultation. At the end of the consultation, which is currently available via GentleRainCoaching .com, one of three things happens:

1. The client loves the ideas but decides to implement them on their own.
2. The client loves the ideas and hires me to implement them. In that case, the consulting fee is applied to whatever project they decide to have us implement.
3. In the unlikely and unprecedented event that they feel like I've wasted their time, I refund their consultation fee immediately. No questions asked.

The result of this change was that the number of people who requested consultations dropped dramatically. However, two out of three of the consultations turn into clients. Obviously this is quite an improvement over my earlier results.

This system works well for me because I have a lot of people in my funnel. In the beginning, when I didn't have as many prospects, it wouldn't have worked. All of which underscores the fact that any marketing system, or any business, is a continually evolving entity. You will change. Your business will change. Your marketing will change.

Personally, I think that's what keeps this stimulating and interesting.

So with that I will bid you adieu and offer my sincere thanks for taking the time to read this book. The One Week Marketing Plan has worked extremely well for me and for my clients. I believe that it will work well for you, too. Something that gives me enormous satisfaction is hearing about the success others achieve by implementing this system. I hope, as you move forward, you'll drop me an email about your successes or even any speed bumps you hit along the way. I can be reached at mark@gentlerainmarketing.com.

I wish you much continued success.

MARK SATTERFIELD
Alpharetta, GA

Appendix A

OUTSOURCING

THE ONE WEEK MARKETING PLAN is easier when you out-source at least some of it. I highly recommend you hire someone to do your website design, and you may want to outsource some of the other activities as well. The biggest issue is going to be your budget.

Let's spend a few minutes talking about different resources you can use to outsource some or all of your marketing, and some tips on how to make it a productive relationship.

The least expensive resource is Fiverr.com, where freelancers take jobs for five dollars. There are certain jobs that make a lot of sense to farm out to Fiverr. I've mentioned them throughout the book, particularly in the chapters on blogging and video.

The one strategy I would recommend with Fiverr is to give your first job to three people. Then you can develop an ongoing working relationship with the person you decide is the best. You can also try to use the advice below for the other outsourcing services I recommend, though people who are working for just five dollars may not be as likely to give you as many answers as those who you are paying significantly more money to.

For more substantial projects, the two companies I like best for hiring freelancers are Elance (Elance.com) and Guru (Guru.com). They make it easy to hire people for fixed fees, instead of hourly, and they offer escrow programs that protect both you and the freelancer. That makes it easy to get your project started without having to pay the freelancer up front. Instead, you put the money into an escrow account managed by the service, and they release it when the freelancer reaches a particular milestone. If there is a dispute, there is a process to help you resolve the disagreement. You are also able to rate your freelancers on a scale of one to five, with five being the best. That gives you another tool to make sure they treat you fairly.

Your first step is to join one of the services. My personal recommendation would be to only use one service at a time. If you don't get the quality of freelancer you want, then try the other one. The reason I recommend this approach is that you'll probably get a lot of responses to your listing, so if you post on both sites, it's really easy to get overwhelmed.

The next step is to develop a budget for the project. You can search on either of the sites for jobs similar to yours, which will give you a rough sense for the going rate. You can also search freelancers in a variety of categories without posting a job. If you look at their profiles in detail, you'll be able to see what they charge and what they've been paid. The particulars are a bit different between Guru and Elance, but with a little research you should be able to develop a very appropriate budget.

You'll notice that talent overseas tends to be less expensive than comparable resources in the United States. There are pros and cons to hiring vendors from other countries. The advantages are that you'll spend less money, the quality is generally quite good, and the person you interface with will have a decent command of English. However, there's a difference between being decent and being fluent in English. My experience with overseas vendors is that they are frequently extremely direct and literal when it comes to English. It can require an enormous amount of patience to communicate with them, and you have to be willing to convey your instructions in great detail. If you're the type of person who says, "You know what I mean," you'll likely get frustrated. If, however, you can say, "I want this in blue, and I want this box moved from the upper right-hand corner to the lower left," you'll be fine.

While I've found that the people I've hired from overseas have strong technical skills, most of them have great difficulty in writing persuasive copy. I wouldn't outsource writing sales copy to them. Some people do, and when you read what's on their website, you can usually tell.

Next you need to come up with a job description. The more detailed you can be, the better. Here's an example: "I'm looking for a WordPress site that includes a squeeze page with a form for prospects to input their name and email address, and a tab for a blog. The form will be attached to 1ShoppingCart as the autoresponder. Familiarity with Google Analytics will be important as well. Here are some websites that are close to what I want." Then list two or three examples.

I've added one sentence to job postings that significantly increases my response rate. That sentence is, "I'm looking for a long-term partner." The truth is, people who use Elance and Guru are not that good at marketing themselves. Once they complete a project for a client, they have to find another job, so they continually have to respond to posts for work. If you communicate that you are looking for a long-term relationship, you're likely to see an increase in both quality and quantity of applications. (It should go without saying, but I'll mention it anyway: You shouldn't say you're looking for a long-term partner if you're not.)

You will find that some freelancers send out the same canned response to everyone, without regard for what your job posting says.

That's why I add the following sentence to all my jobs: "If you just use a cut-and-paste response, it will be obvious and I'll delete your submission immediately." Adding that sentence will cut down considerably on the "spammy" responses that you'll tend to get otherwise.

Once you finish writing your job description, Elance offers you the opportunity to make it a featured job by paying $25 extra. (Guru doesn't have this feature.) This supposedly gets you more responses. My experience is that it doesn't make a difference, so I'd save the $25.

One technique that increases the quality of the responses is to search for freelancers and invite them to bid on your job. Each site lets you pick categories to search in. When you find freelancers who do the kind of work you need, look at what they typically charge. If it's in your budget, check out their portfolio of work and also their ratings. If you like both of these items, invite them to bid on your job. Each of these sites lets you do this quite easily—just follow the steps they give you. If you have trouble, they both have terrific technical support services you can call.

When people bid on your job, if you like what you see, you can contact them by phone or email on Guru or via a message board on Elance.

When you interview them, I suggest you ask:

- How long does it take to complete a project like this?
- How do they work with clients?
- What types of projects do they most enjoy?
- What projects are their least favorite?
- What was their best client like?
- What was their most difficult client like? (You can get a lot of interesting information out of this question. For example, if their worst client was too picky, and you're extremely detail oriented, the two of you are not a match.)
- How soon can they start?

If you still like them, make sure you check out the feedback that's posted on the site. For freelancers in the website development field (the busiest area on both Guru and Elance), take the time to examine their portfolio of work. You may discover that the websites from one designer all look pretty much the same. If that design is what you're looking for, then there's no problem. If, however, you want something different, this should be a caution flag that creativity is not this designer's strong suit. Again, the more examples you can provide the designer with of websites that you like, the better a job he or she will do for you. Most of the designers you'll find on these sites are excellent mimics.

Another great question to ask a prospective web designer is *"How do you test for multiple browsers across several platforms?"* You want to make sure your website works across Internet Explorer, Firefox, Chrome, and Safari as well as iOS and Android, which are the two platforms for mobile phones. As more people are accessing your site via various mobile devices, it's increasingly important that your site be designed to accommodate them.

If you're hiring a graphic designer or writer, you want to ask how many revisions you can request for the artwork or text. This is often negotiable, but you want everyone on the same page before the project begins. Remember, never assume anything when you're negotiating the parameters of the project.

If You Have a Problem After You Hire Someone

Both Elance and Guru have features where you can resolve disputes. Elance in particular has done a very good job in adjudicating differences in a way that's fair to both parties.

I also like the ability that both sites give you to provide feedback. Vendors who receive the majority of their business from these services know that a negative review can severely hurt their business. This is something you can use to your advantage.

In one instance, I had a problem with a vendor, and I said, "You can keep the money, but I'm going to write a negative review about you, or you can refund it to me and I won't say anything." Not surprisingly, they dropped their claim for payment. The escrow account and the recommendations feature enable you to use these services with a lot of confidence that you won't get ripped off.

A SHORT PRIMER
ON SEARCH ENGINE
OPTIMIZATION

WITHIN THE MAIN PORTION of this book, I talked about paid search advertising. When you're getting started, the quickest way to get traffic to your website is by advertising on one of the search engines. As your business matures, you may want to begin to focus on having your site appear high in the natural search listings. Let's take a minute and explain how you accomplish that.

As you may recall, when you do a search on Google, two different types of results appear. Typically, the results at the very top of the page and down the right-hand side are the ads. Those that appear in the middle are the natural search results. Search engine optimization (SEO) is a set of techniques you can use to increase your visibility in the natural search results.

It's important to keep in mind that the rules governing SEO change on a regular basis. What I'll be covering here are the basics that you'll want to make sure you're implementing. In order to keep up to date on the latest changes Google makes, I encourage you to become a subscriber to my newsletter, which you can do by visiting GentleRainMarketing.com. Another resource I'd recommend is to join the SEO community at Moz.com.

Google's primary objective is for the most helpful web pages on a particular topic to appear on the first page of the search results. Every day Google has "spiders" that crawl the Internet searching for the most relevant websites for every conceivable search term. Not surprisingly, this is in Google's best interests. If we search for something and are taken to pages that are irrelevant or mostly promotional, it's likely that we'll start to use a different search tool. However, as business owners with websites that are primarily designed to encourage people to opt in to receive some free information, we have a somewhat different agenda than Google's. Thus, the challenge becomes, what can we do to make our site very appealing to the Google spiders?

Although nobody outside of Google knows precisely why one web page gets on the first page and another does not, we do know that there are a number of factors that have a lot of influence. Thus as you continue to build your website or make changes to it, you want to make sure of the following:

- **Are the keywords you most want to rank for included in the text on the page?** The general rule of thumb is that you want your keywords to appear two to three times on the page. Repeating the words too often is considered keyword loading, and you'll actually get penalized for that.
- **Do your top keywords appear in the title tag for the page?** The title tag is the HTML code that shows up along the top of your browser (next to the "Maximize" and "Minimize" buttons) and in browser tabs. It won't guarantee that you will rank high for the words, but it's a

basic step that you need to make sure your web designer
includes when he or she is developing your site.

- **Do your top three keywords appear in the meta tags?**
  These are also sections of HTML code that appear on the
  very top of your website but they're really only "seen" by
  the spiders that are continuously crawling the Internet.
  Just ask your website designer to make sure they're added,
  and you can check this box off.

There are several other factors that influence how your page
ranks.

Links: A few things to keep in mind about links. (For those
who are unfamiliar with the term, "links" are simply which websites you are connecting to and vice versa.) First, all the SEO
benefit comes from the websites that link *to you*, not vice versa.
Unfortunately, it doesn't help your page ranking by linking your
site to other credible websites.

Second, it's all about the credibility of the site that's linking to
you. If you have a site about résumé preparation and a related article on CNN's site links back to you, your search ranking will be
elevated. If an unrelated site links to you, that won't help you out.
If, God forbid, a porn site links to yours, it will hurt your natural
search rankings (unless you're in a certain type of business).

A few years ago, getting on the first page in the natural search
results was easy. The more people who linked to your page, in
Google's view, the more credible it was. You could get ten thousand links pointing to your site and they all counted equally.
People started getting junk links from places like the Lichten-
stein Board of Tourism and the Association of Romanian Puppy
Farmers. There were link farms that you could pay a hundred
dollars and have thousands of links coming to your site in less
than a day. It wasn't long before Google saw that people were able
to game the system, so they changed their rules.

If you want to try to elevate your ranking by getting more links, make sure you're focusing on sites that have a lot of credibility. Personally, I'd be very wary of the email solicitations you receive from foreign lands promising you a first-page ranking. It's likely to backfire on you.

Popularity on social media: This is becoming increasingly important, but you need to be aware about how the search engines define "popularity." It doesn't refer to how many followers you have on the various social media sites, but rather whether or not people are talking about you. Are you being mentioned on Google+, LinkedIn, Facebook, and Twitter? Are people posting about your perspective on forums or blogs? If people are talking about your site, then its ranking will go up. This is why some level of visibility on Twitter makes sense for most everyone. Granted, your ideal prospect may not be on Twitter, but if people are retweeting what you're posting, it will help your natural search rankings.

The size of your site: Google likes big sites with lots of pages. It used to be that a one-page site could get a high ranking in the search results. Those days are gone. This is the reason why you want to make sure you build your site on WordPress, so you can create a blog and add lots of pages with updated content about your keyword topic. Every new blog is an additional page on your site. Additionally, Google loves sites that are updated regularly. Again, each blog post refreshes your site with new content. If you want to do one thing to increase your search rankings, I'd recommend blogging on a regular basis.

How long people spend on your site: Google assumes that if a site is relevant to the search term, visitors will spend a lot of time there. If people are coming to your site only to leave it after a few seconds, this will hurt your rankings.

For example, with many search results, a Wikipedia page shows up at the very top. This makes sense since the page is highly focused on a specific search term or topic, and people spend a significant amount of time reading the information. The more information on your page, the longer they'll stay and the more "Google credit" you'll get. This is also why video is a powerful tool. Once people start watching a video, they tend to stick around.

Making the First Page

The reality is that Google comprises extremely smart people, and we (unfortunately) are not going to be able to trick them into ranking our site higher than it should be. If you want to be on the first page, you have to make your site as relevant as possible.

Mike Volpe, chief marketing officer at HubSpot, suggests a helpful exercise. Google a term you would like to be ranked for and take some time to analyze the websites that appear on the first page of results. Then ask yourself, "Can I do something as good as or better than this?"

If the answer is yes, keep going. If it's no, pick another keyword or keyword phrase to rank for.

There are lots of keywords. You have to pick your spots where you think you have the greatest chance of success.

THE RELUCTANT MARKETER'S TOOLKIT

MOST PEOPLE I KNOW have a curious relationship with marketing their products or services. On the one hand, they know they need to market. On the other, there's this inner desire for people to just "discover" them and flock unbidden to their website. I think that this dual mindset is one of the reasons why people get stymied when trying to implement a marketing plan.

However, when you break through that resistance, it's very likely that you'll wonder why you turned something so simple into something so frightening or difficult.

My wife, who works with people on overcoming these issues (MarianMassie.com), says there are lots of reasons that we unconsciously sabotage ourselves, sometimes having to do with messages that were passed on from our parents. For example, some men receive unconscious messages not to outdo their fathers; some women are given unconscious messages that business success will make them less attractive to men and therefore unlovable.

It doesn't matter what the message is, only that something is holding you back. The quickest way around them involves what I call "brain geography." These messages are held in certain parts of your brain, and if you can move your thinking into another part of your brain's geography, you'll stop resisting the task at hand.

I'm about to show you several techniques that will help you do that.

Remember What Success Felt Like

This is a technique Marian taught me. It's very simple, but it works like a charm. When you notice that you are stuck and resisting what you *should* do, stop whatever it is you're doing—reading Facebook, playing Words with Friends, answering email, or whatever you do when you're procrastinating—and close your eyes.

Take a second to remember one of your bigger accomplishments in the past. See that result in your mind's eye. Then begin to recall how that accomplishment made you feel. Did it make you proud? Did you feel powerful? Was there a sense of joy or peace or a simple sense that you brought something worthwhile to the world? Did it feel good?

Of course it did. Now imagine doing the task at hand and feeling that good again when you finish it.

When you open your eyes, take that feeling with you and start working on whatever you were avoiding. It will feel much easier.

Focused Breathing

I'm increasingly becoming a believer in the power that breathing techniques can play during times of stress or conflict. The old adage "Take a deep breath and count to ten before you say anything" really is good advice (although I'll admit I don't always follow it).

Breathing can also be a very effective tool for breaking through procrastination and resistance.

The most calming portion of focused breathing is the pause between breathing in and breathing out. This next technique emphasizes that:

1. Breathe in, preferably through your nose, for four counts.
2. Hold your breath in for four counts. (You don't have to make a dramatic movement or sound to hold your breath. Just don't breathe out.)
3. Breathe out for four counts.

Repeat this five to ten times.

Whenever I do this I almost immediately feel calmer and more focused. Whenever I find myself procrastinating, this technique gets me back on track.

As I've mentioned on numerous occasions, while reading about marketing is helpful, ultimately it all comes down to implementation. Unfortunately, we are often our own worst enemy, and procrastination is the single biggest culprit. I'm always interested in what others do to help themselves get over these inevitable periods, so if you've got something that works, I hope you'll share it with me.

Acknowledgments

A MARKETING SYSTEM is much like a mosaic. You take bits and pieces from many sources, and combine them into a system that works for you. The One Week Marketing Plan would never have been possible without the insights, perspective, and assistance from many people, including the following:

Jay Abraham

Andrea Albright

Erin Alli

Matt Bacak

Annette Bau

Larry Benet

Bob Bly

Ali Brown

Jimmy D Brown

Brendon Burchard

John Carlton

Hollie Clere

Terry Dean

Dave Dee

Ryan Deiss

John Doerr

T. Harv Eker

Roxanne Emmerich

Ken Evoy

Mike Filsaime

Vinnie Fischer

Michael Fortin

Bryan Franklin

David Fry

Michael Gerber

Jeffrey Gitomer

Bill Glazier

Bill & Steve Harrison

Jeff Hayzlett

Greg Herlean

Sally Hogshead

David Horsager

John Jantsch

Andy Jenkins

Sheree Keys
Dan Kennedy
Frank Kern
Nate Kievman
Jeffrey Lant
Mitchell Levy
Christina Littrell
Alex Mandossian
Perry Marshall
Ann McIndoo
Rick Miller
Brian Mittman
Armand Morin
Alexis Neely
Eben Pagen

Natalie Petouhouff
John Rees
Jennifer Russell
Marlon Sanders
Lisa Sasevich
Greta Schultz
Mike Schultz
Joey Smith
Alicia Tucker
Chris Vandersyden
Mike Volpe
Jeff Walker
Alan Weiss
Jane Wesman
Al Zuckerman

Mahesh Grossman and the Authors Team for their invaluable help in organizing this work.

And finally to Glenn Yeffeth, Jennifer Canzoneri, and the team at BenBella Books for their suggestions, advice, and support.

About the Author

MARK SATTERFIELD is the founder & CEO of Gentle Rain Marketing Inc. For the past 20 years, he's advised entrepreneurs, consultants, advisors, and business owners on how to attract consistent streams of brand new prospects and turn large percentages of them into paying clients.

Mark's the author of eight previous books, including the best selling *Unique Sales Stories: How To Get More Referrals, Differentiate Yourself From The Competition & Close More Sales Through The Power of Stories.*

Prior to founding Gentle Rain Marketing, Mark held executive positions with PepsiCo and Kraft Foods, in addition to having served as the Director of Career Services for the Graduate School of Business at Emory University.

To receive weekly email tips for growing your business please visit:

www.GentleRainMarketing.com